Palgrave Texts in Counselling and Psychotherapy

Series Editors
Arlene Vetere
Family Therapy and Systemic Practice
VID Specialized University
Oslo, UK

Rudi Dallos
Clinical Psychology
Plymouth University
Plymouth, UK

This series introduces readers to the theory and practice of counselling and psychotherapy across a wide range of topical issues. Ideal for both trainees and practitioners, the books will appeal to anyone wishing to use counselling and psychotherapeutic skills and will be particularly relevant to workers in health, education, social work and related settings. The books in this series emphasise an integrative orientation weaving together a variety of models including, psychodynamic, attachment, trauma, narrative and systemic ideas. The books are written in an accessible and readable style with a focus on practice. Each text offers theoretical background and guidance for practice, with creative use of clinical examples.

Susan Sisko
Editor

Culturally Responsive Psychotherapy, Counselling & Psychology

Practices for Inclusion and Accountability

palgrave
macmillan

Editor
Susan Sisko
School of Health
University of Canberra
Canberra ACT, NSW, Australia

ISSN 2662-9127 ISSN 2662-9135 (electronic)
Palgrave Texts in Counselling and Psychotherapy
ISBN 978-3-031-81830-1 ISBN 978-3-031-81831-8 (eBook)
https://doi.org/10.1007/978-3-031-81831-8

Cover illustration: Sergey Ryumin

This Palgrave Macmillan imprint is published by the registered company Springer Nature Switzerland AG.
The registered company address is: Gewerbestrasse 11, 6330 Cham, Switzerland

Preface

Focus of the Book

The overall aim of this project has been to create a contemporary book drawing on international perspectives and principles that underpin cultural responsiveness in psychotherapy, counselling and psychology and put those into *practice*.

The importance of including multicultural perspectives in the field is widely accepted yet approaches on how to develop culturally responsive practices are varied or, in some cases, fundamentally ignored. There have been many multicultural competence frameworks developed over the past decades for use in psychotherapy, counselling and psychology, but these frameworks are often informed by the dominant paradigms of Eurocentric ideals. These ideals are influenced by systems and structures that fail to recognise the impacts of social constructs for all groups including those who are not part of the dominant or privileged group in society.

We have positioned this book with a postmodern framework, understood as incredulity towards meta-narratives (Rorty, 1984). This position allows the authors to explore core issues within the professions of psychotherapists, counsellors and psychologists that have contributed to limited understanding and practice. The book is articulated in ten chapters with topics of cultural responsiveness in education, research, supervision, clinical practice, school counselling, rehabilitation counselling, relationship counselling and community counselling. Each chapter will include historical background of the topic, issues and concerns, application of postmodern frameworks and case study material to demonstrate how knowledge and understanding develop into practice. Drawing the book to a close, the last chapter will highlight final thoughts related to key principles for cultural responsiveness in psychotherapy, counselling and psychology.

Canberra, ACT, Australia Susan Sisko

Reference

Rorty, R. (1984). *Habermas and Lyotard on postmodernity*. Blackwell Publishing Ltd.

Contents

Notes on Contributors

Jude Bergkamp, PhD is the chair of the Clinical Psychology Program at Antioch University Seattle, as well as clinical faculty in the Department of Psychiatry and Behavioural Sciences at the University of Washington. He is the president of the National Council of Schools and Programs of Professional Psychology (NCSPP), representing over 100 doctoral programs. He serves on the American Psychological Association (APA) BEA/BPA Task Force on Doctoral Competencies in Health Service Psychology. His current research interests include the decolonization of psychology, the exploration of social privilege as the flip side of oppression, and the role social privilege plays in psychotherapy.

Dax Bevly, PhD is full-time faculty for the Clinical Mental Health Counselling program at Antioch University Seattle. Dax received his master's and doctorate degrees in counselling and counsellor education from the University of North Texas. Dax worked full-time in private practice providing individual, family, group, play, and couples therapy to children, adolescents, and adults. He served adults and families with co-occurring mental health and substance use disorders at a psychiatric hospital at the inpatient, partial hospitalization, and outpatient level. Although Dax teaches remotely for the CMHC program in Seattle, he lives in his home state of Texas.

Diana Camilo, Ed.D., LCP, NCC is an assistant professor in the Counselling Program at Cal State University, San Bernardino. Her teaching and research interests include culturally responsive practices and supervision, school counselling, the college and career readiness of minoritized populations, and stress management. Dr. Camilo is co-director of the Centre for Equity and Postsecondary Attainment (CEPA) at San Diego State University. She also founded the Supporting Access to Higher Education for Immigrant and Undocumented Students conference and was a member of the UndocuResearch Collaborative.

John A. Conteh, Ed.D is an associate professor in the Master of Education in Counselling (MEd) Program at University of Puget Sound, Tacoma, Washington. He has been a mental health counsellor for over 20 years. Dr. Conteh began his higher education full-time teaching journey in 2012. He was the 2023 Research Award winner for the Western Association for Counsellor Education and Supervision (WACES) Region.

Katherine Fort, PhD holds a PhD in Counsellor Education and Supervision Program and has nearly 20 years of experience in higher education. She has been instrumental in developing and accrediting programs, including curricula that emphasize social justice and inclusivity. Dr. Fort's research explores resilience, international counselling practices, and the experiences of marginalized students and faculty in academia. She has contributed to numerous publications and presentations in counsellor education, advocating for accessible and equitable counselling practices. Dr. Fort mentors future counsellors and scholars, encouraging thoughtful community engagement. She is dedicated to advancing practices that uplift underrepresented voices and promote holistic well-being.

Mariaimeé Gonzalez, PhD "Maria" Gonzalez (she/her/ella) is a licensed professor counsellor, clinical supervisor, co-founder of the Latinx Social Justice Mental Health Institute and the executive director, Clinical Operations and Community Outreach at Antioch University Seattle. With an extensive leadership background, she has held prominent positions, including president of the American Counselling Association (ACA) of Washington, president for the Western Association for Counsellor Education and Supervision (2023–2024), chair of the ACA International Committee (2021–2022), ACA Foundation Member (2022–2025). Born in San Juan, Puerto Rico, and raised in the states within the United States, Mariaimeé is a first-generation Latiné college graduate who is passionate about liberation and human rights.

Sravya Gummaluri PhD candidate, (she/her) is a Licensed Associate Counsellor in New Jersey and a National Certified Counsellor. She is a Counselling PhD Candidate at The George Washington University in Washington, DC, pursuing a cognate in multicultural counselling leadership and social justice advocacy. She is a 2022 NBCC Doctoral Minority Fellow and has utilized this opportunity to serve diverse and historically marginalized communities through leadership, advocacy, scholarship, and research. Her professional and research interests center on anti-oppressive counsellor education, supervision, research, leadership, and advocacy for BIPOC and migrant communities in navigating socio-political and cultural stressors to promote overall wellness and liberation.

Andrea Hampton Hall, PhD, C.R.C is Assistant Professor in counsellor education at the University of Kentucky in Lexington. Dr. Hall has worked for and with people with disabilities since 2014. Her research interests include decreasing barriers to mental health services for those with marginalized identities, disability justice, and conducting qualitative research that increases community engagement and awareness.

Debra A. Harley, PhD, CRC, LPCC-S is the Wallace Charles Hill Professor of Counselor Education and a Provost's Distinguished Service Professor and at the University of Kentucky (UK). Her research interests include cultural diversity, substance use disorders and addiction, LGBTQ+ populations, ethics, and offender populations. Dr. Harley has published over 90 articles in refereed journals and 91 book chapters, is co-editor of six books, and has authored a series of book reviews, editorials, and conference proceedings.

John J. S. Harrichand, PhD LPC-S, LMHC, NCC, CCMHC, ACS, CCTP, is an assistant professor at The University of Texas at San Antonio. He is a US resident and Canadian scholar of Chinese and East Indian heritage from Guyana, South America. He holds a Hons. BSc. in Psychology and Integrative Biology from the University of Toronto, an MA in Counselling from Providence Theological Seminary, and a CACREP-accredited PhD in Counsellor Education and Supervision from Liberty University. His research focuses on culturally responsive counselling, counsellor education and supervision andragogy, and counselling leadership and professional advocacy. He supports minoritized clients, communities, and ethnic minority counselling leaders.

Joy M. Mwandwa, PhD is an associate professor in the Department of Counsellor Education and Family Studies at Liberty University. She holds a PhD in Counsellor Education and Supervision from Old Dominion University. With over two decades in the counselling profession, her work settings have included a college counselling center, community mental health, churches, and internationally in Kenya, Tanzania, and Malawi. As an LPC (VA), she mostly works with women of color, immigrants, and international students and international professionals. Her research interests are on qualitative and indigenous research methodologies, the development of the profession of counselling internationally, and the multicultural competence.

Laura Owen, PhD is the executive director, Centre for Equity and Postsecondary Attainment at San Diego State University. A prior school counsellor and district school counselling manager, she is a passionate advocate for closing opportunity gaps, investing in strategies that promote equity and attainment and conducting research to discover new and innovative approaches that strengthen postsecondary advising P-16.

Keisha Grayson Rogers, PhD, CRC, LCAS, LCMHC, QS, ACS is Professor of Rehabilitation Counselling at Winston-Salem State University. Keisha has published and presented research on disability-related issues, co-occurring disorders, clinical supervision, multicultural issues in counselling and has facilitated trainings locally and internationally in these areas. She is the 2022 recipient of the Dr. Bobbie Atkins Research Award presented by the National Association of Multicultural Rehabilitation Concerns and 2022 recipient of the Professional Writing and Research Award presented by the North Carolina Counselling Association. Both awards recognize her contributions to the profession through significant writing and research.

Maxine Rosenfield, MRes has been a radiation therapist, community sector manager, author, educator, and clinical supervisor. Teaching at universities and colleges for the past 14 years, Maxine's Master of Research thesis was about supervision in different modes. A Board member of the Australasian Association of Supervision 2005–2022, she supported the development of supervision in Australasia. A clinical member and accredited supervisor of the Psychotherapy and Counselling Federation of Australia (PACFA), Maxine sat on the training standards committee

(2011–2016), ethics committee (2014–2020), and Accreditation Standards committee (2024), being awarded Honorary Life Membership for services to counselling and supervision.

Keiko Sano, PhD is a counsellor educator, licensed mental health counsellor, nationally certified counsellor, and state-approved supervisor. Born and raised in Japan, she worked in Japan, Australia, and Hong Kong before moving to the United States. She values relationships and has worked closely with her students, clients, and local community members, including expatriates, immigrants, and their families. Her passion for global contexts in counselling has fueled her research interest in exploring myths around the universality of counselling theories and practices. She focuses on the diversity of counsellors, counsellors-in-training, supervisors, and counsellor educators, unfolding cultural mismatches of traditional theories and practices.

Yun Shi, MS, PhD is a Licensed Marriage and Family Therapist (LMFT) with 20 years of experience serving individuals, relationships, and families. With a strong interest in culturally responsive counselling approaches for diverse client populations, she conducts research and trains mental health professionals both in the United States and internationally. She is Assistant Professor of Counsellor Education and coordinator of the Marriage, Couple, and Family Counselling Program at Portland State University, Oregon, United States.

Susan Sisko, PhD is a full-time academic at the University of Canberra, Australia. Susan is a researcher and author with over 20 years of clinical experience in the counselling and psychology fields. Susan has lived and worked across multiple countries including Australia, Hong Kong, and USA. She holds a BA and Post-Graduate Diploma in Psychology and an MA in Counselling Psychology. Susan holds a PhD in Counsellor Education with research interests in cultural responsiveness, diversity, anti-racism, and clinical supervision. Susan maintains a private practice where she specializes in psychodynamic work as a therapist and supervisor.

Lindsay Vik (she/her), PhD, LPC, is an assistant professor of Counsellor Education at Portland State University. She works as a Licensed Professional Counsellor and currently resides in Oregon (United States). Passionate about systems perspectives within counselling, Dr. Vik teaches relational counselling and works with clients experiencing a range of mental health and relational challenges. Dr. Vik enjoys working with counsellors-in-training to expand their understanding of and integration of culturally responsive counselling practices to better meet diverse and evolving client needs and finds the balance in working clinically and educationally enriching to both practices.

List of Tables

CHAPTER 1

Cultural Responsiveness in Counselling and Psychology

Susan Sisko

Introduction

It has been a deep personal and professional privilege to have worked as a therapist in Hong Kong, the United States, and Australia. I am a second career academic and still, most ardently identify as a therapist and clinical supervisor. I have worked in many and varied settings with a broad demographic of people with complex stories. Fortunately, this is one profession where longevity garners respect with an assumption that wisdom follows. I have a longitudinal scope of my own education, work experiences, and now as an educator and researcher. As I developed my clinical practice over the years, I have become more reflective in my work—this happened over time and with intention. However, constructs of the therapist self-awareness were not part of my early training. It has become much more commonplace in counsellor education that the therapist is required to possess qualities of self-awareness, for example, "Counsellors are aware of and avoid imposing their own values, attitudes, beliefs and behaviours"

S. Sisko (✉)
School of Health, University of Canberra, Canberra ACT, NSW, Australia
e-mail: Susan.Sisko@canberra.edu.au

S. Sisko (ed.), *Culturally Responsive Psychotherapy, Counselling & Psychology*, Palgrave Texts in Counselling and Psychotherapy,
https://doi.org/10.1007/978-3-031-81831-8_1

(American Counselling Association, ACA Code of Ethics, 2014, p. 5). One of Australia's peak professional bodies describes self-awareness as "recognising our own values and perspectives and understand both our biases and insights and the impact of these on clients and others" (Psychotherapy and Counselling Federation of Australia, PACFA Code of Ethics, 2017, p. 3). As an educator, being mindful of supporting students to develop self-awareness is ever present but often elusive. Being in educational settings there are structures and parameters that can limit our work from this type of student development, though it is both required and important to becoming a therapist. We often use tools such as journal writing hoping somehow, that ah-ha moments or revelations will happen, resulting in deeper self-awareness or insights for students. In my experience, it has been fairly rare that such epiphanies occur from simple journal writing.

Where the work of self-awareness of the therapist started to make sense and really change was the advent of including cultural competence as part of the core curriculum. In particular, the work of Sue et al. (1992): this paper contextualised the significance of self-awareness and made sense as it related to being a therapist. This was also the first multicultural framework that addressed the significance of the beliefs and attitudes of the therapist as part of cultural competence, which I will expand on further in this chapter. Prior to this, the focus had remained on frameworks with roots in traditional Eurocentric theory, that encouraged therapists to adapt their attitudes and beliefs by comparing individual differences to existing norms, inevitably reinforcing stereotypes of individuals and groups. This was a big ah-ha moment for me as a therapist and as an educator.

Through my teaching career I developed courses related to multicultural perspectives and cultural responsiveness for psychotherapists and counsellors. I aimed to develop meaningful assessment tasks underpinned by transformational learning pedagogy. At times this was difficult because of student complaints, suggesting I had ideologies that were questionable. It was difficult working within higher education institutes recognising that the time and structure of transformational learning practices were not readily adapted within the function and systems of the university. There have also been limited contemporary resources available. In fact, publishing textbooks in higher education does not get the status of publishing other forms of research, but without contemporary textbooks, cohesive postmodern material will not be available to support students to evolve into culturally competent and responsive therapists. To quote Churchill, it is a riddle wrapped in a mystery inside an enigma, but perhaps there is a key.

I've recently read Anne Funder's book, *Wifedom* (2023). It is about the wife of George Orwell. What struck me most was a term attributed to Orwell, which was 'doublethink'. Orwell described this as

> The power of holding two contradictory beliefs in one's mind simultaneously, and accepting both of them ... The process has to be conscious, or it would not be carried out with sufficient precision, but it also has to be unconscious, or it would bring with it a feeling of falsity and hence of guilt...it is a vast system of mental cheating. (p. 221)

Throughout his work, Orwell described power imbalances in society and politics. However, interestingly, Orwell himself all but erased his wife, Eileen O'Shaughnessy, from history despite her significant contributions to his life and his work, demonstrating how very skilled he was at mental cheating himself. Egregious, yes, but legions of women have been written out of history. Issues related to race, gender, age, and disability (to mention a few) have allowed seemingly good people to do terrible things to others while holding a belief of decency. In psychological terms this would be defined as cognitive dissonance. It holds significance to understand how these processes of mental cheating are influenced by Eurocentric and historic systems and structures that fail to recognise the impacts of social constructs for all groups including those who are not part of the dominant or privileged group in society.

Call it what you might, mental cheating, double-thinking, colonialism or oppression, these beliefs and behaviours are still present in society. As therapists it is critical to look at the historic and present influences that impact the profession and ultimately, our practices and the client experiences. In doing so we need to explore how systems and structures, including education, research, and policy, need to change and as importantly how we need to change to become not just self-aware, but critically reflective practitioners. This is vital in developing cultural responsiveness.

The following sections will give a brief history of psychology and where we have come from as a profession—to then scaffold where we are at and where we need to go as it relates to cultural responsiveness. This chapter will demonstrate the importance of developing culturally responsive psychotherapy, counselling, and psychology practices.

A Brief History of the Psychology and Theory Development

The history and development of psychological theories is vast and an intricate tapestry that spans centuries, evolving from early philosophical curiosity to modern scientific approaches. Psychological thought traces back to ancient civilisations including Egypt, China, Greece, and India. Early philosophers like Plato, Confucius, and Aristotle wrestled with questions about the mind, body, and soul. Later philosophical roots included thinkers such as Descartes, Locke, and Kant, who contributed ideas about consciousness and the mind. The emergence of modern psychology is credited to Wilhelm Wundt, who was a physiologist and philosopher, and who established the first psychological laboratory in Germany in 1879. Wundt's focus was on introspection and structuralism with an aim to identify basic elements of consciousness. This was followed by Edward Titchener's work that was focused on identifying the structure or mental processes. At the same time William James, heavily influenced by Darwin, focused on the consciousness of mental life. James first coined the term "stream of consciousness" and developed functionalism, which focused on understanding the biological processes behind human consciousness.

In the early twentieth century, Sigmund Freud introduced psychoanalytic theory, delving into the unconscious mind, and proposing that human behaviour is largely driven by unconscious desires and internal conflicts. Freud's ideas heavily influenced the development of clinical psychology, where previously this had not been considered. Freud and his work were products of his time. His ideas emerged during the Victorian era where strict social norms and repressive attitudes towards sex were prevalent. Freud was also influenced by the rationalists and empiricists of European Enlightenment. He sought to apply scientific principles to the study of the mind and behaviour bringing forward the work of Nietzsche and Schopenhauer and the concepts of the unconscious and instinctual drives.

The rise of Behaviourism (early to mid-twentieth century) followed, focusing on observable behaviours rather than internal mental processes. Behaviourism's early development started with Ivan Pavlov and the tenets of classical conditioning. Operant conditioning was spearheaded by John B. Watson and later B. F. Skinner, who rejected the study of internal mental processes, and focused solely on observable behaviour. These approaches dominated psychology for several decades. Behaviourism emerged during a period when scientific method was gaining prominence across disciplines. Influenced by positivism, behaviourists sought to establish a rigorous science focused and observable psychology rather than the previous focus on subjective mental processes. Industrialisation and urbanisation were on the rise which was reflected in the practical application of psychological principles of efficiency and productivity. The development of standardised psychological tests and measurement techniques were prevalent and supported by technological advances.

In the 1950–1970s the field of psychology experienced a cognitivism revolution which was an intellectual movement that marked a shift back to the study of mental processes, emphasising topics such as memory, perception, language, and reasoning. Influential figures here include Noam Chomsky, Jean Piaget, and Ulric Neisser. The combined cognitive and behaviour therapies (CBT) emerged with Albert Ellis developing Rational Emotive Behaviour Therapy (REBT) and then Aaron Beck and Albert Bandura contributing to further cognitive behavioural theory and treatments. CBT is rooted in American psychology which tended to emphasise individualism and personal responsibility with the idea of empowering individuals to change their thought patterns and changes in behaviour will follow. CBT was widely practised and was perceived as being adaptable to cultural contexts.

Humanistic psychology (1950s–1960s) was led by Carl Rogers and Abraham Maslow and these theories emphasised individual potential, self-actualisation, and subjective experiences. Humanism provided an alternative to the more deterministic views of behaviourism and psychoanalysis. At the same time there was significant social unrest with the Countercultural Movements of the 1960s including the civil rights movement, challenging existing racial norms, as well as the second wave of feminism and other significant social changes post-WWII. Humanistic psychology resonated with these values prioritising the individual's subjective experience and potential for self-actualisation. Humanistic psychology embraced themes emphasising the importance of personal agency, freedom, and shaping one's own life.

The aforementioned psychological theories are the main historical and theoretical influences in the discipline, and not a comprehensive list of all individual therapies but they are the mainstays in foundational knowledges. In fact, theories and perspectives continue to evolve and influence psychology, contributing to a diverse understanding of human nature and behaviour. Historical context has played a significant role in shaping the profession of psychology. Overall, the foundational knowledges of counselling are steeped in cultural factors of the time that impacted theories, methods, practices, and have shaped how psychological phenomena are conceptualised, studied, and applied. Recognising and understanding the role of cultural and contextual influences is essential for developing a more inclusive and comprehensive understanding of culturally responsive practice.

Contemporary Frameworks in Cultural Competence

In the 1960s and 1970s, criticisms emerged within the field regarding the lack of attention to issues of race and cultural diversity. The development of multicultural counselling frameworks sought to address the limitations of traditional theories and expand the understanding of human behaviour across diverse cultures. Early attempts to understanding cultural competence in the counselling profession focussed on frameworks grounded in traditional Eurocentric theory that encouraged counsellors to adapt their knowledge by comparing individual differences to existing norms. I remember some early textbooks with titles such as 'Counselling the Culturally Different' highlighting a focus on *difference* to the existing norms and other books framing culture as an issue to be solved, such as, 'Multicultural Issues in Counselling'. These early textbooks included material focusing on *special populations* for example, working with First Nations, African, and Asian peoples and included information about differing communication styles, worldviews and types of therapy best suited for these special populations, inevitably reinforcing stereotypes of individuals and groups. They frequently upheld binary positions to simplify the categorisation of 'others'. Early multicultural textbooks tended to primarily focus on race and did not include other diverse individuals or groups. I remember feeling encouraged when my students complained about the textbooks—we all knew something was wrong but could not fully name it nor could I find other teaching resources.

In the late twentieth century, white privilege concepts began to emerge. Peggy McIntosh's influential essay, 'White Privilege: Unpacking the Invisible Knapsack' (1989), highlighted the unseen advantages that white individuals may experience in society. The concept of white privilege shifted the focus from overt racism to the more subtle ways in which systemic advantages are conferred upon individuals based on their racial identity. At the same time Critical Race Theory (1980s), was developed and examined the intersection of race, power, and law. It challenged traditional legal and psychological theories and emphasised the role of social structures in perpetuating racial inequalities. White Identity Model (1998) was developed by Janet E. Helms who is an African American psychologist who has been influential in understanding how white individuals navigate issues of race and privilege, and this has been widely used in education and counselling settings to promote awareness and social justice. At this significant juncture in history perspectives and frameworks for cultural competence in counselling were further developed.

In 1991 the Association for Multicultural Counselling and Development (AMCD) approved a document with rationale for a multicultural perspective in counselling. Following that the Professional Standards Committee proposed 31 multicultural counselling competencies and encouraged the American Association for Counselling and Development (AACD) to adopt these competencies within the accreditation criteria (Sue et al., 1992). Thereafter, the *Multicultural Competencies and Standard: A Call to the Profession* was published (1992). The multicultural competencies model provided a comprehensive framework for understanding and developing cultural competence in counselling and psychotherapy practice. The design of the framework was a three-by-three matrix that included the following characteristics: (1) counsellor awareness of their own assumptions, values, and biases; (2) understanding the worldview of the culturally different client, and (3) developing appropriate intervention strategies and techniques and each characteristic was described as having three dimensions: (1) beliefs and attitudes, (2) knowledge, and (3) skills (Sue et al., 1992). For the first time—the requirements for cultural competency of the counsellor included becoming aware of their own assumptions, values, biases as well as their beliefs and attitudes putting the onus squarely on the counsellor to develop knowledge and skills in becoming culturally competent, accountable, and responsible. This was truly ground-breaking in the profession.

The focus on cultural competency had begun to shift from mastery in understanding 'others' to a framework that required [counsellor] personal accountability in recognising and challenging individual and institutional barriers that impact marginalised communities (Fisher-Borne et al., 2015). Further, Gorski and Goodman (2015) suggest that multicultural frameworks in counselling may only be meeting a minimal bar of cultural competence rather than a transformative multicultural responsiveness unless grounded in the ideals of equity and social justice. Goodman et al. (2004) define "social justice work of counselling as scholarship and professional action designed to change societal values, structures, policies and practices, such that disadvantaged or marginalised groups gain increased access to these tools of self-determination" (p. 795). The counselling profession was becoming more intentional in developing cultural competence but the limitations of simply ticking multicultural competency boxes in training was lacking in genuine cultural transformation in practice and more was needed to develop transformative cultural responsiveness. Hernández-Wolfe (2011) describes multiculturalism and a decolonising stance as not merely about cultural differences or group identities but also understanding relationships to power, access, and opportunity.

Postmodernism and Counselling

Postmodernism is a critical response to dominant paradigms. I like the expression—*challenging the grand narratives.* Significant influences in postmodernism included philosophers such as Foucault, Derrida, and Lyotard who questioned the foundations of modernist thought, including notions of rationality, progress, and truth. Modernist grand narratives in psychology refer to overarching, universal theories or paradigms that aim to provide comprehensive explanations for human behaviour and mental processes. These narratives emerged during the modernist era, including Psychoanalysis, Behaviourism, Cognitivism, and Humanism. The modernist narratives in psychology provided frameworks for understanding and explaining human behaviour and mental processes during a particular time in history and social context. Often, the people developing modernist psychological theory were overrepresented and W.E.I.R.D., as my students describe it, Western, educated, industrialised, rich, and democratic. Most likely privileged in society and limited by the cultural context in which they developed theories. Therefore, we need to ask how or if these grand narratives of modernist psychological theory, methods, and practice provide frameworks for understanding and explaining a broad spectrum of human behaviour and mental processes inclusive of diverse cultural or social constructs—then or now.

Racism, sexism, classism, heterosexism, ageism, religious hegemonism, and ableism are linked because all these categories are social phenomenon that oppress people. These oppressions have material effects on people's lives through shaping experiences, access to resources and social positions. These are contingent phenomenon, emerging from specific historical and social processes. Therefore, these categories are a product of social history and context, and they can be transformed. Postmodern approaches are responsive social movements borne from real and contingent experiences. Some examples of postmodern approaches include Feminism, Social Justice, Critical Race Theory, Postcolonial Theory, Queer Theory, and Critical Disability Studies. In brief, Feminism aims to address gender inequality, sexism, misogyny, and patriarchy which manifests in various forms of discrimination and marginalisation against women and other gender identities. Social Justice is rooted in the value and belief that individuals deserve fair and equitable treatment and that every individual should have equal access to resources, opportunity, and human rights, and seeks to address systemic injustices that perpetuate discrimination, marginalisation, and oppression. Critical Race Theory examines how race intersects with other forms of power and identity. It emphasises the social construction of race and explores how race operates through cultural norms, institutions, and everyday practices. Postcolonial Theory applies contemporary insights to colonialism and imperialism. It challenges Eurocentric perspectives and colonial discourses that marginalise and dehumanise non-Western people and cultures. Queer Theory challenges fixed categories of sexual identity and normative assumptions about sexuality. It explores fluidity and complexity in human sexual desire and gender identity. Queer Theory critiques heteronormativity and advocates for recognition and acceptance of all sexual orientations and gender expressions. Finally, Critical Disability Studies challenges ableist assumptions and practices. It examines how disability intersects with other axes of identity such as race, gender, sexuality, and class. Critical Disability Studies also seeks to challenge discrimination and oppression of differently abled individuals. These are not the only postmodern approaches, but these are examples of how race, gender, socioeconomic status, and disability, to mention a few, had been excluded from the foundational knowledges of psychology including theories, methods, and practices. Several postmodern approaches later included an understanding of intersectionality in postmodernism.

Rodó-de-Zárate (2014), described intersectionality as developing out of a growing recognition that it is not possible to separate out gender, race, class, and sexuality identities and then to explain them through a singular framework. Intersectionality shares some theoretical principles with postmodernism, but it is not inherently a postmodern approach. Some scholars trace the earliest articulations of intersectionality to the manifesto of the Combahee River Collective, where a group of Black, lesbian-identified feminists, who in 1977, said: “We ... find it difficult to separate race from class from sex oppression in our lives they are most often experienced simultaneously" (Eisenstein (1978) as referenced in Timothy, 2019). The women were highlighting that they had multiple interrelating components of their identity, each component intersects with others to produce a nuanced and multidimensional lived experience. The term intersectionality has most significantly been attributed to legal race scholar Kimberlé Williams Crenshaw (Crenshaw et al., 1996). The concept aimed to address the limitations of mainstream feminism and antiracist frameworks in understanding the experiences of marginalised individuals who faced overlapping forms of oppression. Crenshaw's concept of intersectionality emphasises that individuals hold multiple social identities such as race, gender, age, sexuality, culture, religion, nationality, class, ability, and so forth. These identities intersect, interact, and are cumulative in shaping their experiences and vulnerabilities.

Exercise:

Take a moment to consider the intersections that make up who you are. How have these impacted you, in positive and negative ways and how have you been impacted over time?

This will allow you to consider where you have privileges, for example, higher education opportunities or having financial stability and where you might experience oppressions, for example, being a person of colour or with a disability.

Understanding the interconnected and cumulative effect of various social identities and how they intersect to create unique experiences of oppression or privilege is imperative. In addition to individual intersections, understanding how societal structures and institutions also intersect and contribute to oppression and privilege of individuals and groups. It is paramount to recognise and understand the limitations of the contextual influences of the foundational knowledges of psychology in training and practice. It is of further importance to understand postmodern approaches and intersectional principles to the foundational knowledges of psychology to become culturally responsive—but how?

The Baby and the Bathwater

The idiomatic expression, 'don't throw the baby out with the bathwater', was derived from a German proverb. It is an expression in which something of value might be eliminated when trying to get rid of something unwanted. This idiom has had me thinking about the history of psychology as the foundations of education and training of counselling practice and the limitations of this same foundational knowledge. We cannot eliminate the value of this history nor the knowledges, but we need to explore what is helpful or unhelpful and wanted or unwanted positioning in psychotherapy, counselling, and psychology. It is incumbent on us that we analyse and integrate our understanding with observable realities including the experiences, access to resources, social positions, and disparities in people's lives and the deeper structures that produce and sustain those realities. Using tools such as postmodern approaches and intersectional principles are valuable in the process. These postmodern approaches need to permeate a) education and training, b) various levels of systems and structural oppression, and c) and self-awareness and critical reflection of the therapist. This is not a simple task, but it is possible.

Therapist Training and Practice

One pedagogical approach that I have developed as an educator is a Postmodern Umbrella (Illustration 1) which includes the image of an umbrella of postmodern approaches arranged above the foundational knowledges of psychology. Thus, not throwing the baby out with the bathwater, per se, but overlaying postmodernism atop the foundational knowledges and applying this to training and practice. The application of postmodern approaches in education includes integrating postmodern material throughout the entirety of a training programme and not relegating this to a single course. In every course, for instance, theory, skills practices, ethics, assessment, and case conceptualisation, to mention a few, the content should integrate postmodernism and intersectionality into foundational knowledges. To illustrate, a theory course would include reviewing all theory within the historical and social context of when it was developed, it would be reviewed by looking at what is known about who developed the theory and where they were placed in society. Theory would then be discussed within the contemporary social and cultural contexts identifying the strengths and limitations by filtering each theory through postmodern approaches. A case in point is Roger's Person-Centred Theory which was developed in the 1950–1960s during a significant antiestablishment period in the United States. The theory prioritises the individual's subjective experience and potential for self-actualisation but how might this work for a more collectivist culture? What might need to be adapted or changed in the theory and practice? Additionally, include theory developed independent of early foundational knowledges such as White and Epston's Narrative Therapy developed in the 1980s. This approach views people as the authors of their own stories and focuses on supporting individuals re-author their narratives to create new meanings and possibilities. Another model is the Social Emotional Well-Being model (Gee et al., 2014) which has developed from Australian Aboriginal and Torres Strait Islander communities and underscores the importance of nurturing holistic health by attending to social, emotional, and psychological dimensions of well-being (Illustration 1.1).

To illustrate integrating postmodern approaches in practice this would include how a counsellor conducts intake and assessment processes by exploring the client's cultural background, experiences, and values, recognising the influence of culture on mental health, and tailoring their approach to counselling accordingly. For instance, working with an individual with anxiety where cognitive behaviour therapies often have high efficacy but if this individual is neurodiverse or has developmental delays—it is incumbent on the counsellor to consider and adapt the most culturally appropriate interventions.

Systemic and Structural Oppression

Mental health and well-being do not reside solely within the individual. Rather, they can be dependent on, and shaped by social, economic, and political aspects of a person's environment (Dulaney, 2018). Addressing systemic and structural oppression for non-dominant and diverse individuals and groups seeking mental health support requires comprehensive efforts to dismantle discriminatory practices, promote inclusive policies, and ensure equitable access to culturally competent and responsive care and resources. This involves developing an understanding of issues and concerns and then advocating for systems changes and fostering collaboration between communities, policy makers, and mental health professionals.

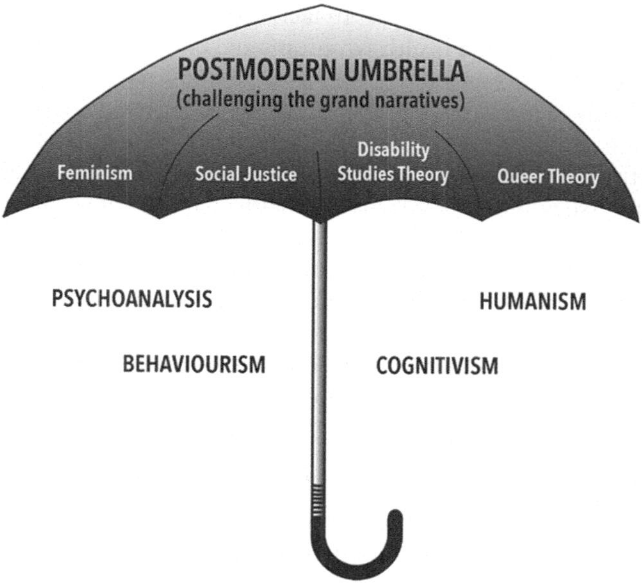

Illustration 1.1 Postmodern Umbrella

Some of the social determinants include discrimination, healthcare disparity, institutional bias, economic inequities, and criminalisation of mental illness. Non-dominant and diverse individuals and groups often face stigmatisation and discrimination in various aspects of their lives, including healthcare, housing, employment, and education. This can lead to social exclusion and limited opportunities. Structural barriers within healthcare systems can exacerbate mental health disparities for diverse populations. Limited access to culturally competent care, language barriers, and disparity in healthcare insurance coverage can prevent individuals for receiving timely care and appropriate mental health support. Further, institutional bias and systems may perpetuate stereotypes against diverse individuals, including individuals of colour, or who identify as LGBTQ+ or who live with disabilities. These individuals might receive differential treatment based on their identity, leading to disparity in access to care, diagnosis, and quality of treatment. Socioeconomic factors, such as poverty, unemployment, lack of access to transportation or affordable housing, disproportionately impact non-dominant and diverse individuals adding to mental health concerns. In fact, economic disparity can contribute to and worsen mental health symptoms and create barriers to accessing quality care.

To develop cultural responsiveness, counsellors need to consider the determinants of health in the ways that they work. Fisher (2021) suggests that practitioners need to consider the individual's circumstances rather than seeing issues as purely internal to an affected individual. Practitioners need to consider the role these circumstances may play as contributory causes of the problem. Fisher continues that it may be useful to focus on mental *health* and ask how people might be supported to act in ways likely to improve well-being. Counsellors also need to consider where they can advocate for policy, programs, and resources that address the determinants of well-being at individual, community, and societal levels.

Self-Awareness and Critical Reflection of the Counsellor

As I previously mentioned, the importance of counsellor self-awareness grew in significance as this related to cultural competence (Sue et al., 1992). Broadly speaking, self-awareness refers to an individual's ability to understand one's own thoughts, feelings, and behaviours. It involves being introspective and developing insight which can then enable individuals to better understand themselves and their impact on others. Cultivating self-awareness involves practices such as mindfulness, seeking feedback from others, journaling, and reflection. Self-awareness relies on introspection, which is inherently subjective and can be limited as a result. My experience has been that typically people have to have an experience or encounter that might evoke a response or reaction to generate a means of developing self-awareness and insight. Something new or different might cause this—for instance, travelling to different countries and immersing oneself in different cultural experiences such as foods, language, and events. In those moments an individual might reflect on their own traditions and wonder about them. This process might enforce one's original beliefs or open space for something new. This can be experienced as exciting or threatening, depending on the individual's outlook and openness. Another example could be education and new learning that might challenge what you have previously known or held as factual, again this can be experienced as exciting or threatening. When an individual's values are challenged, their reactions can vary significantly depending on the importance of the values to their identity. Reactions can include defensiveness, denial, anger, reflection, openness, and seeking confirmation. Self-awareness is shaped and informed by cultural norms and values, which can limit a counsellor's understanding of clients from different cultural backgrounds to themselves. Even with high self-awareness, counsellors may still have biases and blind spots that can affect their judgement and interactions with clients. In short, self-awareness alone is not sufficient for the counsellor's development of cultural responsiveness. Counsellors need external feedback from clients, supervisors, and peers to gain a more comprehensive understanding of their professional behaviour and effectiveness. Counsellors also need to develop critically reflective practice, which is underpinned by many theoretical frameworks.

Critically reflective practice is a way of understanding and engaging with the interconnections of an experience, making meaning, and considering the influences of the social context of the experience (Gardner, 2014). Critical reflection in this manner highlights the intrinsic interconnectedness among all aspects of the self, as well as the relationship to the social context. In Gardner's book, *Being Critically Reflective* (2014) she describes the four theoretical underpinnings of critical reflection. First, *reflective practice* identifies feelings, values, thoughts, and assumptions that influence practice. Second, *reflexivity* generates an understanding of how we perceive others and how we are perceived by others. Third, *post-modernism* challenging modernism and limiting people to binary categories and finally, *critical social theory* which identifies the interrelationship between cultural and social values and emphasises a social justice approach. The four theories "reinforce the importance of bringing what we are not aware of into awareness, making what is unconscious, conscious" (Gardner, 2014, pg. 36).

From Theory to Practice

How would an individual, couple, or group know that you are a culturally responsive counsellor?

Clients can assess whether a counsellor is culturally responsive through various observable behaviours, interactions, and the overall therapeutic environment. Here are some qualities, characteristics, and indicators of a culturally responsive counsellor.

1. Cultural Competence Statement:

   - A culturally responsive counsellor may explicitly address their commitment to cultural competence in their professional statement, indicating an awareness of the importance of cultural sensitivity in the therapeutic relationship.
   - Social media
   - Website
   - Forms

2. Intake and Assessment:

   - Culturally responsive counsellors conduct thorough intake assessments that explore the client's cultural background, experiences, and values. They recognise the influence of culture on mental health and tailor their approach accordingly.

3. Reflective Listening:

   - A culturally responsive counsellor practises active listening, demonstrating genuine interest in the client's unique experiences and perspectives. They validate the client's feelings and acknowledge the impact of cultural factors on their well-being.

4. Open Dialogue:

   - Culturally responsive counsellors foster open dialogue about cultural identities, experiences of discrimination, and the intersectionality of various cultural factors. They create a safe space for clients to discuss issues related to their cultural background.

5. Inclusive Language:

   - A culturally responsive counsellor uses inclusive language that respects and affirms the diversity of the client's cultural identity. They avoid making assumptions based on stereotypes and strive to understand the client's unique experience.

6. Cultural Humility:

    - Cultural humility involves an ongoing commitment to self-awareness and critical reflection and a willingness to learn from clients. A culturally responsive counsellor acknowledges their own cultural biases, engages in continuous education, and adapts their approach based on client feedback.

7. Tailored Interventions:

    - Effective counsellors tailor interventions to align with the client's cultural background, values, and beliefs. They recognise that a one-size-fits-all approach may not be suitable for clients with diverse cultural experiences.

8. Awareness of Intersectionality:

    - Culturally responsive counsellors understand and consider the intersectionality of various cultural identities (e.g., race, gender, sexual orientation, socioeconomic status) that contribute to the client's experiences and challenges.

9. Cultural Knowledge:

    - A culturally responsive counsellor demonstrates knowledge of diverse cultures, traditions, and cultural norms. They are open to learning about cultures that may differ from their own and seek to understand the cultural context of the client's life.

10. Feedback and Collaboration:

    - Clients should feel encouraged to provide feedback about the counselling process, including whether they feel their cultural needs are being met. A culturally responsive counsellor values client input and collaborates with clients to adjust as needed.

11. Referral Network:

    - If a counsellor recognises the need for specialised cultural expertise beyond their own, they should have a network of referral resources to ensure clients receive the most appropriate support.

Conclusion

In conclusion, cultural responsiveness in psychotherapy, counselling, and psychology practice should emphasise the importance of fostering effective therapeutic relationships and promoting positive outcomes. Cultural responsiveness acknowledges and respects the diversity of clients' backgrounds, including their cultural, ethnic, religious, and social identities. It also emphasises the importance of understanding how these factors influence clients' experiences, beliefs, values, and behaviours. By being culturally responsive, counsellors can improve communication working with culturally diverse clients. This includes using language and concepts that are meaningful and respectful to clients, thus enhancing the therapeutic alliance. Understanding how to tailor counselling approaches to align with clients' cultural contexts can lead to more effective outcomes including positive mental health and well-being.

It is ethically imperative for counsellors to provide services that are respectful and responsive to the cultural backgrounds of their clients. This includes understanding and adhering to professional ethical guidelines related to cultural competence. Cultural responsiveness requires ongoing self-awareness, critical reflection, and sensitivity to one's own cultural biases and assumptions. Counsellors need to continually educate themselves about different cultures and be open to learning from their clients. Most importantly, cultural responsiveness is a journey of continuous learning and growth. Counsellors should engage in ongoing training, supervision, and reflection to enhance their cultural responsiveness and effectiveness in practice.

Integrating cultural responsiveness into counselling practices is not just about being politically correct; it is about honouring the humanity and dignity of every client. It enhances the quality of care provided and contributes to more inclusive and equitable mental health services.

Culturally responsive work can be challenging but it is deeply rewarding for clients and counsellors, educators, and researchers.

The following chapters will offer a deep dive into more specific areas of cultural responsiveness including education, research and clinical supervision as well as addressing specific streams within the disciple including Clinical Practice, School Counselling, Rehabilitation Counselling, Relationship Counselling, and Community Counselling.

References

American Counseling Association (ACA). (2014). Code of ethics. https://www.counseling.org/

Crenshaw, K., Gotanda, N. T., Peller, G., & Thomas, K. (1996). *Critical race theory. The key writings that formed the movement.* The New Press. ISBN: 978-1-56584-271-7.

Dulaney, M. (2018). Mental illness and poverty: How class get 'under our skin and into our brain'. *ABC News.* https://www.abc.net.au/news/2018-04-13/is-your-class-status-making-you-depressed-mental-health/9598170

Eisenstein, Z. (1978). The Combahee River collective statement. In R. Timothy. (Ed.). What is intersectionality? All of who I am. *The Conversation.* https://theconversation.com/what-is-intersectionality-all-of-who-i-am-105639

Fisher, M. (2021). Classism. In V. Hutton & S. Sisko (Eds.), *Multicultural responsiveness in counselling and psychology, working with Australian populations* (pp. 106–112). Palgrave.

Fisher-Borne, M., Montana Cain, J., & Martin, S. L. (2015). From mastery to accountability: Cultural humility as an alternative to cultural competence. Social Work Education. *The International Journal, 34*(2). https://doi.org/10.1080/02615479.2014.977244

Funder, A. (2023). *Wifedom, Mrs Orwell's invisible life.* Hamish Hamilton.

Gardner, F. (2014). *Being critically reflective.* Palgrave.

Gee, G., Dudgeon, P., Schultz, C., Hart, A., & Kelly, K. (2014). Aboriginal and Torres Strait Islander social and emotional well-being. In P. Dudgeon, H. Milroy, & R. Walker (Eds.), *Working together: Aboriginal and Torres Strait Islander mental health and wellbeing principles and practice* (2nd ed.). Australian Government Department of the Prime Minister and Cabinet.

Goodman, L., Liang, B., Helms, J. E., Latta, R. E., Sparks, E., & Weintraub, S. R. (2004). Training counseling psychologists as social justice agents: Feminist and Multicultural Principles I Action. *The Counseling Psychologist, 32*, 793. https://doi.org/10.1007/978-1-4939-1283-4

Gorski, P. C., & Goodman, R. D. (2015). Introduction: Toward decolonized multicultural counselling and psychology. In R. D. Goodman & P. C. Gorski (Eds.), *Decolonizing "Multicultural" counseling through social justice.* Springer. https://doi.org/10.1007/978-1-4939-1283-4

Helms, J. E. (1998). Toward a model of white racial identity development. Routledge. ISBN: 9781315051888

Hernandez-Wolfe, P. (2011). Decolonization and "mental" health: A Mestiza's journey in the borderlands. *Women & Therapy, 34*(3), 293. https://doi.org/10.1080/02703149.2011.580687

McIntosh, P. (1989, July). Invisible knapsack. In *Peace and freedom magazine* (pp. 10–12). Women's International League for Peace and Freedom.

Psychotherapy and Counselling Federation of Australia (PACFA). (2017). Code of ethics. https://pacfa.org.au/

Ratts, M. J. (2011). Multiculturalism and social justice: Two sides of the same coin. *Journal of Multicultural Counseling and Development, 39*, 24–37. https://doi.org/10.1002/j.2161-1912.2011.tb00137.x

Rodó-de-Zárate, M. (2014). Developing geographies of intersectionality with relief maps: Reflections from youth research in Manresa, Catalonia. *Gender, Place & Culture, 21*(8), 925–944. https://doi.org/10.1080/0966369X.2013.817974

Sue, D. W., Arredondo, P., & McDavis, R. J. (1992). Multicultural counseling competencies and standards: A call to the profession. *Journal of Multicultural Counseling and Development, 20*(2), 64–88. https://doi.org/10.1002/j.2161-1912.1992.tb00563

Sue, D. W., & Sue, D. (2016). *Counseling the culturally diverse: Theory and practice*. John Wiley & Sons.

CHAPTER 2

Cultural Responsiveness in Education

Mariaimeé Gonzalez, Katherine Fort, Jude Bergkamp, and Keiko Sano

Introduction

Culturally responsive teaching, also referred to as culturally relevant teaching, is a pedagogy that honors the cultural experiences of the students as individuals, but also honors the students as a cultural community within the classroom (Gay, 2018). This cultural response in teaching allows the teacher to co-create a learning space with students that promotes equity, inclusivity and belonging in the classroom, engages one another in the course materials, encourages critical thinking, and honors students' sense of their cultural identity as an individual and as a group. Culturally responsive teaching has many shapes and forms, which allows room for integration, innovation, adaptably, and cultural reflectivity (Gay, 2018).

M. Gonzalez (✉) • K. Fort • J. Bergkamp
School of Applied Psychology, Counseling and Family Therapy, Antioch University, Seattle, WA, USA
e-mail: mymae78@hotmail.com; kfort@antioch.edu; jbergkamp@antioch.edu

K. Sano
Counselor Education, Antioch University, Seattle, WA, USA
e-mail: ksano@antioch.edu

S. Sisko (ed.), *Culturally Responsive Psychotherapy, Counselling & Psychology*, Palgrave Texts in Counselling and Psychotherapy,
https://doi.org/10.1007/978-3-031-81831-8_2

Historical Foundations of Educational Theory

In seeking to understand the relevance and imperative of educational processes conducted from a culturally responsive stance, the history and function of education itself should first be considered. The broader philosophical function of education includes several transcultural attributes across history. Primarily, these include the development of more economically, politically, spiritually, and morally robust societies, as well as improved critical thinking, holistic awareness, balance and the passing of cultural heritage over generations, where both non-Western and Western philosophers have stressed the importance of these attributes in the educational process (Dewey, 1916, 1938; Kant, 2003; Li, 2012; Noddings, 1995; Tan, 2016). Plato and Aristotle investigated the process of human knowledge acquisition, otherwise known as *epistemology* (Plato, 1997; Aristotle, 1984).

Within the disciplines of counseling, education and psychology, specific learning theories most commonly stem from either *constructivism* or *postmodernism*. These include the theories of Piaget, Kegan, Kohlberg, and others who posit slightly different epistemologies or ways of knowing that describe the process of learning (McAuliffe & Eriksen, 2011). In considering each, it can be helpful to consider the following questions for personal reflection:

How do we "know" something to be "true"?
Who teaches us what we "know"?
When do we know something "for ourselves"?
How is the learning process culturally laden?
Who and what challenge(s) us to grow in our thinking and how is this done effectively?

From the philosophical stance of constructivism, individuals actively create the world as they experience it and meaning takes place within a social construction of reality (including personal, political, cultural, historical). The following questions are considered from a constructivist point of view:

What meaning can be derived from this time and place in history, as counselor educators? Whose experiences are more widely represented and whose are not?
What is the impact on learning systems?
What social constructions inform your assumptions?

Further, constructivism seeks to reject absolutes, consider power dynamics, celebrate differences, and consider not just the what, but the how of knowledge and the learning process (McAuliffe & Eriksen, 2011).

Post-modernism guides the educator to consider the context of the learning environment, the social locations and intersectional identities of the educator and the learner, and seeks learning outcomes where transformational interpretations exist, taking in multiple perspectives at once (McAuliffe & Eriksen, 2011). Paolo Friere (1970) was foundational in developing this critical stance in educational theory, where students are encouraged to critically think about social issues, power dynamics, and systems of oppression in order to become agents of change in their communities. From this, more specific culturally responsive teaching strategies have been recognized as critical in order to positively leverage the strengths that individual students bring to the learning environment (Howard, 2010). Additionally, more intentional awareness of racial and cultural dynamics was brought to the foreground as imperative attributes to consider, highlight and give voice to within the classroom setting. In order to operationalize these aims, inclusive curriculum development practices have grown more and more fundamental within these related disciplines. This includes designing educational materials that reflect the cultural backgrounds, histories, and experiences of students from various ethnic, racial, and socio-economic backgrounds as well as assessment methods that allow students to demonstrate their understanding and skills in ways that are culturally relevant to them (Gay, 2010; Wiggins & McTighe, 2005).

The following table (Table 2.1) comprises a non-exhaustive list of some of the most commonly utilized culturally responsive practices in educational environments:

Impact in the Counseling Profession

Culturally responsive teaching aligns with the counseling profession's ethical codes. Counselor educators have a professional duty to guarantee inclusion and representation of diverse global perspectives, as outlined by our ethical guidelines (American Counseling Association, 2014). Culturally responsive teaching, such as illuminating student's cultural assets, creating a contextual learning experience, activating students' prior knowledge, creating spaces rooted in collectivism, provide an opportunity

Table 2.1 Common culturally responsive practices in education

Educational Approach/ Activity	*Culturally Responsive attributes*	*Non-inclusive Attributes*	*Additional Notes*
Curricular Revision	Reflecting, gathering critical feedback from various voices and diverse constituents that aid in revising course content and delivery practices and include more diverse representation.	Can be problematic in a "check box" format and provide a false sense of security or proof of actual decolonization/ impactful/ representative revision.	This is a reflexive and iterative process that should involve communities of educators and learners.
Diversifying Faculty	Recruiting and retaining more diverse faculty voices and experiences in order to improve representation.	Faculty may not experience true support and/or community within the academic system, as well as possibly experience harm/ microaggressions.	This process should be student centered; students should be a part of the faculty hiring process and decision-making. Incoming faculty should be carefully supported and potentially mentored in affinity with other minoritized faculty.
Critical Pedagogy	Reading and implementing work by critical pedagogy theorists like Paulo Freire, bell hooks, or Henry Giroux.	Current political climate that pushes back against Critical Race Theory (CRT) and unjustly vilify faculty who implement equity strategies grounded in CRT ideology.	Special attention should be given to include many theoretical stances within historical context so that students are fully informed of socio-political and historical underpinnings impacting theory development and utilization.
Community Engagement	Community-engaged scholarship or service learning.	Universities should make special effort to provide budget for such engagement practices.	There is a danger in tokenizing minoritized groups if proper long-term support and follow-through is not budgeted and/or planned.

(*continued*)

Table 2.1 (continued)

Educational Approach/ Activity	*Culturally Responsive attributes*	*Non-inclusive Attributes*	*Additional Notes*
Language Justice	Including resources from organizations like the Center for Applied Linguistics or the American Council on the Teaching of Foreign Languages that promote language diversity and equity.	Language evolves quickly and is a part of many layers of academic evaluation, which should be carefully considered.	It is important to include educational support staff in these practices, such as library staff, tutors, etc.
Decolonizing Research	Including materials that discuss decolonial methodologies in research.	Many institutions do not fully recognize "non-traditional" methodologies.	Inclusion of cross-disciplinary research practices may be helpful.
Institutional Accountability	Implementing outcomes evaluation and reporting practices and/or policy documents within programs/ universities/ organizations that outline diversity and inclusion initiatives or address discrimination.	Many institutions struggle to shed light on their more negative histories that have caused harm to individuals or communities. In order to best practice such accountability, it may be imperative to bring in external support programs.	Accreditation considerations should be included in this process.
Reparative Justice	Practices and scholarly works or reports on reparations, memorialization efforts, or indigenous rights movements.	This should be an intentional process that is not rushed.	A collective lens should be used.
Global Solidarity	Work that discusses transnational activism, global social movements, or postcolonial theory.	This can be difficult to execute without budget and/or intentional networking.	Partnering with other educational programs around the globe, even in exchange for ideas, can be a good start.

(*continued*)

Table 2.1 (continued)

Educational Approach/ Activity	*Culturally Responsive attributes*	*Non-inclusive Attributes*	*Additional Notes*
Self-interrogation	Work by critical theorists or practitioners in higher education who emphasize self-reflection and critical consciousness.	Risks being conducted in a silo if not approached collectively.	This is a reflexive process that should unfold ecologically over time.
Social Justice	Reflection and utilization of ecological models that look at systems of privilege and oppression within an ecological context and enact change through action.	Some students and educators shy away from social justice with the misconception that one must be an extroverted advocate.	There are many forms of advocacy and working in community to highlight the best options for each individual can help to social justice come alive in education.
Cultural Reflexivity	Constant comparison and evaluation of program effectiveness in relation to DEIJ experiences and subjects.	This requires a certain level of insight and self-awareness.	Literature should be consistently reviewed and social locations revisited.

for diverse experiences and viewpoints to be represented in the classroom community (Gay, 2018). Additionally, the Council for the Accreditation of Counseling and Related Educational Programs (CACREP, 2016) illuminates the value of teaching about social and cultural diversity in section 2.F.2. CACREP (2016) recognizes social and cultural diversity as one of the "eight common areas [that] represent the foundational knowledge required of all entry-level counselor education graduates" (2.F.) To stay congruent with the profession's ethical and accreditation standards, Counselor Educators can highlight the power of diversity, inclusion, and belonging through culturally responsive teaching within their classrooms (Ramsay-Seaner et al., 2022).

Teaching Through Modeling

Experiential learning, application, and teaching styles are identified as the first, second, and third prominent themes in effective teaching in counselor education (Hurt-Avila et al., 2020). Examples of experiential learning include case studies, role-play, and reflective practice (Fernandez, 2013). By facilitating culturally responsive teaching, instructors can create unique and meaningful learning experiences for students by engaging them in invaluable "here-and-now" moments of learning. To facilitate these experiences, instructors need to demonstrate their skills and competence in identifying teaching opportunities, as well as the goals and purposes of using these opportunities for students' learning experiences. However, modeling can often be more challenging than presenting teaching materials or sharing knowledge through dialogue.

Barriers to Modeling Culturally Responsive Teaching

In counselor education, teaching and modeling are two different approaches. Unlike directive instructional learning in teaching, modeling can include demonstrating empathy, professional communication skills, cultural awareness, and ethical practices, which can go beyond demonstrating knowledge or counseling skills. Modeling can occur in the relationship with the students, which relies on students' observations and subjective experiences. In the meantime, modeling culturally responsive teaching can be challenging for instructors for various reasons.

Educational and Theoretical Perspectives

The medical model (Teem, 2022) and Eurocentric perspectives influence the theories of counseling and psychology, as well as theories in teaching and supervision (Durrah et al., 2022). Traditionally, theories of counseling and psychology were developed in Western contexts, and counselor education and training are facilitated within Western values (Interiano & Lim, 2018). Due to the differences in culturally influenced values and perspectives, practical approaches in modeling cultural responsiveness can be difficult to apply globally without deconstructing those Eurocentric views.

For instance, cognitive behavioral therapy [CBT], developed by Beck in the 1960s, is often discussed as one of the most empirically studied psychotherapy forms (Butler et al., 2006). Because CBT emphasizes the shift of clients' thoughts, feelings, and behavior, this theory expects clients to talk about their feelings with their clinicians. However, it is important to be aware of the fundamental cultural differences in expressing feelings. Unlike Western approaches, which value direct verbal expressions (Enns & Kasai, 2003), individuals from certain cultures value non-verbal communication (Iwakabe, 2008) and do not verbalize their feelings. Instead of assuming talking about feelings is universal, respecting culturally unique communication styles is essential.

Just like this example, perspectives or traditional theories can be incongruent with individuals from the values and perspectives of individuals. Therefore, teaching traditional theories by assuming their universality results in failing to demonstrate cultural considerations and can harm clients. Similarly, instructors' teaching philosophy is influenced by their theoretical perspectives, developmental aspects, learning strategy facilitation, beliefs about education, and student learning goals (Hall et al., 2021). When an instructor's own counseling theories or teaching philosophy are developed within the Western context, their fundamental approaches are often associated with those Western values and perspectives. Especially because traditional theories do not consider the diversity of clinicians or instructors, discussing cultural considerations within that framework can be skewed to the ideas of multiculturalism within the Western context.

Physical and Environmental Challenges

Challenges in Classrooms. A sense of safety is a fundamental component of learning, yet developing and maintaining a safe learning environment is not always guaranteed. Regardless of the instructor's effort or awareness, students do not always express or report when they are not feeling safe or comfortable participating in the classroom because they lack the safety to do so. Microaggressions in the classrooms can be difficult to identify and become even more difficult in a larger classroom. Also, although being uncomfortable is a critical part of counselor training, this experience can be misunderstood or dismissed to further exploring or discussing when there is another agenda, such as covering the course curriculum or focusing on the course materials.

Challenges in Program. Counselor education programs often face various limitations, including time and funding constraints, while maintaining compliance with accreditation-required curricula (Budesa & Barrio Minton, 2022). The accreditation criteria and licensure requirements determine the course contexts and students' competence. Time constraints also pose challenges in balancing coverage of required course contents and facilitation of community or relationship building, experiential learning, or meaningful discussions exploring students' perspectives further.

For example, discussing real-time social events can help students practice reflective self-explorations or learn about local systems or resources. Even though the instructor believes continuing these discussions with the students is more relevant than discussing the given materials, they have limited time to cover those. As a result, the discussion time is cut short and immature.

Furthermore, the students' in-class experiences can be invaluable learning opportunities for them to understand the group dynamics and its development, as well as to increase self-awareness. Their learning opportunities can extend outside of the classroom, such as student groups, community activity, and professional organization engagement. However, in addition to the time constraint in the classrooms, instructors face challenges in finding time to support those students' learning opportunities because of their other professional obligations, such as meeting tenure requirements or administration work for accreditation, regardless of their willingness to spend more time directly with their students.

Challenges in Institution. Working in an institutional culture where diversity is not truly emphasized or respected can block instructors and students from engaging in culturally relevant teaching and learning. Although modeling cultural responsiveness can begin with an individual, developing an inclusive community or culture in the classroom or the institution is extremely challenging to advocate alone without collaboration or support from colleagues or the institution. When the institution is structured with leaders from dominant populations, ignores students' voices, or is unwilling to recognize or respect diversity, the organizational system and culture negatively influence and deliver incongruent messages from what counseling and psychology programs are aiming at in modeling inclusion and cultural sensitivity.

Historical and Sociocultural Experiences

Our culture and experiences can form specific narratives, values, biases, stereotypes, and assumptions and influence our perspectives. They can also block self-awareness, reduce our ability to take risks, and/or overlook critical moments. For example, when a student has difficulty engaging in a clinical skill practice session with another student, some instructors may perceive the situation as the student's lack of preparedness or competence, whereas other instructors may perceive it as cultural dynamics or interpersonal issues. Some instructors may not notice the situation, and other instructors may be aware of the situation but rely on the students' accountability. These differences are usually influenced by their previous experiences in facing similar situations or culturally influenced narratives they have internalized. Biases and assumptions associated with previous challenging experiences, including cultural norms and trauma, can create hesitation in modeling culturally relevant approaches as well.

Emotional Challenges
Guilt and shame have been studied well in clinical practice to be influential on individuals' behaviors through the self-reflection process (Heflin, 2015). Similarly, guilt and shame influence teaching because they are experienced in the relationships with their students, particularly in self-awareness, self-exploration, and emotional stability. Guilt and shame can manifest as distress, low compassion, and low self-esteem, and can likely lead to engaging in unethical decision-making.

When a student states their instructor engaged in microaggression in the classroom, the instructor may feel they made a huge mistake and harmed the student because the class frequently discusses microaggression. These concerns can increase their anxiety associated with their shame and guilt. Those emotional experiences can create blockages from the instructor's seeing the situation objectively. The student may take a risk to practice their confrontation skills, they may feel comfortable enough to call in the instructor, or they may have a different meaning or purpose through their statement. However, it is difficult for the instructor to pay attention to various possibilities because of their inner dialogues.

Understanding possible barriers to demonstrating culturally relevant teaching and learning is as important as understanding strategies for learning and modeling them. However, these barriers are not always recognizable, and increasing self-awareness can be limited to thinking about, processing, or reflecting on experiences alone.

Foundational Concepts in Culturally Responsive Counselor Education

The ghosts of colonization throughout the fourteenth to nineteenth centuries are haunting the globe today, and lurk within counselor education. Colonial techniques of exploitation, dehumanization, caste, and cultural manipulation have been consistent across time, place, and situation. Specific colonial strategies include mass violence, the concept of property, laws, taxes, racialized medicine, and for this chapter, education. Each colonized region was stripped of indigenous ways of knowing and being, along with earned intellectual, relational, and physical resources. Yet, within an international context, the colonial process has been diverse and the impact distinct. Colonized regions have unique cultures, geography, social structures, and psychology. Each region also had differing colonizing forces ranging from the Portuguese and Spanish to the English and Dutch. Thus, the unique combination of colonizer and colonized, as well as the recency of colonization and the process of feigned independence produces a specific dynamic for each region.

While the dominant discourse represents colonization in historical terms, the techniques and consequences are still very much a contemporary force; possibly the most powerful force inspiring the structural oppression of our daily lives across the globe. The field of psychology has seen revolving calls toward diversity, multiculturalism, cultural competency and humility, and social justice and social responsiveness (Bergkamp, 2022). Counseling education is in a pivotal moment in which it needs to both aspire to these values while simultaneously reconciling its own part in colonial oppression over history and into the present. We use the same terms without a clear understanding of the distinctness and recency of colonization that we have been ingrained and educated within. Could it be that when counselors utilize these terms in one region, it means something very different in another, due to the historical forces of the colonial combination? How might these terms be contextualized in North America versus Africa versus Australia? Could the colonial ghosts continue to haunt us, separate and confuse us, despite our best efforts?

In this section, the authors will define colonization, colonialism, and colonial mindset. Then, contemporary concepts of social privilege awareness, dysconsciousness, and principles of critical race theory will be introduced. Finally, implications for decolonial and liberatory education will be articulated.

Colonization, Colonialization, and Coloniality

Colonialization refers to the historical large-scale expansion of nation-states by taking control of foreign land and the indigenous populace utilizing supremist philosophy. Colonization refers to the process of establishing outpost colonies that centralize these efforts. Thus, colonization is the act, while colonialization is the intention and rationale motivating the behavior. The most profound example of mass colonialization is that of the Colonial Era in which Western European countries, such as England, France, Spain, Prussia (Germany), and the Netherlands, traveled to lands that were considered "discovered" or "new," including Africa, Latin America, Australia, North America, and Asia. These European countries' expansionist efforts were supported by an ideology of supremacy instrumentalized through the institutions of religion, science, economics, and the military. This ideology was driven by the European Enlightenment and the coming of modernity, including capitalism, urbanization, the decentralization of the home as the center of industry, and militarization. Both the U.S. and South Asia have been influenced and formed by colonial forces, primarily the British, yet in dramatically different ways.

Distinct from historical acts of colonialization are the powerful remnant forces of coloniality. Coloniality refers to the often-unspoken, hierarchical system of influence and power that has governed interactions between countries since the beginning of the colonial era. This hierarchy places formal colonies at the bottom of the global power structure and the most vigorously colonizing states at the top. Although specific countries have formed, changed, and disintegrated throughout history, thereby altering the ordering of states within the hierarchy of coloniality, the hierarchical framework itself persists. In today's globalized society it can be seen across the realms of politics, economics, and cultural influence, where many of the most influential countries are also former colonizing powers (Quijano & Wallerstein, 1992). This dynamic results in the active reenactment and reification of colonial worldview and practice that permeates our education, relationships, economics, and psychology. Coloniality is a powerful influence on Western psychology's definition of what is functional, normal, and healthy. To reiterate, while colonialization is not a metaphor, and instead refers to historical atrocities, coloniality is the current manifestation that permeates our daily lives (Bhatia, 2018).

Socially Conferred Privilege

The contemporary manifestation of historical colonialism is socially conferred privilege (Bergkamp et al., 2022). Black and Stone (2005) provide an accessible definition of social privilege: First, privilege is a special advantage; it is neither common nor universal. Second, it is granted, not earned or brought into being by one's individual effort or talent. Third, privilege is a right or entitlement that is related to a preferred status or rank. Fourth, privilege is exercised for the benefit of the recipient and to the exclusion or detriment of others. Finally, a privileged status is often outside of the awareness of the person possessing it (p. 244).

Social privilege is tied to the ranks of an individual's positionality, also called social location, which "offers that all persons have a position in relation to others within a society" (Hearn, 2012, p. 42). An individual's positionality is socialized by their overlapping social identities of race, sex, class, gender, ability, age, religion, sexual orientation, indigenous heritage, and nationality, and the meanings these identities have within society (Hays, 2022). These socialized positionalities contribute to an individual's beliefs, attitudes, biases, and preferences. An individual might occupy a rank of social privilege in some of these identity domains, thus being afforded special rights in society, and a rank of social oppression in others, thus being denied special rights. This also varies depending on the legacy of geographic colonial context.

Dysconsciousness

A psychologically descriptive explanation for why privilege awareness is so elusive is dysconsciousness concept of King (1991). Although Goodman (2015) links privilege and oppression generally, King connected Black and Stone's final condition of privilege to the cognitive and subsequent behavioral reinforcement of systems of oppression when she described dysconsciousness: Dysconsciousness is an uncritical habit of mind (including perceptions, attitudes, assumptions, and beliefs) that justifies inequity and exploitation by accepting the existing order of things as given. This lack of critical judgment against society reflects an absence of what Cox (1974) refers to as "social ethics"; it involves a subjective identification with an ideological viewpoint that admits no fundamentally alternative vision of society (1991, p. 135). This last aspect of dysconsciousness is the primary obstacle for agents (individuals with privilege) to consider its implications.

Principles of Critical Race Theory

Critical Race Theory (CRT) is a culmination of critical theory, Black feminism, and legal studies focused on the paradoxical results of colorblind laws enacted during the post-civil rights era (Taylor et al., 2009). U.S. legal scholars asserted that racial discrepancies were only increasing, despite, or possibly because of, laws that feigned racial equality but resulted in the resegregation of schools, falling economic outcomes for BIPOC workers, and increasing the number of BIPOC individuals stuck in the criminal justice system. Over time, CRT has developed into a multidisciplinary field of study with contributions from scholars in legal studies, education, sociology, and psychology. Notably, it has recently come under criticism from politicians claiming reverse racism and the degradation of American values.

CRT's pillars include social construction, differential racialization, the norms of racism, institutionalized racism, interest convergence, and intersectionality (Delgado & Stefancic, 2001). The following is only a cursory summary of these important concepts. CRT asserts that the biogenetic notion of race was refuted in the late twentieth century and holds no true genotype/phenotype. Yet race is a social construct, and racism is constantly established and reinforced through social norms and interactions. Thus, while race itself is not a valid scientific phenomenon, racism very much exists through social agreement and is operationalized through institutions.

Differential racialization is the instrumental use of dynamic stereotypes that fit the needs of white supremacy. A common example is the move from slave-era attributions of African Americans as childlike, helpless, simple-minded, and in need of guidance and direction to the post-civil rights era attributions as deviant, dangerous, and parasitic. Despite the change in stereotypes over time, essential notions of inferiority, immorality, and biological deficiency persist.

Another pillar of CRT is directly refuting the common and convenient misconception that racism is an occasional incident of prejudice or discrimination perpetrated by ill-intentioned, racist individuals, usually occurring in an interpersonal context. Instead, CRT asserts that racism is a norm in America, and it is perpetually occurring at multiple levels and directions. While the dominant discourse in America might appear less racist, especially for white individuals, racial disparities continue to persist and increase despite the civil rights laws of decades ago.

A related pillar is the fact that racism is inherently baked into the institutional structures of America. While America was founded on an overt rejection of colonial structures, it ironically recapitulated the systems it claimed to disown. An institution has been defined as an established organization, custom, law, or principle that serves a particular purpose in society. Our governmental and societal institutions include law, economy, education, military, medical, infrastructure, religion, media, and society. CRT asserts that these institutions are based on systems of white supremacy that are inherently designed to benefit some and exclude others. The focus on "racist individuals" serves as a bypassing distraction, meant to draw attention away from the actuality of structural and institutional racism.

Interest convergence is a sophisticated CRT pillar that contends that social and legal change that seemingly benefits people of color only occurs when it also serves the white majority (Bell, 1980). A common example is the Brown vs. Board of Education landmark decision to desegregate schools. While on the surface, this appears to exemplify values of racial equality, legal scholars claim that this decision occurred during the Cold War with Russia in order to refute any Russian claims that the U.S. engaged in racial oppression (Dudziak, 1988). Interest convergence lasts only as long as the dominant group benefits and will inevitably shift back to oppression.

One of the most popular CRT pillars is intersectionality. This concept, born out of Black Feminism, brings attention to the tendency to minimize Black women to either being Black or a woman, but not both. It serves the purposes of white supremacy to focus on isolated identity domains instead of acknowledging the exponential ramification of embodying multiple oppressed domains simultaneously (Crenshaw, 1989). Recently, the term has been diluted from its original formulation to infer any intersecting identity domain, despite the dynamics of socially conferred privilege and historical oppression. Caution is advised to ensure the core meaning of the term is not co-opted into a white supremacist frame.

Case Study Example of Cultural Responsiveness in Practice

Background

Dr. Muniz is Professor of Counseling teaching a master-level counseling course. Her university is an urban school with a highly diverse student population. Her students come from various cultural backgrounds, including Black, Latine, Asian, and Middle Eastern communities. They are a diverse cohort of students with varying cultural backgrounds such as race, ethnicity, relational orientation, gender, age, ableism, economic status, religion, spiritualty, languages, and more. Dr. Muniz attended professional development workshops on cultural humility, decolonization, and anti-oppression. She learned about different cultural norms, values, and communication styles. This training helped her understand her students' backgrounds better. She revised her curriculum to include content that reflected the diverse cultures of her students. For example, in her counseling lessons, she incorporated stories and contributions from various cultural groups from the global community.

Dr. Muniz adopted a student-centered approach by incorporating students' cultural references in her teaching. She invited students to co-create classroom community guidelines focused on creating brave spaces, and different ways for them to share their cultural experiences and perspectives during class discussions. This made the lessons more relatable and engaging for the students. Recognizing that students learn in different ways, Dr. Muniz employed various teaching methods to cater to different learning styles. She used visual aids, group projects, and hands-on activities to make learning more accessible to all students. Dr. Muniz adapted her assessment methods to be more culturally relevant. She used a variety of assessment tools, including oral presentations, projects, and group work, to evaluate students' understanding. This approach acknowledged the diverse ways students demonstrate their knowledge. By recognizing and valuing the diverse cultural backgrounds of her students, she was able to engage them more deeply in their education and improve their academic outcomes.

Culturally Responsive Strategies

Inclusive Curriculum Design can help set up the community with diverse theoretical perspectives: The curriculum can includes theories and practices from various cultural contexts, such as African American psychology examples include Ubuntu Philosophy, African Self-Consciousness (ASC), Spirit-Centered Psychology, Sankofa (African American Psychology), or African Indigenous Knowledge Systems (AIKS), Latinx psychology theories such a liberation psychology and the Multidimensional Ecosystemic Comparative Approach (MECA), Indigenous psychology such as Kaupapa Māori (Māori Psychology), Hózhó (Navajo Psychology), or Dadirri (Aboriginal Australian Psychology), and Asian psychology such as Confucian Psychology, Taoist Psychology, Japanese Psychology (Naikan and Morita Therapy), or Buddhist Psychology. Case Studies and Research are other methods which highlight cultural considerations in psychological practice, emphasizing the impact of culture on mental health and therapeutic outcomes.

Contextualized Learning

Cultural humility training can be benficial in courses focused on cultural competence and multicultural counseling. These courses cover topics like cultural humility, biases, microaggressions, and the importance of culturally sensitive therapeutic approaches. Would be helpful to get guest lecturers and experts from diverse cultural backgrounds to share their experiences, and insights enhance students' understanding of cultural nuances in psychological practice.

Practical Application

Diverse practicum placements can be helpful for students to get real life experience. Students are placed in practicum settings that serve diverse populations. The practicum experience allows them to apply their knowledge in real-world contexts and develop cultural humility and competence. Placement to help with cultural experience can include but not limited to; work in community health centers that serve diverse populations including immigrants and refugees, university counseling centers focusing on supporting international students and students from diverse backgrounds, non-profits that focus on mental health services for specific cultural groups, such as Black, Latine, LGBTQIA, Asian, or indigenous communities, cultural centers that offer support services to specific ethnic or cultural communities, schools that serve culturally diverse student populations, or hospitals or clinics that serve a diverse patient population. Supervision and Mentorship: Supervision and mentorship are provided by faculty members who emphasize the importance of cultural responsiveness and guide students in navigating cultural issues in their clinical practice. Placements not only provide practical experience but also enhance cultural competence, making future counselors better equipped to serve diverse populations.

Reflective Practice

Students maintain journals and write reflection papers on their experiences with cultural issues in their coursework and practicum placements. This encourages ongoing self-awareness and critical reflection on their cultural biases and assumptions. Regular self-assessment exercises help students evaluate their cultural competence and identify areas for growth.

Community and Student Engagement

Educator and students co-create community guidelines rooted in liberation. These guidelines can include processes for accountability and healing, and acknowledge the emotional labor which can take place in a community. Emotional labor is the need for one group to regulate their emotions to satisfy another group, usually the group holding the most power. In the classroom community, the community should want to acknowledge the diversity present, and not present. As a result of these acknowledgments, it is a goal of this group for the folks that do not tend to hold the weight of emotional labor, to accept the complexity and pervasiveness of emotional labor.

Another method of engagement for students is community outreach projects that address mental health needs in diverse communities. These projects foster a deeper connection with the community and provide practical experience in culturally responsive practice. Clear expectations and thoughtfulness of one's cultural intersections are important when working in the community, and supervision or mentorship can be a helpful approach with the students while they engage in the community.

Research and Scholarship
Students are encouraged to conduct research on culturally relevant topics and to consider cultural factors in their research design and analysis. This includes understanding the cultural context of psychological phenomena and developing culturally sensitive measurement tools. Opportunities for students to publish their research and present at conferences, particularly those focused on multicultural and international psychology, would be helpful for students to engage and share about their research.

Inclusive Learning Environment
Educators are encouraged to co-create brave space for dialogue with the students. This entails creating brave spaces for students to discuss cultural issues, share personal experiences, and learn from each other's perspectives. Facilitated discussions and support groups can help build an inclusive community. A brave space is when a community works together to create an environment with intentionality around sensitive topics and takes culture power, privilege, and oppression into consideration when discussing these topics. The community fosters individual and community accountability and responsibility, and honors the experience of vulnerability when folx share. Creating a brave space includes establishing clear policies and practices for addressing microaggressions and discrimination within the program. This includes training faculty and students on how to recognize and respond to such incidents.

By integrating these culturally responsive strategies into graduate psychology and counseling programs, educators can prepare students to become competent, empathetic, and effective practitioners who are attuned to the cultural dimensions of mental health and well-being.

Conclusion

Cultural responsiveness in education is not just an additive approach to teaching; it is a fundamental shift in how we perceive and engage with diversity in the learning environment. It recognizes and values the rich tapestry of backgrounds, experiences, and perspectives that students bring to the classroom community. By embracing cultural responsiveness, educators can create more inclusive, equitable, and effective learning experiences for all students.

Key Points:

1. **Enhancing Engagement and Learning Outcomes:**
   - Culturally responsive teaching connects curriculum content to students' lives, making learning more relevant and engaging. This approach acknowledges students' cultural references in all aspects of learning, which enhances their motivation, community connection, and academic success.
2. **Promoting Equity, Inclusion, and Belonging:**
   - It addresses and aims to eliminate the achievement gaps between different student groups by acknowledging, celebrating, and valuing diversity. Culturally responsive education fosters an inclusive environment where all students feel respected and valued with a sense of belonging.
3. **Developing Critical Thinking and Empathy:**
   - This approach encourages students to understand and appreciate diverse perspectives, fostering critical thinking skills and empathy. It prepares students to function effectively in a multicultural world by promoting understanding and respect for differences and similarities.
4. **Preparing Culturally Competent Graduates:**
   - In professional fields, such as psychology, counseling, counseling education, and healthcare, cultural competence is essential. Programs that integrate cultural responsiveness prepare graduates to work effectively with diverse populations, ensuring they are equipped to address the needs of all individuals they serve.

5. **Strengthening Community Connections:**
   - Culturally responsive education builds stronger connections between schools and communities. It involves collaboration with families and community members, creating a supportive network that enhances students' learning experiences and outcomes.

The path forward to fully embrace cultural responsiveness in education, institutions, and educators must commit to continuous learning and reflection. This includes:

- **Professional Development:** Investing in ongoing training for educators to develop cultural competence and inclusive teaching practices.
- **Curriculum Review:** Regularly reviewing and revising curricula to ensure diverse perspectives are represented and valued.
- **Policy Implementation:** Establishing policies that promote equity and inclusion at all levels of the education system.
- **Community Engagement:** Building partnerships with communities to ensure that education is responsive to the needs and aspirations of all students.

In conclusion, cultural responsiveness in education is a crucial pathway to creating more inclusive, equitable, and effective learning environments. It empowers counseling and psychology students, enriches the educational experience, and prepares individuals to contribute positively to a diverse and interconnected world. By committing to cultural responsiveness, educators and institutions can play a pivotal role in co-cultivating a more just and inclusive society.

References

American Counseling Association. (2014). 2014 ACA code of ethics. https://www.counseling.org/resources/aca-code-of-ethics.pdf

Aristotle. (1984). Posterior analytics. In J. Barnes (Ed.), *The complete works of Aristotle* (Vol. 1, pp. 114–166). Princeton University Press.

Bell, D. A. (1980). Brown v. Board of Education and the interest convergence dilemma. *Harvard Law Review, 93*, 518.

Bergkamp, J. (2022). Tugging at the root of oppression: Infusing social justice across doctoral level clinical psychology curriculum. *Journal for Social Action in Counseling & Psychology, 14*(1), 37–52. https://doi.org/10.33043/JSACP.14.1.37-52

Bergkamp, J., Olson, L., & Martin, A. (2022). Before allyship: A model of integrating awareness of a privileged social identity. *Frontiers in Psychology: Personality and Social Psychology, 13*, 993610. https://doi.org/10.3389/fpsyg.2022.993610

Bhatia, S. (2018). *Decolonizing psychology: Globalization, social justice, and Indian youth identities.* Oxford University Press.

Black, L. R., & Stone, D. (2005). Expanding the definition of privilege: The concept of social privilege. *Journal of Multicultural Counseling, 33*, 243–255. https://doi.org/10.1002/j.2161-1912.2005.Tb00020.x

Budesa, Z., & Barrio Minton, C. A. (2022). Enhancing counselor education and supervision through deliberate practice. *Teaching and Supervision in Counseling, 4*(1), 5. https://doi.org/10.7290/tsc04k3n1

Butler, A. C., Chapman, J. E., Forman, E. M., & Beck, A. T. (2006). The empirical status of cognitive-behavioral therapy: A review of meta-analyses. *Clinical Psychology Review, 26*(1), 17–31. https://doi.org/10.1016/j.cpr.2005.07.003

Counsel for Accreditation of Counseling and Related Educational Programs. (2016). 2016 CACREP standards. http://www.cacrep.org/wp-content/uploads/2018/05/2016-Standards-with-Glossary-5. 3.2018.pdf

Cox, G. O. (1974). *Education for the Black Race.* African Heritage Studies Publisher.

Crenshaw, K. (1989). Demarginalizing the intersection of race and sex: A Black feminist critique of antidiscrimination doctrine, feminist theory and antiracist politics. *The University of Chicago Legal Forum, 140*, 139–167.

Delgado, D., & Stefancic, J. (2001). *Critical race theory: An introduction.* NYU Press.

Dewey, J. (1916). *Democracy and education: An introduction to the philosophy of education.* Macmillan.

Dewey, J. (1938). *Experience and education.* Macmillan.

Dudziak, M. L. (1988). Desegregation as a cold war imperative. *Stanford Law Review, 41*(1), 61–120. https://doi.org/10.2307/1228836

Durrah, E., Hall, A. H., & Vajda, A. J. (2022). The importance of culturally responsive and Afrocentric theoretical frameworks—A call for more inclusive curriculum in counselor education. In K. Johnson et al. (Eds.), *Developing anti-racist practices in the helping professions: Inclusive theory, pedagogy, and application.* https://doi.org/10.1007/978-3-030-95451-2_3

Enns, C. Z., & Kasai, M. (2003). Hakoniwa: Japanese Sandplay Therapy. *The Counseling Psychologist, 31*(1), 93–112. https://doi.org/10.1177/0011000002239403

Fernandez, M. A. (2013). A model of pedagogy for beginning counselor educators, *VISTAS 2013.* https://www.counseling.org/docs/default-source/vistas/a-model-of-pedagogy-for-beginning-counselor-educators.pdf?sfvrsn=8

Freire, P. (1970). *Pedagogy of the oppressed*. Herder and Herder.
Gay, G. (2010). *Culturally responsive teaching: Theory, research, and practice* (2nd ed.). Teachers College Press.
Gay, G. (2018). *Culturally responsive teaching: Theory, research and practice* (3rd ed.). Teachers College Press.
Goodman, D. J. (2015). Oppression and privilege: Two sides of the same coin. *Journal of Intercultural Communication, 18*, 1–14.
Hall, D. P., Waalkes, P. L., & Smith, P. H. (2021). A content analysis of counselor educators' teaching philosophy statements. *Journal of Counselor Preparation and Supervision, 14*(1) https://digitalcommons.sacredheart.edu/jcps/vol14/iss1/3
Hays, P. A. (2022). *Addressing cultural complexities in practice: Assessment, diagnosis, and therapy* (4th ed.). American Psychological Association.
Hearn, M. C. (2012). Positionality, intersectionality, and power: Socially locating the higher education teacher in multicultural education. *Multicultural Education Review, 4*, 38–59. https://doi.org/10.1080/2005615X.2011.11102893
Heflin, S. (2015). *Attachment and shame-coping style: A relationship mediated by fear of compassion?* (UMI No. 371240) [Doctoral dissertation, University of Missouri-Kansas City]. ProQuest Dissertations and Theses database.
Howard, T. C. (2010). *Why race and culture matter in schools: Closing the achievement gap in America's classrooms*. Teachers College Press.
Hurt-Avila, K. M., Barrio Minton, C. A., & Dunbar, E. T. (2020). Exploring counselor educator dispositions related to teaching. *Journal of Counselor Preparation and Supervision, 13*(2). https://doi.org/10.7729/42.1375
Interiano, C. G., & Lim, J. H. (2018). A "Chameleonic" identity: Foreign-born doctoral students in U.S. counselor education. *International Journal of Advance Counseling, 40*(3), 310–325. https://doi.org/10.1007/s10447-018-9328-0
Iwakabe, S. (2008). Psychotherapy integration in Japan. *Journal of Psychotherapy Integration, 18*(1), 103–125. https://doi.org/10.1037/1053-0479.18.1.103
Kant, I. (2003). *On education*. (A. Churton, Trans.). Dover Publications. (Original work published 1803).
King, J. E. (1991). Dysconscious racism: Ideology, identity, and the miseducation teachers. *Journal of Negro Education, 60*, 133–146. https://doi.org/10.2307/2295605
Li, J. (2012). *Cultural foundations of learning: East and West*. Cambridge University Press.
McAuliffe, G., & Eriksen, K. (Eds.). (2011). *Handbook of counselor preparation: Constructivist, developmental, and experiential approaches*. Sage/ACES.
Noddings, N. (1995). *Philosophy of education*. Westview Press.
Plato. (1997). *Theaetetus*. In J. M. Cooper & D. S. Hutchinson (Eds.), *Plato: Complete works* (pp. 157–234). Hackett Publishing Company.

Quijano, A., & Wallerstein, I. (1992). Americanity as a concept, or the Americas in the modern world-system. *International Social Science Journal, 44*(134), 549.

Ramsay-Seaner, K., Sandusky, B., Heckmann, C., Knippling, K., & East, C. (2022). Culturally responsive teaching recommendations for the inclusion of multimedia in counselor education. *Journal of Creativity in Mental Health, 1–14*, 1–14. https://doi.org/10.1080/15401383.2022.2151718

Tan, C. (2016). Beyond 'either-or' thinking: John Dewey and Confucius on subject matter and the learner. *Educational Philosophy and Theory, 48*(12), 1243–1252.

Taylor, E., Gillborn, D., & Ladson-Billings, G. (Eds.). (2009). *Foundations of critical race theory in education*. Routledge.

Teem, M. E. (2022). *Influence of the medical model on counseling identity: Counselor educators' experience* (29992842) [Doctoral dissertation, Mercer University]. Proquest.

Wiggins, G., & McTighe, J. (2005). *Understanding by design* (2nd ed.). Pearson.

CHAPTER 3

Cultural Responsiveness in Research

Katherine Fort, John A. Conteh, and Mariaimeé Gonzalez

Introduction

Research is a science that involves the systematic quest for knowledge (Ponterotto, 2005). In considering the critical need for culturally responsive research practices, it is important to first unpack the function and philosophical foundations of research, as it pertains specifically to the discipline of counselling. Numerous scholars have described counselling research and notable themes include: the science-practitioner model of research, understanding practical research skills, the importance of establishing a clear research theoretical identity and framework, the direct and indirect impacts of research on counsellor development, the evolution of evidence-based practice, counsellor-education, outcomes, and public policy (Heppner et al., 2008; Ponterotto, 2005). Heppner et al. (2016)

K. Fort (✉) • M. Gonzalez
School of Applied Psychology, Counseling and Family Therapy, Antioch University, Seattle, WA, USA
e-mail: kfort@antioch.edu; mgonzale3z@antioch.edu

J. A. Conteh
School of Education, University of Puget Sound, Tacoma, WA, USA
e-mail: jconteh@pugetsound.edu

S. Sisko (ed.), *Culturally Responsive Psychotherapy, Counselling & Psychology*, Palgrave Texts in Counselling and Psychotherapy,
https://doi.org/10.1007/978-3-031-81831-8_3

describe research as "a never-ending process of successive approximations in which the scientist has a tolerance for ambiguity, a willingness and ability to question, and an ability to entertain competing answers, and conduct empirical tests among them" (p. 5). In this process, the researcher tests certain approximations step-by-step, seeking to uncover "truth" (Heppner et al., 2008).

Research in Counselling: Philosophical Foundations of Human Behaviour

Various research paradigms exist that orient the individual researcher to specific questions and processes of inquiry. A paradigm consists of an interrelated set of assumptions about the social world that provide a philosophical and conceptual framework for organised study (Heppner et al., 2008; Ponterotto, 2005). In the field of counselling, the most commonly described paradigms are *Positivism, Post-Positivism, Constructivism*, and *Critical Theory* (Ponterotto, 2005).

Positivism is a research paradigm traditionally used in the physical sciences where one reality exists, and the researcher is seen as objective (Ponterotto, 2005). It considers research to be a linear process where "the nature of the universe can be known and the scientist's goal is to discover the natural laws that govern objects in the universe" (Ponterotto, 2005, p. 6). In the field of counselling, positivistic research seeks a universal "truth" that best describes specific mental health phenomena.

Similarly, the paradigm of *post-positivism* posits that a "real" reality exists, yet in this framework, the researcher is likely biased from specific lived experiences. Researchers attempt to discover reality, while remembering to consider the impact of known biases, inferences are based on probability (*p*-value in statistics represents probability) (Ponterotto, 2005). A null hypothesis is identified to be tested against. In this framework, all research is viewed as inherently flawed, thus possibly affecting the research process (Ponterotto, 2005).

Constructivism is a paradigm in which there is no absolute truth and where the researcher is an investigator in the world of the subject (Ponterotto, 2005). Research is thus a recursive process in which truth and reality are constructed within the minds of individuals. These constructions are based on experience, social context and may be idiosyncratic, where meaning is created by those in the system of an event. Constructivism utilises the practice of hermeneutics, or the interpretation of data, as well as dialectics, the interactions between researcher and participant (Ponterotto, 2005). Data is meant to lead the researcher on a journey of new knowledge rather than testing previously constructed hypotheses.

The paradigm of *Critical Theory* digs under the fabric of societal "norms" to both check their impact and to create new systems. Through the lens of Critical Theory, one's social constructions are based within political, cultural, social, historical, economic contexts that are created and impacted by people and systems of power (Ponterotto, 2005). Such societally constructed concepts are not "absolute truth" but socially constructed beliefs. Outcomes of Critical Theory include raising consciousness, social action, radical change, and replacing problematic social structures.

Additionally, the paradigm of *Critical Realism* warrants consideration here. Critical Realism was developed by Bhaskar and Hartwig (2010) and it is a philosophical approach to understanding reality that combines a realist ontology with critical epistemology. Critical Realism asserts that while the world is structured and governed by causal mechanisms, our understanding of it is limited by our subjective experiences and scientific enquiry. Critical Realism is often applied in social sciences to examine how deeper structures influence observable events, encouraging researchers to uncover and understand underlying causes in society, which is significant in understanding cultural responsiveness in research.

When it comes to culturally responsive research paradigms in counselling, Constructivism, Critical Theory, and Critical Realism are widely utilised due to the attention given to cultural, intersectional, and contextual factors. In this framework, the researcher is not the expert, but rather an instrument in the process of better understanding. This aligns with the counselling profession itself, where the client is viewed to be the expert on their identity and lived experience.

Counselling Research Methods and Design

Heppner et al. (2008) describe three components comprising the "research trinity" (p. 118). These include design, measurement, and analysis and together are the "backbone" of all research (Heppner et al., 2008, p. 118). It "provides the conceptual framework from which the study is structured and executed" (Heppner et al., 2008, p. 118). Choosing the appropriate research design helps the researcher to best understand the phenomenon or construct and works in tandem with the chosen measurement, analysis and theory—each informing the other (Heppner et al., 2008).

In the field of counselling, several research methods are commonly utilised to explore various aspects of counselling theory, practice, pedagogy, and andragogy. The most frequently used methods include: quantitative research, qualitative research, mixed methods research, action/participatory research, case studies, and programme evaluation (Creswell & Creswell, 2018; Heppner et al., 2008).

Quantitative Research involves the collection and analysis of numerical data to identify patterns, relationships, and trends. Surveys, experiments, and statistical analyses are typical quantitative research methods used in counsellor education to investigate phenomena such as the effectiveness of counselling interventions or factors influencing counsellor development.

Qualitative Research focuses on understanding human experiences, beliefs, and behaviours in depth. Techniques such as individual interviews, focus groups, and observations explore various issues in the field of counselling, such as counsellor identity, the impacts of relational and cultural factors, or the experiences of clients in therapy. The most commonly utilised qualitative approaches include narrative research, phenomenology, grounded theory, ethnography, and case studies (Creswell, 2007). Case studies provide detailed analysis of individual cases, groups, or communities to explore specific experiences in great depth.

Mixed Methods Research combines both quantitative and qualitative approaches and aims to create a comprehensive understanding of a particular research question, linked questions, or phenomenon. Mixed methods studies in counselling typically involve collecting and analysing both numerical data and narrative accounts to explore diverse perspectives and enrich the findings.

Action/Participatory Research involves collaboration between researchers and practitioners to address current problems existing in the real-world. In counselling, action/participatory research may involve counsellors working together with community stakeholders to implement specific strategies, interventions, or programmatic changes.

Programme Evaluation research assesses the effectiveness, efficiency, and outcomes of counselling programmes, interventions, or services. Utilising a variety of more specific research methods, programme evaluation in counsellor education helps provide evidence-based information in order to improve the quality and impact of counselling programmes and services.

When choosing a research method, it is important to deeply consider which method or combination of methods is best suited to the specific research questions, goals, context(s), and available resources. Each method offers distinct advantages and challenges. However, beyond the research method itself lies the greater importance of how the researcher approaches their question, their positionality, the context of the research problem and population, and the impact of the research process on the participants and related communities, past, present, and future. This reflexive process and relational approach are critical in developing trust and in conducting culturally responsive research. To conduct research that is ethically sound and culturally responsive, the researcher must consider the impacts of historically unjust research practices.

The following grid describes some of the most utilised research methods, their pros and cons related to cultural responsiveness, and what we recommend (Table 3.1):

Critical Changes Made to Research Practice

Before the development and implementation of institutional or ethic review boards, many historical research studies in the fields of psychology and counselling were conducted with culturally minoritised communities without ethical guidelines or protection of human participants (Heppner et al., 2016). Studies that enacted extreme abuse of participants include the Tuskegee syphilis experiment, the Nazi medical experiments, the Stanford prison experiment and countless sterilisation experiments on African slaves, and indigenous, Puerto Rican, and African American women (Briggs, 2002; Heppner et al., 2008; Kelm, 1999; Washington, 2008; Zimbardo, 2008). Many important lessons from the history of unethical research practices, such as the advent of ethical guidelines and standards, the practice of informed consent, the intentional protection of vulnerable populations and the consideration of cultural sensitivity, critical reflection, and accountability. Each of these pillars of ethical research practice comprises the components of the institutional review board (IRB) application process when researching human subjects. Researchers are expected to report their findings accurately, avoid conflicts of interest, and uphold the highest standards of scientific integrity.

Ethical Guidelines and Standards

The history of unethical research practices has led to the development of rigorous ethical guidelines and standards for research involving human

Table 3.1 Research methods

Method	*Quantitative/ Qualitative*	*Pros*	*Cons*	*Recommendations*
Single subject design	Quantitative	Detailed analysis of the effect of an intervention; practical; flexible	Not generalisable; external validity is limited; hard to replicate	Pay close attention to individual differences due to unique personal and contextual factors
ANOVA	Quantitative	Comparison across many groups; looks at interactions; controls Type 1 Error; flexible	Potential exploitation	Do not use with small sample groups
Phenomenological	Qualitative	Efficient	Not generalisable	Consider a larger sample size; pay close attention to language and nuance; member checking is critical
Grounded Theory	Qualitative	Saturation of data	Time intensive, participants may fatigue impacting validity	Pay close attention to language and nuance; member checking is critical
Participatory Action Research/ Critical Participatory Research	Mixed Method	The needs of participants and their communities are at the forefront	Time intensive and participants may experience fatigue impacting validity; added pressure to implement results	Member checking is critical
Photo Voice	Qualitative / Mixed Method	Collaborative. Consideration of participant voices. Can be community-based and participatory.	Meaning can be difficult to verify	Consider theming with another method for added validity

Delphi	Mixed Method	Multiple data collection points expands research lens of participants. Recursive process.	Time intensive	Member checking is critical
Black Storytelling	Qualitative	Collaborative. Consideration of participant voices. Reciprocity and exploitation are carefully considered.	Added pressure to implement results; can be subjective	Member checking is critical
Indigenous	Qualitative	Collaborative, consideration of participant voices. Reciprocity and exploitation are carefully considered. Can be community-based and participatory.	Added pressure to implement results; can be subjective	Member checking is critical
Interpretive Phenomenological Analysis (IPA)	Qualitative	Participant centred, flexible	Can be subjective; small sample size; complex analysis	Consider theming with another method for added validity; Member checking is critical

participants. Professional organisations such as the American Psychological Association (APA) and the American Counseling Association (ACA) have established codes of ethics that outline principles for conducting research and providing therapy in an ethical and responsible manner. The principles of beneficence (acting in the best interest of participants) and non-maleficence (avoiding harm) are central to ethical practice in psychology and counselling. Both researchers and clinicians are reminded to consider the potential consequences of their actions and strive to maximise benefits while minimising harm.

Informed Consent

Both researchers and therapists must ensure that participants and clients are fully informed about the nature of the research or therapy, potential risks and benefits, and their right to withdraw at any time without consequences. Typically, participants are given the opportunity to participate or not to participate in the research process. All language included in the informed consent process should be very simple to ensure the understanding of all participants within their reading grade level. In some cases, where participants may not be able to read, this requires an additional translation of the informed consent or translation support to facilitate understanding. Researchers should also be careful with colloquial terms to avoid potential misunderstanding.

Protection of Vulnerable Populations

The history of exploitation of vulnerable populations has emphasised the need for special protections for these groups. Ethical guidelines now emphasise the importance of minimising harm and ensuring equitable treatment for all participants and clients. The fields of psychology and counselling have become more attuned to the importance of cultural sensitivity and diversity in research and practice. Researchers and clinicians must consider the cultural backgrounds, values, and beliefs of their participants and clients and to adapt their approaches accordingly.

Critical Reflection and Accountability

Finally, the history of unethical research practices serves as a reminder of the importance of critical reflection and accountability. Professionals are encouraged to continuously reflect on their own practices, seek feedback from colleagues and supervisors, and hold themselves accountable to ethical standards and principles. Ultimately, the history of unethical research practices has prompted the fields of psychology and counselling to prioritise ethical conduct, promote the well-being of participants and clients, and uphold the highest standards of integrity and professionalism. In doing so, culturally responsive researchers must consider and acknowledge the traumas of historical injustice, colonisation, and participant distrust.

A Framework for Culturally Responsive Research

Cultural responsiveness in research refers to the acknowledgement, understanding, and incorporation of diverse cultural perspectives and values into the research process. It involves recognising the cultural backgrounds, beliefs, practices, and experiences of the individuals or communities being studied, and ensuring that research methods, protocols, and interpretations are sensitive and respectful to these cultural factors. Furthermore, cultural responsiveness in research involves recognising, respecting, and incorporating the cultural contexts and perspectives of participants into all stages of the research process. Understanding Cultural Contexts: Researchers need to understand the cultural backgrounds, beliefs, values, and practices of the communities they study. This understanding helps in designing research that is respectful and relevant (Sue & Sue, 2016) and promotes cultural competence and humility. Researchers should strive to be culturally competent and exercise humility, meaning researchers are open and curious to learn more about cultural knowledge, skills, and attitudes to effectively participate in research with diverse populations. This involves ongoing learning and self-reflection.

Ponterotto (2005) describes fundamental philosophical branches that explore various aspects of the human experience and related inquiry of such. Of these, ontology describes the nature and reality of being, epistemology is the study of knowledge, axiology is the role and place of values in the research process, rhetorical structure is the language and presentation of the research, and finally, methodology, which is the process and procedures of research (Ponterotto, 2005). Each of these philosophical components come together to comprise the overall research framework with which a researcher seeks to design their research and create new knowledge. The foundational research design is the catalyst of scientific inquiry that creates evidence-based knowledge in the counselling profession. Therefore, culturally responsive research must originate from a place of ontological flexibility, epistemological curiosity, and ideologically inclusive and respectful of cultural differences and values. An ecological approach to a culturally responsive research framework is crucial, as it recognises the interconnectedness of individuals, communities, and their environments. Such a perspective aids in creating a more comprehensive and nuanced understanding of values that considers the multiple layers of influence and interaction within a given system or context.

Holism and Reflexivity

In the field of counselling, this is especially important in that a culturally responsive research framework emphasises a holistic approach and view regarding how values are formed, sustained, and transformed. It deepens contextual sensitivity, highlights dynamic interactions, promotes sustainability and resilience, furthers systemic thinking, allows for more interdisciplinary collaboration, and better ensures that marginalised and vulnerable communities are included in knowledge building and decision-making processes. "The researcher is an individual whose influence on the research is inextricably connected to each phase" (Heppner et al., 2016, p. 362) where researchers "recognize that science cannot be value free and instead seek to identify and utilize the social location of the researcher" (Heppner et al., 2016, p. 362). For example, "Researchers recognize that their specific contexts are shaped by their personal histories and identities" (Heppner et al., 2016, p. 363) and are "expected to engage in a thorough process of reflexivity and to openly acknowledge their positions, including in the written manuscript" (Heppner et al., 2016, p. 363).

Reflexivity in research refers to the researcher's awareness of their own influence, biases, and assumptions throughout the research process. It is impossible for a researcher to be a neutral observer—we are active participants whose perspectives shape research outcomes. This concept is particularly significant in qualitative research methods, where the researcher's subjectivity can greatly influence data collection, analysis, and interpretation (Finlay & Gough, 2003). Thus, it is critical for a researcher to acknowledge their positionality. Factors such as background, experiences, beliefs, and social identities all can influence how we perceive and interpret the world. For example, a researcher's cultural background may affect how they understand and interact with participants from different cultural backgrounds, potentially impacting the data they collect (Harding, 1991).

Reflexivity is a process of critically examining and reflecting on personal beliefs, challenging assumptions, and seeking diverse perspectives to ensure a more comprehensive understanding of the research topic (Hammersley & Atkinson, 2007). It extends to the research process itself, including decisions regarding methodology, data collection techniques, and analytical frameworks. Researchers should continuously reflect on how these choices may shape the research outcomes and consider alternative approaches to enhance the validity and reliability of their findings (Charmaz, 2006). In qualitative research, researchers utilise methods such as memo-writing, journaling, and member checking to document their thoughts, feelings, and reflections throughout the research process (Creswell, 2007).

Ultimately, reflexivity enhances the rigour and credibility of research by promoting transparency, self-awareness, and critical engagement with one's own biases and assumptions. It reminds us that research is a subjective endeavour conducted by individuals with their own perspectives and biases, and that actively considering and reflecting upon these factors is essential in order to produce meaningful, trustworthy scholarship.

When thinking through one's development of a culturally responsive framework, it may be helpful to consider the following questions as a practice of reflexivity:

1. What various sources of knowledge do I align with the most? Human authority, systemic power, intuition, empirical data, direct experience? A mixture of these?
2. What motivates me to create new knowledge?
3. What is present for me from a space of identity and experience? How does that inform my future research identity and practice?
4. What do I currently look for when I gather information?
5. What is needed in our field right now?
6. What does good research look like in today's world? What is the function and purpose of this research?
7. How long does it take to conduct good research? What does saturation look like?
8. How do we advance research in our field at the doctoral level?

Whether it is before the research, during or after, researchers should be thoughtful that individuals may belong to multiple cultural groups simultaneously (e.g., race, gender, sexual orientation, socioeconomic status) is crucial. Intersectionality helps researchers understand the complexity of individuals' identities and experiences (Crenshaw, 1989) and Reflexivity. Researchers should critically reflect on their own cultural biases, assumptions, and privileges throughout the research process. Reflexivity helps minimise biases and enhances the validity of research findings (Finlay, 2002).

Researcher Intersectionality

In counselling and psychology, the concept of intersectionality of the researcher refers to the understanding that an individual's experiences and identities are shaped by multiple factors, such as race, gender, sexual orientation, socioeconomic status, ability, and more. It's essential for researchers in these fields to acknowledge and address the complexities of intersectionality to ensure their work is culturally responsive. Researchers need to recognise that individuals' experiences are shaped by the intersections of various social identities. For example, a Black woman's experiences may differ significantly from those of a White woman due to the intersection of race and gender (Bowleg, 2008). Researchers must be culturally competent and exercise humility to work effectively with individuals from diverse backgrounds. This includes understanding and/or learning about the cultural norms, values, and histories of different communities and being sensitive to how intersecting identities influence mental wellness and help-seeking behaviours (Sue & Sue, 2016).

Intersectionality highlights power dynamics and how they intersect with various identities. Researchers need to be aware of their own power and privilege and how it may influence their interactions with participants. This awareness helps in creating a more equitable research process (Crenshaw, 1991). In addition, researchers should use inclusive methodologies that allow for the exploration of diverse experiences. This might involve qualitative methods such as narrative inquiry or participatory action research, which allow participants to share their stories in their own words and on their own terms. Intersectionality emphasises the importance of advocacy and social justice in counselling and psychology research. Researchers can use their findings to advocate for policies and practices that address systemic inequalities and promote the well-being of marginalised communities (Zane et al., 2024). Researchers should engage in reflexivity, continuously examining their own biases, assumptions, and positions of privilege. Reflexivity helps researchers to acknowledge their own standpoint and how it influences their research process and interpretations (Finlay, 2002). By incorporating these principles into their research, psychologists and counsellors can better understand and address the complexities of intersecting identities, thus providing more culturally responsive and inclusive services.

Cultural Humility in Research

Cultural humility in research involves acknowledging and respecting the cultural diversity of participants, recognising one's own biases and limitations, and engaging in a lifelong process of learning and self-reflection. Researchers need to recognise the power differentials between themselves and the communities they study. Cultural humility encourages researchers to approach their work with a sense of openness and respect for the knowledge and expertise of the communities they engage with (Tervalon & Murray-García, 1998). Researchers should actively listen to the perspectives and experiences of participants, valuing their insights and knowledge. This requires setting aside preconceived notions and being open to learning from others (Hook, et al., 2013). Cultural humility influences research methodologies, emphasising the importance of using approaches that are sensitive to the cultural contexts of participants. This might involve employing community-based participatory research methods or adapting data collection tools to better fit the cultural backgrounds of participants (Israel et al., 2010). Researchers engage in reflective practice, continually examining their own assumptions, biases, and cultural blind spots. This involves acknowledging when cultural misunderstandings or biases may have influenced the research process and taking steps to address them (Hawkins et al., 2017). Cultural humility promotes collaboration and partnership with community members and stakeholders throughout the research process. This ensures that research is conducted in a manner that is respectful, relevant, and beneficial to the communities involved. Cultural humility includes ethical considerations that prioritise the well-being and autonomy of research participants. This involves obtaining informed consent in culturally appropriate ways, protecting participants' confidentiality, and ensuring that the research benefits the communities involved (APA, 2017). By integrating cultural humility into their research practices, researchers can foster more equitable and respectful relationships with participants and produce research that is more meaningful and relevant to diverse communities.

Social Location

Social location refers to the intersecting factors of an individual's identity—such as race, gender, sexuality, class, ability, and nationality—that shape their experiences, perspectives, and access to resources within society. Ignoring or overlooking these dimensions can lead to biased, incomplete, or even harmful research outcomes. Acknowledging social location is imperative in order to expose the power dynamics at play within research settings. Researchers run the risk of bringing their own biases, privileges, and assumptions to their work (Jones, 2001). Acknowledging social location helps unveil these dynamics and fosters a deeper understanding of how researchers' backgrounds might influence their interpretations, methodologies, and conclusions (du Preez, 2008). Research that fails to acknowledge social location risks perpetuating the marginalisation and minoritisation of certain groups. By centring the experiences and perspectives of these communities, researchers can help to amplify their voices, highlight their authentic lived experiences, and build more inclusive, equitable knowledge (Collins, 2015).

Factors such as cultural context, historical experiences of oppression, and systemic inequalities significantly shape individuals' behaviours, beliefs, and responses (Bowleg, 2008). When these factors are ignored, misleading or inaccurate conclusions may be drawn, which ultimately undermines the integrity of the research. Researchers have a responsibility to conduct their work with integrity, respect, and consideration for the well-being of participants (American Psychological Association, 2017). Identifying one's own intersectionality as a researcher, as well as that of the participants, acknowledges that individuals occupy multiple social locations simultaneously and that these intersecting identities shape their experiences in unique ways (Crenshaw, 1991). By acknowledging social location, researchers can conduct more nuanced analyses that account for the intersecting influences of privilege and oppression. In exposing the structural inequalities and injustices faced by oppressed communities, research can inform advocacy efforts, policy reforms, and interventions aimed at addressing systemic barriers and promoting social justice (Hankivsky et al., 2009).

Community Engagement

Community Engagement is a powerful way to conduct cultural responsiveness research. Engaging with the community being studied fosters trust and ensures that research is culturally relevant and respectful.

Researchers can involve community members in the design, implementation, and dissemination of research (Israel et al., 2010). It is also imperative of the cultural adaptation of measures when working with diverse communities. When using measures or instruments in research, it's important to ensure they are culturally appropriate. This may involve translating measures, adapting them to fit the cultural context, or developing new measures altogether (Sperber, 2004). By engaging in communities, using measures and conducting research, researchers must address ethical concerns when conducting research with diverse populations. This includes obtaining informed consent in a culturally sensitive manner, protecting participants' confidentiality, and ensuring that the research benefits the community (APA, 2017).

Adaptation of Methods

Researchers may need to adapt research methods and instruments to be culturally appropriate and relevant. By integrating cultural competence into research design and implementation, researchers can improve both the validity and impact of their findings within specific cultural groups (Gone, 2021). This may include translating materials into different languages, using culturally specific examples or metaphors, or modifying data collection techniques to align with cultural norms. Ethical considerations in research, including issues of informed consent, privacy, and confidentiality should also be considered. Researchers must respect the rights and dignity of participants, particularly when working with vulnerable or marginalised communities. Such adaptations are essential in developing effective interventions that span a variety of cultures (Bernal & Domenech Rodríguez, 2012).

Interpretation, Analysis, and Dissemination

Interpretation and analysis must carefully consider cultural nuances and contextual factors that may influence the interpretation of findings in order to avoid misrepresentations and situate the findings within the appropriate cultural context and framework (Smith, 2019). This includes incorporating culturally responsive theoretical ideology and bringing in community members to aid in the interpretation process (Gone, 2021). It is important to simultaneously recognise the limitations of applying Western frameworks or theories to diverse cultural contexts. Researchers should then communicate findings in a way that is accessible and relevant to diverse audiences, and how to ensure that research contributes to positive social change without perpetuating stereotypes or reinforcing inequalities (Buchanan & Witkin, 2020). Researchers must also consider the implications of generalisability and assumptions thereof. For example, "differences found among cultural groups are erroneously attributed to group membership as opposed to more proximal variables that may actually be responsible for differences (e.g., familiar values, neighborhood characteristics)" (Heppner et al., 2016, p. 201).

Connecting to Multiculturalism and Social Justice

Implementing such culturally responsive research practices impacts the larger counselling field and clientele in many crucial ways. Perhaps the largest impact is on the professions' overall improvement in understanding multicultural perspectives, thus enabling more culturally competent interventions. By studying how various cultural factors, values, communication styles and belief systems impact the counselling experience and outcomes, a greater understanding of necessary therapeutic approaches may be developed or adapted. Such research also has the capacity to address broader health and systemic inequities by examining the impact of cultural, social, and systemic factors on mental health outcomes. Access to mental health services, barriers to treatment, and culturally relevant approaches to prevention and intervention can be highlighted with this research focus and orientation, thus contributing to a more equitable and inclusive healthcare system. Other research topics that include the impact and experiences of discrimination, oppression, trauma, and resilience can promote social change by amplifying diverse voices and perspectives.

Restorative Justice

Restorative justice using culturally responsive research in the counselling field focuses on harm reduction, reparation, and relationship building/rebuilding. Centring accountability, this process may involve a variety of stakeholders such as victims, offenders, and the larger community in the healing process (Zehr, 2002). Researchers can conduct interviews, focus groups, or observations to understand the experiences and perspectives of participants in restorative justice processes. This helps in exploring how restorative justice affects victims, offenders, and communities, ultimately fostering community cohesion (Umbreit et al., 2005). This research can compare different models of restorative justice, such as family group conferencing, victim-offender mediation, victims' sense of justice, healing, and satisfaction, or circle sentencing, to understand their strengths, weaknesses, and suitability for different contexts. It may track the outcomes of restorative justice participants over time to see if there are lasting effects on recidivism, rehabilitation, and community reintegration (Liebmann, 2007). Finally, it may inform public policy by providing evidence-based recommendations for the development, improvement, or expansion of restorative justice programmes.

Equity and Access

When discussing equity and access in the context of culturally responsive education in the classroom, Stembridge (2019) posed a framework for understanding the process as follows: who gets access, who has the capacity to be successful, what groups of people are underrepresented and underperforming relative to others, what are the gaps and how are they understood, the social, historical, and political contexts of under-achieving groups, assumptions made about certain groups and their abilities, and policies and practices impacting assets within communities. The existence of equity gaps undermines the positionality of an individual or group from having access to opportunities. The interplay of historical and contemporary environments of inequality has not been favourable for researchers engaging in not-so-familiar methodological designs. For instance, the idea of student researchers working on a research design that is unfamiliar to the dissertation committee could pose challenges for the marginalised individuals interested in promoting and preserving their cultures of origin and communities.

Similarly, culturally responsiveness in research nurtures equity and access. The use of culturally relevant pedagogy (CRP) (Ladson-Billings, 2021) in classroom settings helps teachers support students who otherwise would traditionally struggle to succeed. Culturally responsive research alongside culturally responsive pedagogies provides students with opportunities to conduct designs that deviate from the traditional norm. When this happens, emerging and seasoned researchers are provided the opportunity to critically examine designs such as Black storytelling, photovoice, and indigenous participatory research focused on creating meaningful outcomes that have neither a top-bottom or bottom-up influence. Rather the focus is on how the actions of the researcher involves the individual or groups in the process in a meaningful way with intentional preservation of the existing status quo, not promises. Paris (2012) espoused the term "Culturally Sustaining Pedagogy" further expanding CRP in a bid to explicitly encourage marginalised groups preserve their linguistic and cultural sovereignty.

Methods that Centre Cultural Responsiveness

Accountability in culturally responsive research involves consideration into research designs' socioeconomic and systemic constructs of marginalised individuals and their communities.

The focus on culturally responsive research in counselling has relational roots from diverse fields such as psychology, leadership, and education. In the field of counselling, the rise of multicultural counselling (Sue & Sue, 2016) ushered in a new wave of examining worldviews of clients as well as counsellors. Over the years, expanding cultural responsiveness into research has become imperative, given that researchers are bound by ethical and legal procedures in their interactions with participants and their environments. Such accountability processes include but are not limited to centring voices (Collins, 2015), unveiling power dynamics (Jones, 2001), and driving social change (Hankivsky & Cormier, 2009). This further gave rise to consideration of a number of research designs such as Black storytelling, photovoice, and indigenous story work.

The use of multicultural competency continues to represent the White and Western framework of traditional ways of conceptualising North American and European ideologies (Singh et al., 2020). The term competency itself has been recently criticised as being more of a top-to-bottom expertise, ignoring the relational power differences. This perspective comes along with limitations as the voices of intended beneficiaries are often left out. One such limitation is exploitation, not often considered in research. Participant data collected with no beneficial reciprocity on the part of the researcher sheds light on the need for reconsideration as Burkhard (2022) puts it. In a bid to address the gaps in cultural responsiveness research in counselling, the *Journal of Counseling and Development* (JCD) has made some bold strides in publishing a number of articles centring the importance of this process. Publications include mental health concerns of international student (Mori, 2000), integrating Hip-Hop culture in social justice counselling (Washington, 2018), impact of racial microaggressions and mental health (Nadal et al., 2014), complicated grief (Crunk et al., 2017), mindfulness interventions (Brown et al., 2013), power of language and labels (Granello & Gibbs, 2016), culturally responsive counselling interventions regarding refugee trauma (Bemak & Chung, 2017), affirmative LGBTQ counsellor education (Whitman & Bidell, 2014), and affirming strengths in men (Englar-Carlson & Kiselica (2013). Collaborative research practices and methods are essential in the field of counselling to ensure culturally responsive practices such as centring, recentring research around diverse needs of communities, and research methods designs tailored to the participant communities.

Centring practices involve a culturally responsive lens to integrating a research reparative justice approach with populations who have been oppressed and harmed by research. For example, as part of the collaborative process of research, O'Hara et al. (2021) recommended counselling researchers endeavour to address power dynamics. This empowering process ensures researchers include participants as co-researchers in the determination of needs, designing, implementation, and dissemination of the research with the goal of shared benefit of knowledge gained in study with participants and their communities. Recent efforts of centring include studies examining the impact of racial microaggression on mental health (Nadal et al., 2014).

The fact remains that cultural responsiveness in research also takes place in the context of older methodologies capturing some foundational semblance of positionality. With the emergence of culturally responsive methodologies, positionality of the researcher as travelling an uncharted territory where unlearning of prior paradigms becomes an imperative deconstruction process (Berryman, et al., 2013; Nevin, 2013) alongside the needs of participant communities. Methods of culturally responsive research include indigenous story work (George et al., 2020), Black storytelling (Phillips & Nguyen, 2021; Toliver, 2021), critical participatory research, photovoice (Black & Faustin, 2022; Smith et al., 2012), and single subject designs (Brown et al., 2024; Kazdin, 2019; Lenz, 2015). In the field of counselling, these are essentially emerging research methodologies, in spite of their resounding contributions towards improving client outcomes. Recentre research around different needs of communities, for example, indigenous stories, photovoice, and narratives is an essential aspect of paths towards culturally responsive research.

Indigenous Story Work

Indigenous research ethics (George et al., 2020) highlighted the importance of reclaiming research sovereignty steering the process away from deficit models with colonial legacy implication and noted a need for sense cultural humility. Similarly, Smith (2012) echoed the need for decolonising research, a process more geared towards recentring the perspectives of participants as collaborators and beneficiaries within the context of needs assessment. Among immigrant communities, qualitative research is faced with varying complexities. For example, Burkhard (2022) invited researchers to consider in their qualitative research interrogation of the local and global contexts of colonialism, race, and migration. In another instance Burkhard (2022) suggested applying a transnational Black feminist lens when working with transnational Black women, one reason being regardless of one's origin, there are commonalities such as racism, misogyny, microaggressions, and oppression. Scholars have long challenged the philosophy of outsiders being vehicles of change in indigenous communities (de Finney et al., 2021; Smith, 2012; Tuck, 2010). For example, Tuck (2010) challenged the flawed thinking that, "assumes that it is outsiders, not communities, who hold the power to make changes" (p. 638), while Kovach (2021) advocated for integration of indigenous methodologies in research.

Black Storytelling

A qualitative research process accounting for the inclusion of Black narratives using alternative methods of data collection, analysis, and representation (Toliver, 2021). Contrary to White-centric qualitative methods, Toliver advocated for a culturally responsive onto-epistemological tool centring of Black storytelling, Afrofuturism, and womanism. Black storytelling has also gained traction in pedagogy (Phillips & Nguyen, 2021).

Critical Participatory Research

Critical Participatory Research (CPR) in counselling is a methodology that engages participants in the research process, ensuring that their voices are heard, and their experiences impact the study's direction and outcomes. Grounded in social justice principles, this approach aims to empower participants by addressing systemic inequalities within counselling practice (Fine & Torre, 2021). CPR is a collaborative process between researchers and participants within a specific community and is bidirectional in mutual learning goals that seek to create actionable change (Kemmis et al., 2014; Leavy, 2022). Counselling practices are then driven to become more inclusive and responsive to diverse needs (Eckhoff, 2019).

Photovoice

Until recently, photovoice began to make its way into the field of counselling as a social justice initiative (Smith et al., 2012). As a form of participatory action research, the authors advocated for use of photovoice as a promising interconnected research design approach focused on critical consciousness connecting youths to their communities. As a centring qualitative research, Black and Faustin (2022) advocated the use of photovoice during the pandemic as a community-based participatory approach with meaningful results via use of authentic engagement and trust building with promising collaboration among participants, communities, and academic partners.

Single Subject Designs

Single-case research designs (SCRDs) are emerging in the field of counselling (Brown, et al., 2024) and their uses in the evaluation of intervention effects are clear in counselling research (Vannest & Ninci, 2015). To address the needs of non-responders, SCRD uses either a smaller scale or modified interventions to personalise treatment (Brown et al., 2024; Kazdin, 2019). According to Brown et al. (2024) "Single- case research is compatible with professional counselling pillars of prevention, development, and wellness" (p. 1). Since 2015, the flagship journal of the American Counseling Association, the *Journal of Counseling and Development* (JCD) provided justification in a special issue for the need for SCRDs to address the gaps between practice and research related to the evaluation of intervention and treatment effectiveness of client outcomes research (Brown, et al., 2024; Lenz, 2015). Since then, there is persistently limited research in assessing SCRD methodological practices (Brown et al., 2024) in spite of its invaluable contribution towards client empowerment. Given that the field of counselling emphasises relationships and collaborations, it makes sense that treatment effectiveness empowering clients evolves within a practitioner-scholar context.

Sample Course Assignment

In a research course classroom assignment, students are engaged to develop a research topic of interest using a line of thinking approach. In the line of thinking, students explore prior research using various search tools ranging from university libraries to Google scholar. Students are asked to develop a research topic with social justice and advocacy in mind. After developing a topic, students are asked to review related literature to explore what has been done and or gaps in the literature surrounding their topic. In this process, students are asked to consider a counselling theory of their choice and to further develop a research question from this perspective. This framework must be conceptualised as a social justice and advocacy lens regarding the intended participant community. In addition, students are required to ensure that a successful literature review includes the following:

1. An identified problem area and its significance, in terms of scope, impact, urgency, etc.
2. A clear research question that can be addressed within the scope of a seven- or ten-page paper.
3. Identification and evaluation of other relevant research that has been conducted and why this body of literature is not sufficient to answer the question at hand (e.g., does existing research not ask the right questions, or measure the right variables? Considering various intersectional identities, do they only focus on a particular age, ability, gender, race, language, socioeconomic status, and sexual orientation?
4. Adequate explanation of concepts and a clear statement of the expectations or research hypotheses.
5. The literature review should proceed logically from the general problem area down to the specific research being proposed.

Conclusion

Over the past thirty years, numerous scholars in the fields of counselling and psychology have posited that all counselling is multicultural in nature (Patterson, 1996; Speight et al., 1991; Sue & Sue, 2016). Given this imperative, it is critical for counsellors to access research that has been conducted through a culturally responsive framework. To implement best practices that originate from evidence-based findings, researchers must bring awareness to their own epistemological and ontological views. First, one must consider their own values, beliefs, positionality, and biases before discerning which research method best suits their question. Then, the methods most often utilised in the field of counselling should be reviewed for their pros and cons related to the research aims and cultural implications. Finally, counsellor educators and scholars should continue to think creatively about how we can push the boundaries of existing research paradigms creating scholarship that considers the specific needs of various populations and issues through a more collaborative approach that partners with the real experts—the communities themselves.

References

American Counseling Association. (2014). *2014 ACA code of ethics.* https://www.counseling.org/resources/ethics

American Psychological Association. (2017). *Ethical principles of psychologists and code of conduct.* https://www.apa.org/ethics/code

Bemak, F., & Chung, R. C.-Y. (2017). Refugee trauma: Culturally responsive counseling interventions. *Journal of Counseling & Development, 95*(3), 299–308. https://doi.org/10.1002/jcad.12144

Bernal, G., & Domenech Rodríguez, M. M. (2012). *Cultural adaptations: Tools for evidence-based practice with diverse populations.* American Psychological Association.

Berryman, M., SooHoo, S., & Nevin, A. (2013). Culturally responsive methodologies. In *EBL* (1st ed.). Emerald.

Bhaskar, R., & Hartwig, M. (2010). *The formation of critical realism.* Routledge. ISBN: 9780415260992.

Black, K. Z., & Faustin, Y. F. (2022). How community-based participatory research can thrive in virtual spaces: Connecting through photovoice. *Human Organization, 81*(3), 240–247. https://doi.org/10.17730/1938-3525-81.3.240

Bowleg, L. (2008). When Black + lesbian + woman ≠ Black lesbian woman: The methodological challenges of qualitative and quantitative intersectionality research. *Sex Roles, 59*(5–6), 312–325. https://doi.org/10.1007/s11199-008-9400-z

Briggs, L. (2002). *Reproducing empire: Race, sex, science, and U.S. Imperialism in Puerto Rico.* University of California Press.

Brown, A. P., Marquis, A., & Guiffrida, D. A. (2013). Mindfulness-Based interventions in counseling. *Journal of Counseling & Development, 91*(1), 96–104. https://doi.org/10.1002/j.1556-6676.2013.00077.x

Brown, C. L., Peltier, C., Smarinsky, E. C., Lewis, O. J., & Lee, D. Y. (2024). A review of counseling research using single-case research design. *Journal of Counseling & Development, 102*(3), 334–349. https://doi.org/10.1002/jcad.12517

Burkhard, T. (2022). *Transnational Black feminism and qualitative research: Black women, racialization and migration.* Routledge. https://www.taylorfrancis.com/books/9781003056621

Charmaz, K. (2006). *Constructing grounded theory: A practical guide through qualitative analysis.* SAGE Publications.

Collins, P. H. (2015). Intersectionality's definitional dilemmas. *Annual Review of Sociology, 41*, 1–20. https://doi.org/10.1146/annurev-soc-073014-112142

Crenshaw, K. (1989). Demarginalizing the intersection of race and sex: A black feminist critique of antidiscrimination doctrine, feminist theory and antiracist politics. *University of Chicago Legal Forum, 1989*(1), 139–167. http://chicagounbound.uchicago.edu/uclf/vol1989/iss1/8

Crenshaw, K. (1991). Mapping the margins: Intersectionality, identity politics, and violence against women of color. *Stanford Law Review, 43*(6), 1241–1299. https://doi.org/10.2307/1229039

Creswell, J. W. (2007). *Qualitative inquiry and research design: Choosing among five approaches* (2nd ed.). SAGE Publications.

Creswell, J. W., & Creswell, J. D. (2018). *Research design: Qualitative, quantitative and mixed methods approaches* (5th ed.). SAGE Publications.

Crunk, A. E., Burke, L. A., & Robinson, E. H. M., III. (2017). Complicated grief: An evolving theoretical landscape. *Journal of Counseling & Development, 95*(2), 226–233. https://doi.org/10.1002/jcad.12134

de Finney, S., Bennett, K., & Adams, C. (2021). Centering Community-Led Indigenous Gender Sovereignty. *Collaborations: A Journal of Community-Based Research and Practice, 4*(1), 1–12. https://doi.org/10.33596/coll.72

du Preez, J. (2008). Locating the researcher in the research: personal narrative and reflective practice. *Reflective Practice, 9*(4), 509–519. https://doi.org/10.1080/14623940802431499

Eckhoff, A. (2019). *Participatory research with young children.* Springer.

Englar-Carlson, M., & Kiselica, M. S. (2013). Affirming the strengths in men: A positive masculinity approach to assisting male clients. *Journal of Counseling & Development, 91*(4), 399–409. https://doi.org/10.1002/j.1556-6676.2013.00111.x

Fine, M., & Torre, M. E. (2021). *Essentials of critical participatory action research.* American Psychological Association.

Finlay, L. (2002). Negotiating the swamp: The opportunity and challenge of reflexivity in research practice. *Qualitative Research, 2*(2), 209–230. https://doi.org/10.1177/146879410200200205

Finlay, L., & Gough, B. (Eds.). (2003). *Reflexivity: A practical guide for researchers in health and social sciences.* John Wiley & Sons.

George, L., Tauri, J., & MacDonald, L. T. A. o. T. (2020). *Indigenous research ethics: Claiming research sovereignty beyond deficit and the colonial legacy* (1st ed.). Emerald Publishing.

Gone, J. P. (2021). The (post)colonial predicament in community mental health services for American Indians: Explorations in alter-Native psy-ence. *American Psychologist, 76*(9), 1514–1525. https://doi.org/10.1037/amp0000906

Granello, D. H., & Gibbs, T. A. (2016). The power of language and labels: "The mentally Ill" versus "people with mental illnesses". *Journal of Counseling & Development, 94*(1), 31–40. https://doi.org/10.1002/jcad.12059

Hammersley, M., & Atkinson, P. (2007). *Ethnography: Principles in practice* (3rd ed.). Routledge.

Hankivsky, O., Cormier, R., & de Merich, D. (2009). *Intersectionality: Moving women's health research and policy forward.* Women's Health Research Network.

Harding, S. (1991). *Whose science? Whose knowledge? Thinking from women's lives.* Cornell University Press.

Heppner, P. P., Wampold, B. E., & Kivlighan, D. M., Jr. (2008). *Research design in counselling* (3rd ed.). Cengage Learning.

Heppner, P. P., Wampold, B. E., Owen, J., Thompson, M. N., & Wang, K. T. (2016). *Research design in counselling* (4th ed.). Cengage Learning.

Hook, J. N., et al. (2013). Cultural humility: Measuring openness to culturally diverse clients. *Journal of Counseling Psychology, 60*(3), 353–366. https://doi.org/10.1037/a0032595

Israel, B. A., et al. (2010). Community-based participatory research: A capacity-building approach for policy advocacy aimed at eliminating health disparities. *American Journal of Public Health, 100*(11), 2094–2102. https://doi.org/10.2105/AJPH.2009.170506

Jones, C. P. (2001). Invited commentary: "Race," racism, and the practice of epidemiology. *American Journal of Epidemiology, 154*(4), 299–304. https://doi.org/10.1093/aje/154.4.299

Kadzin, A. E. (2019). Single-case experimental designs: Evaluating interventions in research and clinical practice. *Behavior Research and Therapy, 117*, 3–17. https://doi.org/10.1016/j.brat.2018.11.015

Kelm, M. E. (1999). *Colonizing Bodies: Aboriginal Health and Healing in British Columbia, 1900–50.* UBC Press.

Kemmis, S., McTaggart, R., & Nixon, R. (2014). *The action research planner: Doing critical participatory action research.* Springer.

Kovach, M. (2021). *Indigenous methodologies: Characteristics, conversations, and contexts* (2nd ed.). University of Toronto Press.

Ladson-Billings, G. (2021). Three decades of culturally relevant, responsive, & sustaining pedagogy: What lies ahead? *The Educational Forum, 85*(4), 351–354. https://doi.org/10.1080/00131725.2021.1957632

Leavy, P. (2022). *Research design: Quantitative, qualitative, mixed methods, arts-based, and community-based participatory research approaches* (2nd ed.). The Guilford Press.

Lenz, A. S. (2015). Using single-case research designs to demonstrate evidence for counseling practices. *Journal of Counseling & Development, 93*(4), 387–393. https://doi.org/10.1002/jcad.12036

Liebmann, M. (2007). *Restorative justice: How it works.* Jessica Kingsley Publishers.

Mori, S. C. (2000). Addressing the mental health concerns of International Students. *Journal of Counseling & Development, 78*(2), 137–144. https://doi.org/10.1002/j.1556-6676.2000.tb02571.x

Nadal, K. L., Griffin, K. E., Wong, Y., Hamit, S., & Rasmus, M. (2014). The impact of racial microaggressions on mental health: Counseling implications for clients of color. *Journal of Counseling & Development, 92*(1), 57–66. https://doi.org/10.1002/j.1556-6676.2014.00130.x

Nevin, A. (2013). Deconstructing my positivistic paradigm: Making room for culturally responsive methodology. In M. Berryman, S. SooHoo, & A. Nevin (Eds.), *Culturally responsive methodologies.* In *EBL* (1st ed., pp. 107–125).

Paris, D. (2012). Culturally sustaining pedagogy: A needed change in stance, terminology, and practice. *Educational Researcher, 41*(3), 93–97. https://doi.org/10.3102/0013189X12441244

Patterson, C. H. (1996). Multicultural counselling: From diversity to universality. *Journal of Counseling & Development, 74*(3), 227–231. https://doi.org/10.1002/j.1556-6676.1996.tb01856.x

Phillips, L. G., & Nguyen, T. T. P. (Eds.). (2021). *Storytelling Pedagogy in Australia & Asia.* Palgrave Macmillan. https://doi.org/10.1007/978-981-16-4009-4

Ponterotto, J. G. (2005). Qualitative research in counseling psychology: A primer on research paradigms and philosophy of science. *Journal of Counseling Psychology, 52*(2), 126–136. https://doi.org/10.1037/0022-0167.52.2.126

Singh, A. A., Appling, B., & Trepal, H. (2020). Using Multicultural and Social Justice Counseling competencies to decolonize counseling practice: The important roles of theory, power, and action. *Journal of Counseling & Development, 98*(3), 261–271. https://doi.org/10.1002/jcad.12321

Smith, L., Bratini, L., & Appio, L. M. (2012). "Everybody's teaching and everybody's learning": Photovoice and youth counseling. *Journal of Counseling & Development, 90*(1), 3–12. https://doi.org/10.1111/j.1556-6676.2012.00001.x

Smith, L. T. (2012). *Decolonizing methodologies: Research and Indigenous peoples* (2nd ed.). Zed Books.

Speight, S. L., Myers, L. J., Cox, C. I., & Highlen, P. S. (1991). A redefinition of multicultural counselling. *Journal of Counselling & Development, 70*(1), 29–36. https://doi.org/10.1002/j.1556-6676.1991.tb01558.x

Sperber, A. D. (2004). Translation and validation of study instruments for cross-cultural research. *Gastroenterology, 126*(1), S124–S128. https://doi.org/10.1053/j.gastro.2003.10.016

Stembridge, A. (2019). *Culturally responsive education in the classroom: An equity framework for pedagogy* (1st ed.). Routledge.

Sue, D. W., & Sue, D. (2016). *Counseling the culturally diverse: Theory and practice.* John Wiley & Sons.

Tervalon, M., & Murray-García, J. (1998). Cultural humility versus cultural competence: A critical distinction in defining physician training outcomes in multicultural education. *Journal of Health Care for the Poor and Underserved, 9*(2), 117–125. https://doi.org/10.1353/hpu.2010.0233

Toliver, S. R. (2021). *Recovering Black storytelling in qualitative research: Endarkened Storywork* (1st ed.). Routledge.

Tuck, E. (2010). Breaking up with Deleuze: Desire and valuing the irreconcilable. *International Journal of Qualitative Studies in Education, 23*(5), 635–650. https://doi.org/10.1080/09518398.2010.500633

Umbreit, M. S., Vos, B., Coates, R. B., & Lightfoot, E. (2005). Restorative justice in the twenty-first century: A social movement full of opportunities and pitfalls. *Marquette Law Review, 89*(2), 251–304. https://scholarship.law.marquette.edu/mulr/vol89/iss2/3

Vannest, K. J., & Ninci, J. (2015). Evaluating intervention effects in single-case research designs. *Journal of Counseling & Development, 93*(4), 403–411. https://doi.org/10.1002/jcad.12038

Washington, A. R. (2018). Integrating Hip-Hop Culture and rap music into Social Justice Counseling with Black Males. *Journal of Counseling & Development, 96*(1), 97–105. https://doi.org/10.1002/jcad.12181

Washington, H. A. (2008). *Medical Apartheid: The dark history of medical experimentation on Black Americans from colonial times to the present.* Vintage.

Whitman, J. S., & Bidell, M. P. (2014). Affirmative Lesbian, Gay, and Bisexual Counselor Education and Religious Beliefs: How do we bridge the gap? *Journal of Counseling & Development, 92*(2), 162–169. https://doi.org/10.1002/j.1556-6676.2014.00144.x

Zehr, H. (2002). *The little book of restorative justice.* Good Books.

Zimbardo, P. G. (2008). *The Lucifer effect: Understanding how good people turn evil.* Random House.

CHAPTER 4

Cultural Responsiveness in Clinical Supervision

Susan Sisko and Maxine Rosenfield

Introduction

Clinical supervision is a compulsory professional activity through which counsellors and psychologists (practitioners) achieve professional accreditation / registration and a requirement (in most jurisdictions) to continue to develop professional competence and skills throughout their careers. It is a working alliance, enabling a practitioner "to gain in ethical competence, confidence, compassion, and creativity in order to give [the] best possible service to the client" (Inskipp & Proctor, 2001, as cited in Creaner, 2013, p. 7). Practitioners often receive supervision from a more experienced, more senior practitioner and it can be individual sessions or in groups. Peer supervision, usually between senior practitioners, may be permitted towards accreditation in some jurisdictions. Supervision can be in person, by videoconference or phone. It is a live interaction to support practitioners who in turn support their vulnerable clients. Assisting

S. Sisko • M. Rosenfield (✉)
School of Health, University of Canberra, Canberra ACT, NSW, Australia
e-mail: Susan.Sisko@canberra.edu.au; maxine.rosenfield@canberra.edu

S. Sisko (ed.), *Culturally Responsive Psychotherapy, Counselling & Psychology*, Palgrave Texts in Counselling and Psychotherapy,
https://doi.org/10.1007/978-3-031-81831-8_4

practitioners to avoid burn-out by debriefing in a safe and supportive environment, to develop more skills, to increase their competence and to ensure they hold ethical and legal boundaries with clients are all desirable outcomes of clinical supervision.

Supervision in the context of this chapter is not a management activity and it is not conducive for it to be conducted by practitioners' managers for obvious reasons such as boundary blurring, lack of willing disclosure of potential or actual errors by the practitioner, and an editing of the details of client interactions to ensure no adverse impact on the practitioner's role.

Historical Background

In January 1925, 367 nurses attended a conference at Mount Sinai Hospital in New York whose topic was Supervision (Schmidt, 1926). Amongst the presentations were topics including "Principles of Supervision" in which the supervisor seeks to put themselves in the supervisee's position to support the supervisee's professional growth and there was a topic about the management of employees as well as the "importance of standardization (sic) of hospital equipment as an aid to better supervision". In 1930, Burton defined nursing supervision as "an expert, technical service designed to improve the efficiency of groups of workers under supervision" (p. 1045).

These considerations of nursing supervision, which suggest a mixture of clinical and managerial functions, are not totally aligned with the principles of clinical supervision of counsellors and psychologists that we practise today to support practitioners, but there is a similarity since they illustrate the desire to provide some oversight of nurses to support their professional development and to provide quality services in patient care.

Early models and discussions about clinical supervision were focused on the student counsellor and their professional development. The evaluative role of supervisors when supervising students of counselling and psychology, for example, has been often explored. In early articles, the debate focuses on what is considered supervision and what is counselling and teaching as discussed by Arbuckle (1965) who points to counsellor congruence, genuineness, and honesty towards clients as being essential to lead to empathy and considers the question of how a counsellor can function as a supervisor of student counsellors. He discusses the importance of building empathic understanding between student and counsellor, such that the student feels the counsellor has their interests at the core, reflecting that this is like their work with clients in which a counsellor conveys being no threat to the client. Students may feel, however, that they cannot be open in supervision where there is an evaluative component to the relationship.

Patterson (1964), writing about supervising counselling students on practicum, discusses the supervisor/student relationship in comparison to a teacher/student relationship, commenting that supervision is "woefully inadequate". Patterson explores the supervisory relationship with the need to use techniques that are similar to counselling or psychotherapy rather than to teaching so that the supervisor listens to the student and supports the student to self-evaluate their performance.

Gurk and Wicas (1979) describe several supervision models from the 1960s to 1977 considering some that are didactic and others that are more counselling focused, commenting that a model that supports supervisees to think for themselves while receiving some guidance is most effective. They conclude that a consultation metamodel for supervision, which is inclusive, supportive, leads to learning and is aligned with psychoeducation will effectively support the supervisee.

The concept of supervision as a reflective practice is described by Tremmel (1993) quoting from Schőn (1987, p. 64) that reflective learning is "a dance-like pattern, simultaneously involved in design and in applying various roles in virtual and real worlds while, at the same time, remaining detached enough to observe and feel the action that is occurring and to respond" (p. 436). Reflective practice is explored by Ward and House (1998) who discuss a reflective model of counselling supervision that supports counsellors in training and with their ongoing development. At the end of their article, Ward and House provide a seven-step reflective supervisory relationship to help the student counsellor to picture a recent unsettling counselling experience, discuss this exploring their feelings and any other affects, to check any assumptions they are making, to consider how they would prefer this experience to be, to check what might prevent them from adapting their approach, to consider what knowledge and skills development are needed and how to evaluate their role and counselling practice (pp. 32–33).

Alongside reflective practice, competency-based learning is now also used in the supervision of counselling and psychology students. Falender and Shafranske (2012) provide a rationale for using strength-based competencies in psychology supervision as a means of bringing more accountability into the profession. Watkins (2014) describes what he refers to as six broad-based, internationally relevant supervision competence areas for use in supervision and these incorporate both reflective practice and knowledge of models, skills, ethical and legal matters as well as attention to diversity and difference. Falender (2014) states that clinical supervision has been an acknowledged professional competency since 2002 but notes that the lack of evidence-based outcome data resulted in low levels of recognition of supervision as a significant and valuable part of beginner psychologists' careers. In counselling, supervision has been a recognised practice since the 1980s. Watkins (2020a) comments that psychotherapy supervision is the signature pedagogy for psychotherapy education, teaching future practitioners to "think, perform and act with integrity" (p. 244).

Training Supervisors

Supervisors who are trained, who have developed boundaries, who are experienced practitioners and who are self-aware, can provide skilled support to practitioners. Training to become a supervisor began to be available in the 1980s (Hess & Hess, 1983). Carroll (1988) writing in the UK, considers the question of how judgemental the supervisor should be, discussing confidentiality and the role of the supervisor in monitoring the professionalism of the supervisee, noting that rarely are counsellors who are working as supervisors trained to be supervisors. He poses questions about the impact of supervision on the client, the counsellor's knowledge, and skills and whether the counsellor has explored personal issues that arise during sessions. Specific training for supervisors was rare at this time; rather a supervisor was usually a more qualified and experienced counsellor. At the end of his article, Carroll considers supervision in 1988 to be in the "adolescent" stage of development (p. 395).

Considering supervision in clinical and counselling psychology, Robiner and Schofield (1990) note that supervision is a significant part of practice, focusing on the internship year but found that less than 20% of those supervising had any training as supervisors. Relatively recently, Whitman et al. (2001), comment that there is little training in how to supervise for psychiatry, psychoanalysis, or social work, although they note that the American Association for Marriage and Family Therapists did have a training programme which included supervision of supervisors.

According to Peake et al. (2002), training in supervision was included in curriculum after the American Psychological Association's Committee on Accreditation updated its guidelines for accrediting doctoral and internship programmes in 1996. Borders (2006) details work carried out in in the US in the 1990s by the Association for Counsellor Education and Supervision (ACES) to create standards for counselling supervisors, curriculum standards for supervisor training, and ethical guidelines specific to supervision practice.

The move to competency-based training for supervisors has been well documented. Olds and Hawkins (2014) described nine competency frameworks for supervision in psychology after consolidating various existing frameworks. These align with Watkins' (2014) six broad based areas of competence. In 2018, Falender explored the broad position of competency-based supervision in psychology and discussed how to bring the teaching of supervision into curricula to ensure supervisors are skilled. She comments that supervision is part of a practitioner's path for all their career and discusses the need for supervisors to have extensive training because supervisors are gatekeepers, evaluators, and support supervisees to become aware of their professional development. It is only within the past decade that accredited training to become a supervisor has been available for counsellors in Australia.

Impacts of Supervision

There is no doubt that training is an essential part of becoming a clinical supervisor to support the supervisee's development and through this to support the client. Due to ethical and legal constraints, practitioners cannot discuss their clients outside of a professional environment. Supervision provides the space in which these discussions can occur. It aids the practitioner's professional development and competency to practice, educating and supporting the practitioner to reflect on the impact of their work on themselves and their clients. Apart from helping to develop the practitioner's identity and skills and providing safety for the clients through the practitioner's competency, supervision also supports the practitioner to avoid burn-out and remain fit to practice.

Wheeler and Richards' (2007) review of research evidence about the impact of supervision from 1980 onwards, concludes that supervision impacts several aspects of a supervisee's professionalism including skills, self-efficacy, and theoretical orientation and that supervision impacts the clients through the supervisee's increased ability to conceptualise and provide different interventions with clients. They comment that practitioner self-awareness is, perhaps not surprisingly, enhanced through supervision.

There is a power differential between supervisor and supervisee, although this may be less evident in peer supervision. In general, a more senior or more experienced practitioner is supervising a less experienced or more junior practitioner and there is an evaluative component so there is an inevitable hierarchy and therefore a difference in power. When the junior practitioner is a student, this might be more pronounced because the student may not yet know what exactly to expect or how to use supervision and this learning relies on the supervisor's competence and personal attributes. Amongst the studies that have considered the impact of supervision on supervisees when trainee practitioners, Wilson et al. (2016) consider the power differential of the roles and note that supervisees who feel safe and supported are encouraged to disclose and be open and this builds confidence. Pepper (2018) and Hooley (2019) also write about power differentials impacting supervision. Pepper discusses the conflict of interest between a training institute's need to treat clinically and to train and teach educationally. This conflict of interest raises ethical issues and can lead to harmful supervision due to abuses of power and the blurring of boundaries for supervisors and supervisees. For Hooley, working with a supervisor she believed was not aware of the power dynamics in their relationship led to confusion and conflict. The supervisor's blurred boundaries, insisting on sharing personal information about his life led to her feeling abused and fearful. She was unable to confront the dynamic because this would have had implications for her continued study; his power could have led to her being forced out of the training. Her self-efficacy was obviously not enhanced during this relationship.

Cashwell and Dooley (2001) conducted a trial of a mixture of recent graduates and longer-term qualified practitioners and divided them into who did and did not receive clinical supervision. They found that support from a supervisor enhanced practitioner self-efficacy regardless of the length of time a practitioner had been qualified and practising. Even senior practitioners continue to benefit from supervision.

Anxiety amongst supervisees is discussed in a phenomenological study by Koçyiğit (2024) who determined three categories of anxiety in novice practitioners who are new to being supervised. These three categories are not surprising: the novice practitioner may not feel competent about working with the client, the supervisor may provide negative and corrective feedback, and group supervision could lead to fear of making mistakes in front of peers. It is noted in this article that the self-efficacy of the practitioners increases with experience.

If a practitioner feels more effective and supported, then it could be reasonably surmised that this has a positive impact on the client/practitioner relationship. There are many studies that consider this, including Bambling et al. (2006) who studied the impact of supervision on the supervisee/client working alliance and symptom reduction for major depression in a randomised control trial. Amongst the findings were that supervision does play a role in developing the working alliance in the counselling relationship thus enhancing the outcome for the clients.

Callahan and Love (2020) highlight positive and negative practices in supervision, according to supervisees' experiences. They summarise that good supervisors are aware of their power and create a warm, accepting, and open atmosphere for supervision, modelling good professional and personal qualities such as cultural humility "while validating and honoring [sic] the intersectional identities of supervisees" (p. 4). Creating relational authenticity and tailoring supervision to the needs and developmental levels of different supervisees are amongst the factors that facilitate positive supervision experiences.

In some countries such as the US, supervisors hold responsibility for the work of the counsellors and client safety. Vallance (2004) writing from UK where this is not the case, supports other literature that ethical practitioners will support client welfare and that an open, egalitarian, supervisory relationship leads to a positive impact on clients.

Supervision Models

Clinical supervision, by definition, is a distinct discipline within the field of counselling requiring additional experience and specific training. Clinical supervision is a complex activity.

> The competent clinical supervisor must embrace not only the domain of psychological science, but also the domains of client service and trainee development. The competent supervisor must not only comprehend how these various knowledge bases are connected, but also apply them to the individual case. (Holloway & Wolleat, 1994, p. 30)

This requires high levels of skills and competence. Let's start with an understanding of clinical supervision models to understand aspects of supervisee development and how to apply them with cultural responsiveness.

There are several models of clinical supervision that provide frameworks for how supervision sessions are structured and conducted. This is by no means an exhaustive list but a cross-section of some commonly recognised overarching models:

Normative-Restructuring Models: These models focus on the supervisor's role in transmitting professional standards and knowledge to the supervisee. These involve teaching, advising, and correcting, aiming to enhance the supervisee's skills and adherence to professional norms. An example of this might include the

Cognitive Behavioural Supervision (CBS) model which integrates principles from cognitive-behavioural therapy (CBT) into the supervisory process. This model focuses on applying CBT techniques not only in client therapy but also in the supervisory relationship to facilitate learning, growth, and effective clinical practice. Here are some key aspects and examples of the CBS model:

Goal-Oriented Approach emphasising setting clear, specific goals for supervision sessions that align with the supervisee's learning objectives and professional development needs. For example, a supervisee might set a goal to improve their skills in conducting cognitive restructuring techniques with clients. *Collaborative Problem-Solving* which encourages supervisees to identify and analyse specific challenges or problems encountered in their clinical work. With the supervisor they then collaboratively explore and apply CBT principles to develop effective solutions. This might involve using techniques such as behavioural experiments or thought challenging exercises to address clinical issues. *Structured and Skills-Based Feedback* whereby supervisors provide structured feedback on the supervisee's clinical interventions and conceptualisations. They focus on linking feedback to specific CBT techniques and principles, such as identifying cognitive distortions or behavioural patterns in client interactions. For instance, the supervisor might provide feedback on how the supervisee could have applied exposure techniques more effectively with a client experiencing anxiety.

Modelling and Role-Playing: Supervisors using CBS will often employ role-playing exercises to simulate client scenarios. This allows supervisees to practise applying CBT techniques under supervision, receive immediate feedback, and refine their skills. The supervisor might role-play as a client while the supervisee practises conducting a cognitive restructuring exercise. *Case Formulation and Treatment Planning* CBS emphasises the development of comprehensive case formulations based on CBT principles. Supervisors assist supervisees in identifying clients' cognitive, emotional, and behavioural factors contributing to their difficulties, and in designing evidence-based treatment plans. They may use tools like cognitive conceptualisation diagrams to illustrate these formulations. *Self-Reflection and Cognitive Awareness* CBS encourages supervisees to reflect on their own cognitive processes and biases that may influence their clinical work. Supervisors help supervisees identify and challenge unhelpful cognitions or assumptions that could impact their therapeutic effectiveness. And finally, *Integration of Evidence-Based Practices* CBS supervisors stay updated on current research and evidence-based practices within CBT. They guide supervisees in integrating new evidence and techniques into their clinical practice, ensuring they are providing clients with the most effective interventions.

Overall, the CBS model aims to enhance supervisees' competence in applying CBT principles, improve client outcomes, and promote continuous professional development through structured, skills-focused supervision sessions.

Developmental Models: These models emphasise the supervisee's growth and development over time. They often draw from developmental psychology and focus on stages of professional growth, encouraging self-awareness, autonomy, and reflection.

Developmental models of clinical supervision focus on the personal and professional growth of the supervisee over time. These models emphasise stages of development, self-awareness, autonomy, and reflective practice. For example, here is a key developmental model of clinical supervision.

Stoltenberg's Developmental Model: Integrated Developmental Model (IDM) (Stoltenberg, 1981; Stoltenberg & Delworth, 1987; Stoltenberg et al., 1998) outlines three levels of counsellor development:

Level 1: Dependency. The novice supervisee relies heavily on the supervisor for

guidance and direction. Often high in motivation higher anxiety related to

performance and evaluation.

Level 2: Autonomy. The supervisee is at mid-level and experiences fluctuating

confidence and motivations, they begin to develop more independence and

confidence in their clinical skills, often linking their experiences with the perceived client success.

Level 3: Mutuality. The supervisee achieves a balanced relationship with the supervisor, demonstrating competence and self-assurance while still benefiting from collaboration and consultation.

Development models recognise that clinical supervision is not just about monitoring and correcting but also about fostering the supervisees' growth as a competent and reflective practitioner. They provide structured frameworks to support supervisees at different stages of their professional development journey.

Integrated Developmental Models: These models combine aspects of both normative-restructuring and developmental approaches. It recognises the need for both skill development and personal growth, providing a balanced approach to supervision.

Bernard's Discrimination Model (1979, 2006) of clinical supervision is a framework that focuses on the supervisor's role in helping the supervisee develop greater self-awareness and clinical competence through a process of discrimination. Here's an overview of Bernard's ***Discrimination Model*** and in this context, discrimination refers to the supervisee's ability to differentiate relevant from irrelevant information in clinical settings. It involves the capacity to recognise and understand the nuances and complexities present in therapeutic interactions.

There are three domains of discrimination, first, *Perceptual Discrimination* which is the ability to accurately perceive and interpret clients' verbal and nonverbal communication cues, emotional states, and interpersonal dynamics. Second, *Conceptual Discrimination* which includes understanding and applying theoretical concepts, principles, and strategies in clinical practice, as well as the ability to analyse and conceptualise case material using theoretical frameworks. Finally, *Executive Discrimination* which is about making informed and effective decisions in clinical practice, including intervention choices, treatment planning, and ethical decision-making. In addition to the domains of discrimination the supervisory tasks include:

Assessment which involves evaluating the supervisee's current level of discrimination in each domain, *Feedback* with the supervisor providing constructive feedback to help the supervisee improve their discrimination skills, *Teaching and Skill Development* where the supervisor offers guidance, teaches theoretical knowledge, and facilitates skill development in perceptual, conceptual, and executive discrimination, and finally *Self-Evaluation* by encouraging supervisees to reflect on their clinical experiences, decisions, and interactions to enhance their discrimination abilities. Bernard's model provides a developmental focus and recognises the supervisee's progress in their ability to discriminate effectively overtime. Supervisors help supervisees navigate through stages of development by providing appropriate challenges and support.

Bernard's Discrimination Model provides a structured approach for supervisors to foster supervisees' development of critical clinical skills, ultimately enhancing their effectiveness as practitioners. It underscores the importance of discrimination across perceptual, conceptual, and executive domains to support competent and ethical practice.

Parallel Process Models: These models emphasise the parallels between the client-counsellor relationship and the supervisee-supervisor relationship. They encourage supervisors to use their relationship with the supervisee to model effective therapeutic techniques and relational dynamics. An example here is psychodynamic clinical supervision which is based on psychodynamic principles and theories, focusing on understanding unconscious processes, relational dynamics, and the therapeutic relationship. Here are key aspects and considerations in psychodynamic clinical supervision:

Unconscious Processes: Psychodynamic supervision emphasises exploring the unconscious processes of both the client and the supervisee. The supervisor helps the supervisee recognise unconscious material that may influence their clinical work, such as countertransference reactions or unresolved conflicts. *Transference and Countertransference* supervisors using a psychodynamic approach pay attention to transference (the client's unconscious feelings and reactions towards the therapist) and countertransference (the therapist's unconscious reactions and feelings towards the client). They help supervisees understand and work through these dynamics to enhance therapeutic effectiveness. Additionally, there is Exploration *of Defence Mechanisms* which is where supervisors assist supervisees in identifying and understanding defence mechanisms employed by clients and themselves. They explore how defences impact the therapeutic process and help supervisees develop interventions that address underlying issues.

Interpersonal Dynamics are key for psychodynamic supervision as it focuses on the interpersonal dynamics between the therapist and client. Supervisors help supervisees recognise relational patterns, enactments, and relational ruptures within the therapeutic relationship. Supervisors guide supervisees in developing psychodynamic case formulations, which involve understanding the client's internal world, conflicts, and developmental history. They assist in formulating psychodynamic interpretations that deepen the client's self-awareness and facilitate therapeutic change. Additionally, supervisors support the development of *Reflective Practice* as supervisees are encouraged to engage in reflective practice, examining their thoughts, feelings, and reactions within the therapeutic context. Reflective exploration helps supervisees gain insight into their own dynamics and enhances their capacity for empathic attunement with clients.

Process-Experiential Models have developed from humanistic and experiential theories, they focus on the emotional and relational aspects of the supervisory relationship. These models emphasise exploration of the supervisee's experiences, emotions, and interactions with clients. For example,

Person-Centred Clinical Supervision is rooted in Carl Rogers' person-centred therapy principles and focuses on creating a supportive and empathetic supervisory relationship that mirrors the therapeutic relationship. Here are key aspects and considerations in Person-Centred Clinical Supervision: *Unconditional Positive Regard* where supervisors offer genuine acceptance, respect, and empathy towards supervisees. This creates a safe and non-judgmental space where supervisees can explore their thoughts, feelings, and experiences openly. *Empathic Understanding* where supervisors strive to deeply understand the supervisee's perspective, experiences, and challenges. They reflect the supervisee's emotions and thoughts, helping them gain insight into their own process. *Congruence/Authenticity* is demonstrated by the supervisors presenting in a genuine and transparent manner in their interactions with supervisees. They model authenticity and encourage supervisees to be honest and transparent about their experiences, concerns, and uncertainties.

Like Person-centred therapy, Person-centred supervision explores the dynamics and feelings within the supervisory relationship. Supervisors encourage supervisees to express their reactions and responses to the supervisory process. Person-centred supervision prioritises the supervisee's subjective experience and personal growth within the supervisory relationship, aiming to cultivate a supportive and empowering environment for supervisees to develop their therapeutic skills and self-awareness.

Each supervision model, and again this is not an exhaustive list, offers distinct advantages and may be more suitable depending on the context, goals, and preferences of the supervisee and supervisor. Clinical supervision in counselling and psychology provides numerous benefits essential for professional growth and effective client care. Firstly, it offers a structured framework for supervisees to reflect on their clinical practice, enhancing self-awareness and refining therapeutic skills. Supervision facilitates ongoing learning and skill development by integrating theoretical knowledge with practical application in client sessions. It also serves as a supportive space where supervisees receive feedback, guidance, and validation, which helps in managing challenging cases and ethical dilemmas effectively. Moreover, supervision fosters a collaborative and consultative approach, encouraging supervisees to explore diverse perspectives and innovative interventions. Ultimately, clinical supervision ensures adherence to ethical standards, promotes continuous professional development, and enhances the quality of therapeutic outcomes for clients, and beyond the fact that it is an ethical requirement—it is indispensable in the development and support of the profession.

Issues

As stated earlier in this chapter, there has been some acknowledgement of a power differential between supervisor and supervisee, however, this is not addressed in the clinical models of supervision. This seems most clearly expressed by the supervisee because of their experiences of anxiety about supervision (Mangione et al., 2011). Clinical supervision has an evaluative component creating an inevitable hierarchy and therefore a difference in power. Interestingly, when I (SS author) facilitate clinical supervision training courses I will start with a brainstorm with the course participants about what they are excited about and what they are concerned about in becoming a clinical supervisor. Not surprisingly, most talk about mentoring, teaching, collaboration, and supporting supervisees. However, it is rare that the participants discuss evaluation components of the role and the inherent power in that role. This cannot be ignored but it certainly seems an uncomfortable aspect in clinical supervision.

Mangione et al. (2011) referred to power from both the supervisor and supervisee perspective and described when supervisors considered power, it was in "the spirit of minimising its significance" (p. 163) or noting their discomfort with it, whereas for the supervisees' "power was affectively charged" (p. 156). Watkins (2014) stated that supervision, by definition is, an evaluative activity and since the exercise of power is involved in any such evaluation, supervisors coming to grips with and accepting power and influence as a necessary part of being a supervisor is requisite.

Awareness of issues around power and collaboration and an eventual reframing of power when needed in cases of correction and evaluation of the supervisee needs to be brought into discussion in clinical supervision. What we do know is that the power differential of the roles and supervisees who are made to feel safe and supported are encouraged to disclose and be open and this builds confidence (Wilson et al., 2016). Incorporating open and transparent discussions about power, evaluation, and processes are valuable. Supervision, as with counselling, happens in the context of the relationship and therefore tools for communication and clarity will be helpful. One very effective working tool is a supervision agreement.

Supervision agreement is a document developed by the clinical supervisor to discuss all aspects of clinical supervision. There are many online resources and designs for a supervision agreement. The justification for a supervision agreement includes:

- Clarifies the methods, goals, and expectations of supervision.
- Encourages professional collaboration.
- Upholds ethical principles.
- Documents services to be provided.
- Aligns supervision with counselling and consultation (two services that currently utilise a written contract with clients).

Components of Supervision Agreement should include:

- Name, contact details, education / training of the supervisor.
- Purpose, goals, and objectives of supervision.
- Your theoretical framework / philosophy.
- Context of services / cost (individual, group).
- Procedural considerations (when, where, and how often).
- Methods of evaluation (self-report, recordings).
- Clarification of responsibilities supervisor / supervisee.
- Supervisor's scope of practice.
- How to resolve concerns/grievance.

Whilst this will not mitigate the experience of hierarchy in clinical supervision this will create a platform for clarity, communication, and processes.

Another issue with clinical supervision is the lack of cultural focus and responsiveness in the models and frameworks that have been developed. What you may have noticed as you read through the section on clinical supervision models was a general lack of inclusion of cultural adaptation or responsiveness as a characteristic of the model. Much like the development of psychological theory, clinical supervision models developed without attention to diversity, and they continue to be slow off the mark to recognise cultural significance to the discipline of clinical supervision.

One could anticipate that competent supervisors address issues of diversity and multicultural matters in their supervision sessions. It appears, however, that this is not the case. Constantine (2001) explored whether the time spent focusing on multicultural issues in supervision had any correlation with counsellors' multicultural self-efficacy. The role of the supervisor as an influence on the supervisee was noted; the study found that those supervisors who discuss cultural issues in supervision encourage supervisees to work more effectively with culturally diverse clients.

Likewise, culturally sensitive supervision enables practitioners to explore their own multi-cultural awareness. Apostolidou and Schweitzer (2017) explored practitioners' perspectives on supervision in their work with asylum seekers and refugees. They found that it was very important that the supervisors have experience of cross-cultural work and can support practitioners to work with clients from different cultural backgrounds.

Watkins (2020b) includes amongst the purposes of supervision that it is a triadic multicultural relationship as client, supervisee, and supervisor personal variables will be part of the supervision process. If a supervisor acknowledges the importance of culture and the clients' cultural background, the supervisee is more likely to enhance their awareness of cultural humility. Hook et al. (2016) had found this to be the case when they considered ways in which supervisors can stimulate supervisees to develop cultural humility. Modelling this in supervision and teaching cultural humility are the areas in which their model is focussed. Taking as a starting point that supervision can support supervisee cultural development, King et al. (2020) found that the supervisory alliance was impacted by the supervisor's cultural humility and willingness or lack thereof to discuss culture in sessions.

To measure the impact of multicultural supervision in counselling and clinical psychology, Tsong and Goodyear (2014) developed a Supervision Outcome Scale (SOS) to be a valid instrument to assess the impact of supervision on cultural competence, decreasing client symptoms and improving supervisees' work with clients as well as multicultural competence. They found that the supervisees were not as aware of changes in their multicultural competence due to supervision as they were of changes in their clinical effectiveness. It seemed that multicultural awareness was not overtly being conveyed to supervisees.

Application of Postmodernism

A Feminist Framework of Supervision can be an approach that integrates feminist principles into the supervisory relationship. Feminist principles aim to empower supervisees by valuing their strengths, experiences, and insights, while fostering a collaborative relationship. The framework highlights the importance of understanding and addressing power imbalances within supervision and the broader context of society. It encourages supervisors to be mindful of how the power dynamic can affect the supervisee's professional development and well-being. Within this framework self-awareness is promoted in both supervisors and supervisees. This includes examining one's own biases, assumptions, and values, and understanding how these influence their professional practice. A feminist framework considers the multiple and intersecting identities (such as gender, race, ethnicity, sexual orientation, socioeconomic status) of both the supervisor and supervisee.

By incorporating these principles, a feminist framework of supervision creates a more inclusive, equitable, and supportive environment for personal and professional development of the supervisee. Applying postmodernism, such as a feminist framework, as an overlay (see Postmodern Umbrella in Chap. 1) with the supervision model will support cultural responsiveness within the supervisor and supervisee relationship as well as informing and modelling within the counsellor and client relationship.

Case Study

Ana James (supervisee) and Dr. Margot Lee (supervisor) using a feminist framework and applying a psychodynamic clinical supervision model.

Background

Ana is a 30-year-old counsellor working at a women's shelter. She has been practising for four years and is currently under the supervision of Dr. Margot Lee, a psychodynamic therapist with a strong feminist orientation.

Presenting Issue

Ana has been working with Maria, a 40-year-old woman who has experienced domestic violence. Maria struggles with feelings of worthlessness and self-blame. Ana feels connected to Maria's story but finds herself becoming emotionally overwhelmed and unsure of how to best support her client.

Supervision Session

Dr. Lee starts the supervision session by asking Ana to describe her sessions with Maria in detail. Ana shares that Maria frequently discusses her feelings of worthlessness and self-blame, which evoke strong emotional responses in her.

Dr. Lee describes the concepts of transference and countertransference from a psychodynamic perspective. They explore how Maria might be transferring her feelings of worthlessness and self-blame onto Ana, possibly viewing her as a judgmental or critical figure. Conversely, Ana's strong emotional responses could be countertransference, reflecting her own unresolved feelings related to her experiences as a woman in a patriarchal society.

Dr. Lee integrates feminist principles by discussing the societal context of Maria's experiences. They explore how patriarchal structures and cultural norms have contributed to Maria's feelings of worthlessness and self-blame. Dr. Lee emphasises the importance of validating Maria's experiences and recognising the external factors influencing her internal struggles.

Exploring Ana's Background

Dr. Lee asks Ana to reflect on any personal experiences or societal messages that might be influencing her reactions to Maria's story. Ana shares that she, too, has faced gender-based discrimination and societal pressure, which might be contributing to her emotional responses and desire to protect Maria.

Developing Strategies

Dr. Lee encourages Ana to support Maria by helping her recognise contributions of the societal roots that may be impacting her feelings, which may foster a sense of agency for Maria. They discuss ways how Ana can support Maria in reclaiming her sense of self-worth and advocating for her own needs and rights.

Dr. Lee and Ana develop strategies to manage the transference and countertransference dynamics. These include maintaining a reflective stance, setting emotional boundaries, and using supervision as a space to process her own feelings. They also discuss ways to incorporate feminist principles into Ana's therapeutic approach, such as validating Maria's experiences and exploring the impact of societal norms on her self-perception.

Ongoing Reflection

Dr. Lee encourages Ana to continue reflecting on her feelings and reactions in future supervision sessions. They agree to regularly revisit this case to monitor progress and address any new challenges.

Outcome

Over time, Ana becomes more attuned to the transference and countertransference dynamics in her work with Maria. She learns to manage her own emotional responses and creates a validating and empowering space for Maria. Maria begins to recognise the societal roots of her feelings of worthlessness and starts to reclaim her sense of self-worth. Ana feels more confident and supported in her role as a therapist.

Key Points

- Integration of Feminist and Psychodynamic Approaches through understanding and addressing transference and countertransference within the societal context.
- Encourage empowerment and advocacy by using a feminist framework to validate the client's experiences and promote agency.
- Self-Reflection for Ana through ongoing exploration of personal and societal influences on the therapeutic process.

- Creating a collaborative and supportive supervision relationship that fosters professional growth and development.

Psychodynamic clinical supervision is tailored to the individual supervisee's developmental stage and learning needs, aiming to foster a deeper understanding of unconscious processes, enhance relational skills, and promote effective psychodynamic practice. Overlaying a feminist framework opens broader aspects of the client's societal context as well as the lived experiences which contribute to the complexity of the client story.

Conclusion

From its early beginnings as a mixed clinical and managerial activity, providing oversight and ensuring that tasks were carried out effectively in nursing environments, supervision has developed by differentiating clinical from task-oriented managerial supervision. When provided by experienced practitioners who have additionally trained to be supervisors, this offers safety and freedom for supervisees to explore and discuss what has occurred in their counselling sessions, to share concerns and where they might feel they have a lack of skill or knowledge without fear. In a supportive, ethical, and boundaried environment the supervisee can grow and develop with confidence and provide the best possible professional service to clients.

In this chapter we have noted the lack of cultural adaptation or responsiveness across several established supervision models. Yet we are hopeful that supervision and supervisor training will continue to evolve, and such responsiveness will become an integral part of every supervisor's career, and in this way also become an integral part of practitioners' awareness and practice.

References

Apostolidou, Z., & Schweitzer, R. (2017). Practitioners' perspectives on the use of clinical supervision in their therapeutic engagement with asylum seekers and refugee clients. *British Journal of Guidance & Counselling, 45*(1), 72–82. https://doi.org/10.1080/03069885.2015.1125852

Arbuckle, D. S. (1965). Supervision: Learning, not counseling. *Journal of Counseling Psychology, 12*(1), 90–94. https://doi.org/10.1037/h0020497

Bambling, M., King, R., Raue, P., Schweitzer, R., & Lambert, W. (2006). Clinical supervision: Its influence on client-rated working alliance and client symptom

reduction in the brief treatment of major depression. *Psychotherapy Research, 16*(3), 317–331. https://doi.org/10.1080/10503300500268524
Bernard, J. M. (1979). Supervisor training: A discrimination model. *Counselor Education and Supervision, 19*, 60–68.
Borders, L. D. (2006). Snapshot of clinical supervision in counseling and counselor education: A five-year review. *The Clinical Supervisor, 24*(1–2), 69–113. https://doi.org/10.1300/J001v24n01_05
Burton, W. H. (1930). Supervision. *The American Journal of Nursing, 30*(8), 1045–1052. https://doi.org/10.1097/00000446-193008000-00028
Callahan, J. L., & Love, P. K. (2020). Introduction to the special issue: Supervisee perspectives of supervision processes. *Journal of Psychotherapy Integration, 30*(1), 1–8. https://doi.org/10.1037/int0000199
Carroll, M. (1988). Counselling supervision: The British context. *Counselling Psychology Quarterly, 1*(4), 387–396. https://doi.org/10.1080/09515078808254224
Cashwell, T. H., & Dooley, K. (2001). The impact of supervision on counselor self-efficacy. *The Clinical Supervisor, 20*(1), 39–47. https://doi.org/10.1300/J001v20n01_03
Constantine, M. G. (2001). Multiculturally-focused counseling supervision: Its relationship to trainees' multicultural counseling self-efficacy. *The Clinical Supervisor, 20*(1), 87–98. https://doi.org/10.1300/J001v20n01_07
Creaner, M. (2013). *Getting the best out of supervision in counselling and psychotherapy: guide for the supervisee*. Sage.
Falender, C. A. (2014). Supervision outcomes: Beginning the journey beyond the emperor's new clothes. *Training and Education in Professional Psychology, 8*(3), 143–148. https://doi.org/10.1037/tep0000066
Falender, C. A. (2018). Clinical supervision—The missing ingredient. *American Psychologist, 73*(9), 1240–1250. https://doi.org/10.1037/amp0000385
Falender, C. A., & Shafranske, E. P. (2012). The importance of competency-based clinical supervision and training in the twenty-first century: Why bother? *Journal of Contemporary Psychotherapy, 42*(3), 129–137. https://doi.org/10.1007/s10879-011-9198-9
Gurk, M. D., & Wicas, E. A. (1979). Generic models of counseling supervision: Counseling/instruction dichotomy and consultation metamodel. *The Personnel and Guidance Journal, 57*(8), 402–407. https://doi.org/10.1002/j.2164-4918.1979.tb05422.x
Hess, A. K., & Hess, K. A. (1983). Psychotherapy supervision: A survey of internship training practices. *Professional Psychology, Research and Practice, 14*(4), 504–513. https://doi.org/10.1037/0735-7028.14.4.504
Holloway, E., & Wolleat, P. L. (1994). Supervision: The pragmatics of empowerment. *Journal of Educational and Psychological Consultation, 5*(1), 23–43.
Hook, J. N., Watkins, J., Davis, D. E., Owen, J., Van Tongeren, D. R., & Ramos, M. J. (2016). Cultural humility in psychotherapy supervision. *American*

Journal of Psychotherapy, 70(2), 149–166. https://doi.org/10.1176/appi.psychotherapy.2016.70.2.149

Hooley, E. M. (2019). Power, diversity, and relational process within supervision. *Training and Education in Professional Psychology, 13*(3), 212–215. https://doi.org/10.1037/tep0000235

King, K. M., Borders, L. D., & Jones, C. T. (2020). Multicultural orientation in clinical supervision: examining impact through dyadic data. *The Clinical Supervisor, 39*(2), 248–271. https://doi.org/10.1080/07325223.2020.1763223

Koçyiğit, M. (2024). Novice supervisees' anxiety in counselling supervision: a phenomenological study. *Studies in Continuing Education, 46*(1), 65–81. https://doi.org/10.1080/0158037X.2022.2161501

Luke, M., & Bernard, J. M. (2006). The School Counseling Supervision Model: An Extension of the Discrimination Model. *Counselor Education and Supervision, 45*(4), 282–295. https://doi.org/10.1002/j.1556-6978.2006.tb00004.x

Mangione, L., Mears, G., Vincent, W., & Hawes, S. (2011). The supervisory relationship when women supervise women: An exploratory study of power, reflexivity, collaboration and authenticity. *The Clinical Supervisor, 30*(2), 141–171. https://doi.org/10.1080/07325223.2011.604272

Olds, K., & Hawkins, R. (2014). Precursors to measuring outcomes in clinical supervision: A thematic analysis. *Training and Education in Professional Psychology, 8*(3), 158–164. https://doi.org/10.1037/tep0000034

Patterson, C. H. (1964). Supervising students in the counseling practicum. *Journal of Counseling Psychology, 11*(1), 47–53. https://doi.org/10.1037/h0045575

Peake, T. H., Nussbaum, B. D., & Tindell, S. D. (2002). Clinical and counseling supervision references: Trends and needs. *Psychotherapy (Chicago, Ill.), 39*(1), 114–125. https://doi.org/10.1037/0033-3204.39.1.114

Pepper, R. S. (2018). The need for safety in clinical supervision. *Group, 42*(1), 55–58. https://doi.org/10.13186/group.42.1.0055

Robiner, W. N., & Schofield, W. (1990). References on supervision in clinical and counseling psychology. *Professional Psychology, Research and Practice, 21*(4), 297–312. https://doi.org/10.1037/0735-7028.21.4.297

Schmidt, E. (1926). Principles and practice of supervision: A course of study in supervision in hospitals and schools of nursing. *The American Journal of Nursing, 26*(2), 119–120. https://doi.org/10.1097/00000446-192626020-00010

Schon, D. A. (1987). *Educating the reflective practitioner*. Jossey-Bass.

Stoltenberg, C. D. (1981). Approaching supervision from a developmental perspective: The counselor complexity model. *Journal of Counseling Psychology, 28*, 59–65.

Stoltenberg, C. D., & Delworth, U. (1987). *Supervising counselors and therapists.* Jossey-Bass.

Stoltenberg, C. D., McNeill, B., & Delworth, U. (1998). *IDM supervision: An integrated developmental model for supervising counselors and therapists.* Jossey-Bass.

Tremmel, R. (1993). Zen and the art of reflective practice in teacher education. *Harvard Educational Review, 63*(4), 434–458. https://doi.org/10.17763/haer.63.4.m42704n778561176

Tsong, Y., & Goodyear, R. K. (2014). Assessing supervision's clinical and multicultural impacts: The supervision outcome scale's psychometric properties. *Training and Education in Professional Psychology, 8*(3), 189–195. https://doi.org/10.1037/tep0000049

Vallance, K. (2004). Exploring counsellor perceptions of the impact of counselling supervision on clients. *British Journal of Guidance & Counselling, 32*(4), 559–574. https://doi.org/10.1080/03069880412331303330

Ward, C. C., & House, R. M. (1998). Counseling supervision: A reflective model. *Counselor Education and Supervision, 38*(1), 23–33. https://doi.org/10.1002/j.1556-6978.1998.tb00554.x

Watkins, C. E. (2014). The competent psychoanalytic supervisor: Some thoughts about supervision competencies for accountable practice and training. *International Forum of Psychoanalysis, 23*(4), 220–228. https://doi.org/10.1080/0803706X.2012.712219

Watkins, C. E. (2020a). Psychotherapy supervision: An ever-evolving signature pedagogy. *World Psychiatry, 19*(2), 244–245. https://doi.org/10.1002/wps.20747

Watkins, C. E. (2020b). The rise and reach of humility in clinical supervision: Reactions to McMahon (2020), Jones and Branco (2020), Gutierrez et al. (2020), and Beinart (2020). *The Clinical Supervisor, 39*(2), 229–247. https://doi.org/10.1080/07325223.2020.1830459

Wheeler, S., & Richards, K. (2007). The impact of clinical supervision on counsellors and therapists, their practice and their clients. A systematic review of the literature. *Counselling and Psychotherapy Research, 7*(1), 54–65. https://doi.org/10.1080/14733140601185274

Whitman, S. M., Ryan, B., & Rubenstein, D. F. (2001). Psychotherapy supervisor training: Differences between psychiatry and other mental health disciplines. *Academic Psychiatry, 25*(3), 156–161. https://doi.org/10.1176/appi.ap.25.3.156

Wilson, H. M. N., Davies, J. S., & Weatherhead, S. (2016). Trainee Therapists' experiences of supervision during training: A meta-synthesis. *Clinical Psychology and Psychotherapy, 23*(4), 340–351. https://doi.org/10.1002/cpp.1957

CHAPTER 5

Cultural Responsiveness in Clinical Practice

Keiko Sano and Dax Bevly

Introduction

In the last decade, multiculturalism and social justice have been discussed as core considerations in clinical practice (Ratts et al., 2016). Traditionally, many counseling philosophies developed within Western individualistic contexts, along with the assumption that counselors are working from privileged social locations while clients are from marginalized backgrounds (Price, 2015). Thus, the literature often emphasizes the demonstration of multicultural skills or competence from the perspective of the majority culture (Ridley et al., 2021; Tittler et al., 2022). Additionally, there is little research offering a clear and concrete operationalization of culturally responsive clinical practice. Culturally responsive counselors use themselves along with their social identities as a therapeutic tool to recognize,

K. Sano (✉)
Counselor Education, Antioch University, Seattle, WA, USA
e-mail: ksano@antioch.edu

D. Bevly
School of Applied Psychology, Counseling and Family Therapy, Antioch University, Seattle, WA, USA
e-mail: dbevly@antioch.edu

S. Sisko (ed.), *Culturally Responsive Psychotherapy, Counselling & Psychology*, Palgrave Texts in Counselling and Psychotherapy,
https://doi.org/10.1007/978-3-031-81831-8_5

reflect, and process their inner experiences with their clients (Al-khodair & Alrawaf, 2023). Thus, in this chapter, the authors seek to incorporate systemic perspectives that highlight diverse clinical schools of thought toward counseling, the therapeutic relationship, diagnosis and assessment, theoretical applications, and ethical considerations by emphasizing counselors' self-awareness in practice from the social location of counselors and clients with various privileged and marginalized cultural backgrounds and identities. A brief case study with examples of applying culturally responsive principles, as well as reflective discussion questions, will offer readers the opportunity to further explore their understanding, awareness, and application of themselves as a therapeutic resource.

Over the past several decades, the counseling field has increased its attention to incorporating a social justice-oriented perspective into clinical practice. The American Counseling Association (ACA) endorsed the Multicultural and Social Justice Counseling Competencies (MSJCC; Ratts et al., 2016) that urged counselors to take action toward reducing injustice and inequity related to clinical work. These multicultural and social justice competencies also called counselors to engage in advocacy at six ecological levels: intrapersonal, interpersonal, institutional, community, public policy, and international/global, using their skills to promote social justice with and on behalf of clients (Ratts et al., 2016). However, there is a lack of information on how counselors can practically apply these principles with clients. Therefore, we discuss how to integrate multiculturalism and social justice attitudes, beliefs, knowledge, and skills into the therapeutic relationship, ethics, assessment and diagnosis, and counseling theory and application. Lastly, we will summarize how to apply the concepts we have discussed to a case study at the end of this chapter.

The Therapeutic Relationship

Within the Western cultural perspective, multicultural counseling literature often assumes the clinical relationship where the counselor is from the majority culture and the client is from a marginalized culture. Thus, scholars may perceive multiculturalism from Western values, which are not aligned with the values and professional identities of counselors from diverse backgrounds and create cultural conflicts with their culture of origin (Interiano & Lim, 2018). This section explores factors of multicultural competence in the context of therapeutic relationships.

The therapeutic alliance has been discussed as a significant aspect of the client's outcome in counseling (Casas et al., 2016; Tao et al., 2015). In fact, they are the most impactful predictors of the therapeutic process (Norcross & Lambert, 2019). On the other hand, counselors' ineffective relational behaviors can be harmful to their clients (Norcross & Lambert, 2018). Traditionally, clinical training emphasizes building rapport within the counseling relationship. Due to the importance of the therapeutic alliance, counselors' development of multicultural competence, particularly multicultural awareness, is considered to be one of the most critical goals in professional training as attention to globalization and diversity of the field of counseling increases (Mollen & Ridley, 2021; Vasquez & Johnson, 2022).

Self-Awareness

In the therapeutic alliance, counselors' self-awareness has been recognized to be an essential element (Pieterse et al., 2013), as well as an essential skill counselors need in order to offer effective clinical interventions (Jack & Miller, 2008). Self-awareness is critical to managing counselors' inner experiences, such as their feelings and thoughts, as well as their nonverbal behaviors (Al-khodair & Alrawaf, 2023). Counselors with strong levels of self-awareness are capable of differentiation and bracketing, putting aside their reactions and the urge to respond to their clients without thoughtful examination first (Campbell et al., 2018) so that they can step back and reflect on the situation as a whole (Al-khodair & Alrawaf, 2023). Counselors practicing self-awareness demonstrate this skill by observing nonverbal communication to formulate an accurate client conceptualization that considers multicultural perspectives while processing their inner experiences to be mindful of possible biases toward certain cultures. Stereotypes are often socially constructed, and the process of moving from self-awareness as a subjective process to self-awareness in the context of multicultural perspectives involves several important steps.

Being Attuned

Counselors paying attention to the body language of clients and/or themselves can be fundamental in forming a meaningful connection in the here-and-now. However, these cues are easily overlooked, disregarded, or misunderstood. For instance, a client's lack of eye contact might be interpreted as respectful in one culture and disrespectful or evasive in another culture. Carefully observing clients' nonverbal communication and discussing these experiences can provide insights and deepen understanding.

Recognizing Stereotypes and Biases

Our subjective experiences and perspectives are uniquely shaped by socio-cultural contexts and previous experiences, which can result in misinterpretations. Because a lack of awareness of the possible biases can cause counselors to impose their own values onto their clients, counselors must continually challenge the manifestation and influence of stereotypes and biases. Asking questions, such as "Through what lens am I seeing and listening to this client?" or "Why do I feel uncomfortable with this client?" can aid in this process.

Cultivating Curiosity

Shifting assumptions from knowledge to curiosity is crucial. Learning may be inhibited when counselors assume they fully know their clients and the meaning of their words. Counselors maintaining curiosity and intent to learn more about clients and themselves is vital in recognizing possible stereotypes and unknown biases. Asking questions, such as "Why do I want to ask this question to this client?" can help reframe the question to be more culturally relevant and enhance the counseling relationship dynamics.

Seeking Feedback

Increasing self-awareness solely as an individual process may have limitations. Reviewing recorded sessions as well as asking peers and supervisors for observation feedback may provide objective perspectives and opportunities to discuss cultural and social justice dynamics and issues. Increasing awareness by seeking corrective feedback is a key strategy for counselors' interpersonal and intrapersonal development regardless of their level of experience.

Despite the emphasis on counselors' self-awareness, novice counselors and counselors-in-training tend to focus on their own level of competence, such as using specific skills and problem-solving. Additionally, they tend to be focused on performance and seek feedback about what the right thing is to say or do to help their clients. There are no universal aspects or manuals for building an effective therapeutic alliance with clients; due to the nature of the work, it is important to note that the client's subjective experience is the most important evaluation of the counselor's competency and relational skills. Because the clients may or may not tell the truth for various reasons, it can be difficult for counselors to know if their intervention was effective for the client. As a result, novice counselors often become uncomfortable with holding the unknown and tolerating uncertainty. In order to increase their sense of comfort and regulation, counselors tend to shift their focus from their inner experience (being) to their performance (doing) to gain their benefit such as satisfaction or self-evaluation, rather than their clients' well-being.

Counselors focused primarily on competency, whether or not they performed the skills and techniques correctly, run the risk of decreased attention and attunement to their self-awareness and the therapeutic alliance; this may impact the counseling relationship in the form of negative treatment outcomes or even harm to clients. Indeed, researchers have highlighted how counselors who prioritize competency performance tend to engage with projection, advice-giving, or interpreting their clients inaccurately (Jensen et al., 2015). These tendencies may stem from unaware biases and/or their need to be seen favorably by clients (Richard et al., 2020). In other words, counselors who demonstrate increased awareness demonstrate their ability to focus on the benefit and well-being of their clients and hold multiple perspectives.

Due to the nature of education and training, developing and modeling counseling skills and professional competency, including ethical and multicultural competence, are fundamental requirements. Competence is assessed by counselor educators, supervisors, clients, and peers, in addition to one's own subjective assessment. However, counselors who are overly focused on prioritizing competence and fulfilling their own agenda over the clients' needs or well-being may cause significant harm to their clients. In the field of counseling, although demonstrating competence undoubtedly ensures quality care, prioritizing self-awareness regarding counselor values and goals in delivering competent practice holds even greater significance.

Before meeting their clients, counselors must clearly establish their client-focused intentions. Some general yet unconscious motives for counselors-in-training and novice counselors who focus on competency include the need for approval, acknowledgment, appreciation, good grades, competition with their peers, and earning the trust of clients, particularly when they are unfamiliar with the clients' cultural backgrounds. Instead of rushing to do or say something, counselors can remain calm and sit with the present as they pay attention to both their and their client's experiences in the here-and-now. Recognizing their own areas of growth, paying attention to internal cues indicates their urge to perform well, and increasing emotional regulation skills to boost levels of differentiation as a counseling professional are all important applications of self-awareness in regard to culturally responsive counseling.

Therapeutic Presence

Geller's (2021) definition of *therapeutic presence* describes counselors' way of being and engaging with their clients, rather than the demonstration of clinical techniques. Counselors attune to the present experiences of themselves and their clients by bringing themselves fully to the here-and-now with their clients (Geller, 2017). It has been well documented that counselors' full presence and engagement with clients supports emotional co-regulation (Geller & Porges, 2014); the counselor's therapeutic presence helps increase clients' emotional safety which enhances the mutual connection, thus strengthening the therapeutic alliance (Geller & Porges, 2014).

For counselors, learning techniques and interventions may be the primary focus of their professional development, especially because graduate courses and training often emphasize obtaining, practicing, and demonstrating clinical skills. This performance-emphasis approach and evaluative aspect within the field of counselor education and training can directly influence the tendency of counselors to lean toward "being good" and "doing it right" as benchmarks of appraisal. However, we the authors advocate for a shift of focus on therapeutic presence, authenticity, accountability, accepting imperfection, and repair, rather than the fear and self-doubt of "doing it wrong" or making mistakes. This focus on the self and the self in relationship could generate more meaningful learning experiences. Counselors modeling to take risks or engage with repairing possible misunderstandings or miscommunications can offer clients opportunities to heal and grow through the counseling relationship. This modeling can contribute to mediating the unnegotiable power balance between the counselor and client to increase the client's sense of safety and trust.

Power Dynamics

In therapeutic relationships, counselors are often considered to be in a position of power within traditional theories and practices. Counselor education research emphasizes that counselors should be mindful of the potential misuse of power as it may negatively influence the therapeutic alliance as well as outcomes (Astramovich & Scott, 2020; Clark et al., 2022; Kress et al., 2018). However, the literature often assumes counselors are in privileged social positions while their clients have marginalized identities; this assumption ignores situations where the counselor may have less power and privilege than their clients in the larger system within a particular social identity. For instance, if a counselor is a member of a marginalized community, such as being part of an ethnic minority, having a visible or invisible disability, or a low socioeconomic status, working with a client who holds more social power in that category may experience a lack of power in this context. Indeed, researchers have discussed that counselors with marginalized identities report reversed power dynamics, powerlessness, and discrimination, as well as a lack of respect when working with clients who may have more privilege within that social dimension (Sano, 2019). Although awareness of the granted power is essential, it is also critical to be aware of the power constructed within social contexts, as well as how it manifests within the counseling relationship.

Additionally, cultural differences influence perspectives toward power (Pendse & Inman, 2017; Sato, 2014). In collectivist cultures, clients often perceive and expect their counselor to be an expert and authority figure. They may be confused or have difficulty trusting their counselor who overtly tries to minimize their power or push for client empowerment. Clients from more collectivistic cultures tend to seek advice from their counselor because they may not know what to expect in clinical settings and/or they want to know what to do in their lives, just as they do with their physicians. However, within more individualistic cultures, clients sharing an equal role in the clinical setting is more normative and beneficial (Knox & Hill, 2016); from this perspective it is the client's responsibility to assess their present experiences and needs in therapy, without any assumptions or impositions from the counselor.

For example, seeking advice is a culturally bound behavior that requires much nuance in the form of self-awareness and therapeutic presence. Because many collectivistic cultures value respect, especially for authority figures, some clients with a collectivistic background may ask questions and advice in clinical settings because they want to demonstrate respect and maintain the hierarchy in which the counselor is the expert. If the counselor does not know this intention, they may offer advice to their client to be culturally competent and helpful. However, the client may not follow their advice as the true purpose was to show respect; the counselor may then mistakenly perceive this behavior as resistance or a lack of motivation. On the contrary, if the counselor does not answer the questions or offer advice because they want to cultivate an egalitarian relationship in which power is shared with the client, the client may doubt the counselor is incompetent or unhelpful.

The first author observed and heard this type of dilemma from novice counselors and counselors-in-training working cross-culturally. In many cases, the counselors who experienced difficulty building rapport or trust with their clients often tried to earn the client's approval by offering or doing something to enhance positive relationship dynamics. Delivering psychoeducation seems to be one of the common mistakes counselors make to try and earn this rapport and trust, particularly when they are unaware that their lack of confidence or anxiety stems from sensing mistrust from their client; this is one example of counselors' misuse of their power, which can cause negative influence in various ways. First, the counselor is not aware of the client's cultural values and norms regarding respect to others; second, the counselor lacks awareness of the needs of both the client and counselor in the here-and-now; third, the counselor lacks understanding of the role of psychoeducation; fourth, the counselor has a tendency to jump into an immediate problem-solving approach rather than a careful assessment of the client's experience of the relationship in the here-and-now.

Culturally responsive counselors must be mindful of therapeutic intention by carefully and objectively assessing their experiences, as well as seeking consultations from others to continue increasing awareness. This self-reflective practice can assist counselors in being aware of their inner experiences with their clients at present to use as an effective intervention. Counselors modeling awareness and continuing to invite clients to discuss their authentic perspectives and experiences in the relationship can help build rapport and explore mutual understanding to enhance the therapeutic alliance.

Ethical Considerations

An important component of a culturally responsive therapeutic relationship involves conceptualizing and framing ethics from a multicultural perspective. Professional organizations in the field of counseling dictate their ethics codes that discuss principles and standards of professional practices and clients' welfare (Herlihy & Corey, 2015). Counselors and counselors-in-training continue to learn about the mandates and guidelines that promote ethical compliance and competency. However, ethical codes in Western countries are developed within the individualistic and patriarchal contexts primarily by White male professionals (Rentería et al., 2020). Thus, even though those ethical codes include multicultural considerations, we can mistakenly impose Western values and perspectives by not maintaining awareness of universal assumptions for ethical behavior. Counselors and novice counselors-in-training can face challenges in noticing gray areas in practicing ethical decision-making, which may inhibit the learning and growth of their clients as well as themselves. Said another way, determining ethical practices in terms of the therapeutic relationship can be challenging because one's assessment of behaviors is closely associated with intra and interpersonal relational values of both clients' and counselors. This section aims to deconstruct Western norms and values in therapeutic relationships by practicing increasing a sense of comfort in holding ambiguity and uncertainty in developing effective therapeutic relationships with clients.

Relational Boundaries

Counseling and psychotherapy are considered to be healing practice deeply rooted in cultural contexts, in the sense that it differs from traditional medical models (Wampold, 2001, 2021). The positive relationship between the client and the counselor is one of the critical components of the clients' healing experience. However, traditional counseling theories often ignore multicultural consideration, so counselors are required to use their own awareness and clinical judgment in building relationships with their clients. When the counselor is less familiar with certain cultural values or perspectives of the client, or less aware of their own stereotypes and biases, those counselors may mistakenly assume that their relationship can be built the same with any and all clients. Therefore, when counselors recognize their clients' resistance to openly discuss their presenting concerns or hesitating to disclose certain information, the counselors may assume that those challenges will be resolved when they move forward without exploring cultural considerations.

In a collectivistic culture, it is possible that the client is consciously and unconsciously resistant to healing because individual changes can be difficult to maintain within their family system, sometimes shifting to an unknown dynamic. For example, a child client is raised by parents who often argue, yet both align with each other to support the child client. This may lead to feelings of fear of losing their parents' alignment or support if they no longer feel anxious. Another example is that clients tend to protect their family members by minimizing or withholding their challenges with them to save face or maintain loyalty. Maintaining relationships can be considered more important than their well-being in collectivistic cultures, which can manifest in significant ways within the counseling relationship.

For example, clinical training often teaches counselors-in-training to ask open-ended questions, such as "What are *you* feeling?" or "What do *you* want?" However, for some clients, focusing on themselves is often challenging because they are more oriented toward feeling responsible for what others feel and want. The conflict between clients' perspective of "it is not just about me" and the counselors' focus of "it is about your well-being" can create tension and conflict. As a result, some clients may choose to stay away from the individualistic focus of the clinical practices, or perhaps choose to say what they believe the counselor wants to hear. Additionally, these unique cultural perspectives can create more challenges for the clients in group counseling settings because the client is concerned with other group members, in addition to their counselors and people in their lives. Thus, it is important to consider the client's relational context from the framework of their culture, background, and family of origin when assessing boundaries.

Assessing, determining, and maintaining appropriate professional boundaries is another area of counseling that needs to consider cultural appropriateness. Culture can greatly influence clients' comfort levels with boundaries and boundary setting in their relationships with themselves and others. Furthermore, setting boundaries itself is influenced by their characteristics, previous experiences, and expectations, in addition to cultural contexts. Counselors may notice their clients tend to cross, withdraw from, negotiate, or expand boundaries, either overtly or covertly. Instead of assuming the intentionality of such behaviors or even educating clients on ethical codes, counselors are encouraged to assess their own values around boundaries and empathically confront their observations of client behaviors. For example, when might it be therapeutic to expand or change boundaries? What is your reaction when your client wants to know more about you? What is your value in receiving gifts? How do you see the situation when your teen client wants their parents to know everything about what you are working on with them? Before assessing or analyzing our clients' intentionality, paying attention to our own reactions and perceptions is essential.

Helpful and Harmful Self-Disclosure

Counselors' therapeutic self-disclosure can be an effective and therapeutic experience for some clients. However, novice counselors are often uncertain about what is therapeutic and what is unhelpful or unethical self-disclosure. Below are some examples to distinguish between counselors' self-disclosure that might be therapeutic or unhelpful.

Broaching

Broaching refers to counselors' genuine commitment and effort to openly and consistently invite their clients to explore diverse issues (Day-Vines et al., 2020). Broaching can invite clients to acknowledge and address possible misunderstandings with their counselors. Counselors' ongoing and frequent invitations can help build rapport and increase their awareness and understanding of multiple perspectives (Ganz, 2020). However, because broaching offered without counselors' cultural awareness and sensitivity can damage their therapeutic relationships (Bayne & Branco, 2018), and offering clients effective and culturally sensitive broaching can be often challenging for novice counselors.

Broaching requires counselors' ability to be aware and process various sociocultural identities and power dynamics influencing the clients' experience including their therapeutic relationships. However, counselors' uncertainty, lack of confidence, and discomfort may result in missing an opportunity to broach (Bayne & Branco, 2018). For example, counselors from dominant cultures may feel a sense of urgency to broach earlier in their counseling process whereas counselors from marginalized cultural backgrounds may experience discomfort and uncertainty in which sociocultural identities should be discussed openly with their clients.

Unlike a positionality statement, where a counselor addresses their sociocultural identities and how those identities may influence their work, broaching can be an invitation and dialogue between the counselor and their client. In considering broaching comes from the counselors' self-awareness and is an invitation to the client, we encourage counselors to broach in more general terms, such as:

> We are all from different cultural and family backgrounds, regardless of some of the shared or different identities. My goal is to understand your unique experiences instead of assuming them or imposing my values or beliefs on you. So, please let me know at any time if you feel I don't understand what you said or misunderstand you.

The above statement does not discuss specific identities, such as "I'm a White male" and does not ask questions to their clients, such as "What is your race?" where the counselor determines what identities are important. Instead, counselors can ask their clients:

1. Which identities are important for you in your life and our work together?
2. What similarities and differences do you see between us?
3. What would you like me to know about you in relation to your identities?

Counselors need to be aware that some clients are not used to talking about their identities, and broaching is an ongoing process.

Here-and-Now

Counselors who are fully engaged and attuned with the client may use their insights to describe their awareness in the here-and-now. For example, "I am sensing some tension in listening to your experience. I wonder if this is just my reaction or you might also feel that way." It is important to avoid imposing the counselors' perspectives or experiences on the client, so inviting the client to share their perspectives by checking the counselors' possible biases or assumptions is essential. Clients may disagree or reject the statement, so this type of self-disclosure requires the counselors' professional risk-taking, which can increase the sense of safety and demonstration of trust toward the client.

Shared Experiences
Counselors briefly disclosing their shared challenging experience can balance possible power dynamics. For example, teen clients show hesitation in talking about their experiences of being bullied because of their feeling shameful or fear of being judged by the counselor; counselors may say "I was also bullied for a few years, and I couldn't tell anyone." This type of counselor's self-disclosure may promote safety, trust, and acceptance within the counseling relationship.

Unconscious Hidden Agenda
When counselors feel a lack of trust or therapeutic alliance with their clients, they may mistakenly engage in unhelpful self-disclosure. For example, when a client says they are from Peru, the counselor describes their experience of visiting Peru. When a client says they went skiing last week, the counselor also says they enjoy skiing too. This type of self-disclosure can be risky because the client may think the counselor talks about themselves too much, or may feel hesitant to talk negatively about skilling because the counselor discusses it in a positive way.

Reflective Practice

In sum, there are many important aspects of cultivating a culturally responsive therapeutic relationship. However, in order to orient self-awareness, therapeutic presence, power dynamics, ethics, boundaries, and self-disclosure from a multicultural framework, counselors must engage in reflective practice. Reflective practice is a process to reflect experiences to look at what/how we said and did in our work with our clients and how we can apply our reflections to increase self-awareness and effectiveness of our practice. Reflective practice can be beneficial for clients to feel more satisfied with their counselor, and counselors to increase opportunities to look back at their client sessions, as well as help plan for future sessions. Below are some questions used to support reflective practice.

Questions for Clients

1. How do you see similarities and differences between you and me?
2. How are we doing together?
3. What are your experiences in working with me?
4. What can I do more or less for you?

Questions for Counselors

1. How my culturally influenced values, beliefs, biases, and stereotypes may manifest in my understanding of the client and my interactions with them?
2. How do my family of origin dynamics play in roles?
3. The thing I did/said was beneficial for the client or for me?
4. Why do I feel more comfortable with my client A but not with my client B?
5. Am I regulating enough throughout the session?

Questions for Supervisors and Peers

1. What else do you notice about my possible blind spot or biases?
2. How do you see this client's experience differently from me?

Building a culturally responsive relationship between counselor and client is the core foundation of any therapy modality or treatment. However, the work of multicultural attunement does not stop there. The next section discusses culturally sensitive clinical practices related to assessment and diagnosis.

Assessment and Diagnosis

Historical Background

It is important to acknowledge and understand the sociocultural history of diagnosis and assessment in the mental health field, especially the harm that marginalized clients have experienced at the hands of a healthcare system that is part of the oppressive structure of the world. Counselors who lack awareness and sensitivity to clients who are culturally different risk conceptualizing behaviors that are heavily influenced by social forces specific to the Western cultural context as representative of all human behavior rather than of only one cultural possibility out of many. Said another way, a counselor unfamiliar with the client's cultural background is at risk of inaccurately diagnosing the normal variations in behavior, belief, or experience that are particular to the client's culture as pathology (Guindon & Sobhany, 2001). Counselors, therefore, must understand the implications of culture and its influence in their assessment and diagnosis. For example, individuals and institutions used classifications of mental disorders to pathologize some marginalized populations; homosexuality was considered deviant and pathological until the publication of the *DSM-III-R* (American Psychiatric Association [APA], 1987). Miller and Prosek (2013) described the complicated history of homosexuality and the *DSM*, illuminating the influence of social norms, special interests, and political advocacy. A similar history can be found in regard to the African American population (e.g., drapetomania, the desire to escape slavery).

Furthermore, although clients with marginalized identities remained underrepresented in research examining mental unwellness, Black and Hispanic/Latine clients are more likely to be diagnosed, to receive diagnoses of greater severity, and to experience less effective treatment outcomes than are White clients (Sue et al., 2022). Additionally, women are disproportionately diagnosed with personality disorders (Eriksen & Kress, 2005), lesbian, gay, and bisexual clients are diagnosed 3 times and 4.7 times the rate of heterosexual clients for major depression and panic disorder, respectively (Cochran et al., 2003), and clients of lower educational levels are diagnosed more often with schizophrenia than with mood disorders (Paniagua, 2005). It is important to note that the aforementioned studies in this paragraph were conducted in the United States.

One oppressive form of possible harm caused during the diagnostic phase is the use of testing and its concomitant test bias. Guindon and Sobhany (2001) argued that the possibility of test bias must be considered in the choice, administration, and interpretation of any assessment. Thus, counselors must consider the context of the cultural characteristics of clients when interpreting test results. Cultural differences can affect appraisal and diagnostic decisions, counseling interventions, and treatment outcomes (Sue et al., 2022). Counselors need to maintain awareness of the potential of such biases and not draw conclusions about clients based on flawed, biased information. Additional issues in assessment bias are the linguistic differences and cultural perceptual variations, which can skew results. Many times, assessments are directly translated into another language from English, without regard to idioms, connotations, and conversational nuances experienced by native speakers. Lack of attention to these translation details may cause clients to misinterpret or misunderstand the content of the instrument, therefore compromising the content validity of the measure (Guindon & Sobhany, 2001).

With the publication of the *Diagnostic and Statistical Manual of Mental Disorders*, fifth edition revised (*DSM-5-TR*; APA, 2022), issues related to cultural competence in diagnosis and assessment have reemerged. Tomlinson-Clarke and Georges (2014) stated that multicultural counseling integrates culturally specific and universal perspectives in explaining the dynamics of behavior and developing culturally responsive approaches to treatment. However, counselors may struggle to integrate multicultural considerations into clinical work when adhering to a medical model implied by the *DSM-V-TR*.

Despite the aims of revising the diagnostic classification to increase sensitivity to cultural variations in clients' expressions of their concerns (Brown & Lewis-Fernández, 2011), the *DSM-V-TR* has been criticized by many professionals and scholars alike. For example, Ladd (2013) critiqued the *DSM-V-TR* for ignoring the counseling relationship as a critical aspect of treatment, depending on statistically acquired symptoms and specific rules and timelines, and gearing its usefulness toward insurance companies. Although the *DSM-V-TR* provides a common language for presenting problems of the client, the language and assumptions associated with the criteria for diagnosis can be harmful if counselors do not examine and reflect on the sociocultural context of symptoms and behaviors (Ladd, 2013). Maddux (2002) further stated that diagnostic categories used in making biased clinical judgments lead to culturally unresponsive treatment interventions. Inherent in this approach is the basis of the medical model, in which clients are more often treated for pathological behavior (Tomlinson-Clarke & Georges, 2014).

Although fraught with meritorious cultural critiques and capacities to cause harm, many counselors and marginalized clients will interact with systems that readily use the *DSM-V-TR* and reliable and valid instruments and assessments. Despite the necessity of engaging with these systems, it is incumbent to do so as sensitively and ethically as possible. Therefore, we have provided several tools to help increase counselor cultural responsiveness in the diagnosis and assessment process.

Multicultural Adaptations

In order to help counselors increase their cultural contextualization and understanding of behavior and symptoms, Sue et al. (2014) developed a model using four dimensions (biological, psychological, social, and sociocultural) to describe etiological explanations of atypical behavior. Social, cultural, and economic considerations should be acknowledged when identifying and classifying behavior as mental unwellness. Additionally, Sue et al. (2014) distinguished cultural universality from cultural relativity in describing behavior within a sociocultural context. Said another way, important cultural nuances can be misunderstood when viewed by others who are culturally dissimilar. This may lead to labeling culturally typical behavior as atypical or maladaptive. In an unfortunate oppressive cycle, stereotypes and myths associated with atypical behavior have led to the social construction of diagnostic categories, which have been cited as major weaknesses of the *DSM-V-TR* (Maddux, 2002; Sue et al., 2014). Thus, it is essential for counselors to use the client's experiences with systems outside the counseling relationship to ensure culturally competent care in diagnosis and assessment.

Another culturally responsive practice counselors may consider is the use of other codes in addition to the *DSM-V-TR* codes. Psychosocial factors are included by using Z codes from the *International Classification of Diseases*, tenth revision (ICD-10; World Health Organization, 1992), as well as three new terms: cultural syndrome, cultural idiom of distress, and cultural explanation or perceived cause (Pomeroy & Anderson, 2013). The inclusion of psychosocial factors may highlight the relationship between social, cultural, and economic factors and mental health. Consideration of these multicultural factors in diagnosis allows counselors to contextualize and conceptualize how one's lived experiences define their identity and individual cultural characteristics. These characteristics of a client's identity are intersectional; Pomeroy and Anderson (2013) implore counselors to be aware of losing the uniqueness of a client by using group generalizations as represented by the *DSM-V-TR* as the only means of understanding a client's experiences. The importance of understanding how clients and their stories interact with the systems in which they live is crucial to any psychological evaluation process.

Another way to highlight how culture influences mental health diagnosis is through the use of the Cultural Formulation Interview (CFI; Pomeroy & Anderson, 2013). The CFI was developed to improve cross-cultural diagnostic assessment; aligned with multicultural competency models, the CFI provides a way for counselors to explore and understand clients' experiences and worldviews, as well as clients' cultural explanations and interpretations of their concerns. Counselors' ability to develop authentic and caring relationships is essential to accurate diagnosis and relevant counseling interventions. When clients are viewed as unique and counselors understand their experiences, accurate diagnosis and ethical practice are more likely (Tomlinson-Clarke & Georges, 2014).

Furthermore, Guindon and Sobhany (2001) developed a practical conceptual framework for cultural competency in diagnosis, including obtaining a specific and complete understanding of the client's chief complaint; engaging in active negotiation with the client as a therapeutic ally; and utilizing instruments with caution. The authors (Guindon & Sobhany 2001) suggested the following questions for counselors when seeking to obtain a specific and complete understanding of the client's presenting concerns:

1. Does the counselor understand what the problem is?
2. What does the client want to gain from therapy?
3. What are the probabilities that a favorable outcome will be reached?
4. Are there alternative modes of intervention that are as effective, more efficient, or less risky?
5. Will the client perceive the course of intervention and treatment as pleasant or unpleasant?

In regard to engaging in active negotiation with the client as a therapeutic ally, Guindon and Sobhany (2001) created the following questions for clients:

1. What do you think has caused your problem?
2. What caused it to start when it did? What does your problem do to you?
3. How does it work or not work for you?
4. How severe do you think your problem is?
5. What are the complications that your problem has caused for you?
6. What do you fear most about your problem?
7. Will its resolution have a short or long course?
8. What kind of treatment do you think you should receive?
9. What are the most important results you hope to receive from treatment?

Additionally, in a study examining diagnostic variance among counselors, Hays et al. (2010) found that differences in diagnoses could be attributed to cultural characteristics and suggested the following questions upon which counselors should reflect:

1. What cultural characteristics define the client?
2. What symptoms does the client present with?
3. How could the symptoms be caused or perpetuated by cultural characteristics?
4. How might symptom expression be related to environmental factors and situational factors?
5. What assessments fit this client?
6. To what degree do the client's cultural characteristics—or the interface between these characteristics and environmental factors—influence my assessment and understanding of the client story?
7. Would I give the same assessment to a client with different cultural characteristics?

In describing the ethical considerations necessary for a culturally responsive counseling relationship as well as the multicultural considerations for the assessment and diagnosis process, we hope that these core concepts can be applied in the following sections that seek to address how theoretical orientation impacts the relationship between the counselor and the client.

Counseling Theory and Application

Historical Background

The idea of multicultural counseling rose to prominence during the 1960s in North America, along with the formation of the American Counseling Association (ACA) from American Personnel and Guidance Counseling (APGA) in 1955 (Utomo et al., 2022). Because of the post-civil rights movement in emphasizing inclusion and social justice (Mollen & Ridley, 2021) based on the historical context of unequal and poor mental health services for clients from minority backgrounds (Sue, 1977), various multicultural counseling theories were developed, which often emphasized adaptation and adjustment of traditional counseling theories.

Increasing attention to the globalization of counseling and the counseling profession over the last two decades further increased the emphasis on multicultural counseling and competence. There are continued discussions of the integration of the Western counseling practice into the unique culture of clients (Keklik, 2023), but this intention of inclusion can mistakenly cause the exclusion of counselors and clients from various backgrounds. For example, traditional counseling theories and practices assume counselors are from the dominant cultures and clients are from diverse cultural backgrounds, and colonization and organization can continue to occur.

Historically, counseling theories developed within a White and Western framework have potential to perpetuate European and North American biases if not critically examined. Most counseling training programs offer theory courses that survey traditional schools of thought when it comes to psychotherapy such as psychoanalysis, individual psychology, reality therapy, cognitive behavioral, rational emotive behavioral, person-centered, gestalt, and existentialism. However, this model may exclude postmodern frameworks as well as Indigenous approaches to healing (Singh et al., 2020).

Although counselors may practice traditional counseling theories in culturally competent ways, these theories are often from an individualistic perspective that focuses on the client when the source of clinical concerns may stem from oppressive structures within the client's environment that require direct advocacy. Said another way, "classical theories focusing on individuals and/or families were not created with the goal of dismantling systems of oppression" (Singh et al., 2020, p. 261). Additionally, traditional theories of counseling often focus on the individual, one-on-one relationship between the client and the counselor. It may behoove the social justice-oriented counselor to adapt and reconceptualize counseling to a community perspective that holistically embraces the role of advocate and activist (Singh et al., 2020).

In recent years, discourse of decolonizing practices in the clinical practice of counseling has increased. Hernández-Wolfe (2011) described colonizing as the seen and unseen attempts to assimilate those who hold marginalized identities to mainstream cultural values and experiences. The mainstream culture of White, Eurocentric society, if left unchecked, seeks to maintain its structure, power, and privilege while other cultures are supposed to accommodate to and value this structure. However, decolonization is focused on examining these concepts of power and access to resources while disrupting the structures that maintain the status quo (Hernández-Wolfe, 2011).

Although nontraditional theories that have a foundation of social justice and advocacy have existed in the counseling profession for quite some time, many counseling training programs view these theories as supplemental or additional theoretical perspectives rather than comprehensive and sufficiently independent orientations for clinical practice. For example, multicultural and feminist theories (Sommers-Flanagan & Sommers-Flanagan, 2018) are frequently a part of counseling programs theory training but are much less applied as a foundational guiding theory for work with all clients. However, because clients' mental health and lived experiences are directly impacted by these cultural frameworks, counselors who are not grounded in this postmodern framework risk becoming agents upholding these structures rather than disruptors of injustice (Singh et al., 2020).

Although there is a plethora of research for evidenced-based counseling practice utilizing postmodern and social justice-oriented theories, we have decided to focus on relational cultural theory and therapy as well as liberation psychology. We believe these two theoretical orientations provide a solid framework for making space to address social identities and structural injustices within the counseling relationship. It is our hope that this introduction could serve as a starting point for practicing counselors to expand their theoretical horizons to integrate knowledge and skills related to cultural responsiveness and social justice advocacy and activism.

Relational Cultural Theory

Relational Cultural Theory (RCT) is a systemic approach that promotes the conceptualization of clients systemically, rather than individually, which is aligned with the ethical obligation to actively work to understand clients' contexts and worldviews (ACA, 2014; Ratts et al., 2016). Counselors utilizing RCT understand that both problems and solutions must be contextualized within relationships, and that the connection and empathy in the counseling relationship is the mechanism through which healing, and growth take place (Trepal & Duffey, 2016). Scholars have identified that RCT is sensitive and responsive to marginalized individuals who have been pathologized by traditional theories that value separation, according to White, male, middle-class culture (Sackett & Jenkins, 2019). People in social positions that are systematically oppressed have been assessed and treated through a lens constructed by the mainstream Western culture of separation and individualism. Therefore, traditional counseling theories have centered around the individual and on resolving internal conflicts as the mechanism of change and growth.

RCT differs from traditional theoretical orientations in that it emphasizes the role that power dynamics play in mental health and wellness (Haskins & Appling, 2017). We chose to highlight this theory because it operationalizes how counselors can work relationally with culturally diverse clients and facilitate social justice through specific RCT concepts such as mutual empathy and mutual change (Sackett & Jenkins, 2019). Utilizing an RCT approach, the counselor works to decrease emotional and physical separation and increase relational connectedness through a supportive, therapeutic relationship. Furthermore, a key component in RCT is for the counselor to serve as a corrective relationship. Thus, RCT counselors are called to model an equitable and mutually beneficial relationship between themselves and clients by bringing awareness to oppression in the here-and-now during sessions. This acknowledgment can assist clients in learning not to isolate themselves in relationships as counselors approach the discussion of social justice from a stance of genuineness and authenticity while maintaining appropriate boundaries (Sackett & Jenkins, 2019).

Liberation Psychology

Liberation psychology is the second counseling theory espoused by the authors due to its inherent philosophical foundation of understanding and conceptualizing clients within their cultural, societal, political, and historical context. Ignacio Martín-Baró is generally considered one of the foundational scholars in the field of liberation psychology (Martín-Baró et al., 1996). Martín-Baró et al. (1996) maintained that Western psychology was an insufficient framework to address the lived experiences of marginalized clients and argued that the mental health field could only be relevant to oppressed groups if it is reoriented toward the realities of those who have experienced social and political marginalization. Because mental health problems are impacted by structural oppression, a conceptualization of the sociopolitical etiology of unwellness is crucial (Martín-Baró et al., 1996). Another key point within this theory is the historical narrative of cultural groups; many oppressed populations, especially those who experienced colonization and/or genocide, have had their histories written from the perspective of the oppressor or the colonizer (Martín-Baró et al., 1996). Therefore, from a liberation psychology perspective, conceptualizing client issues must start with examination of the current societal structures and the recovery of historical memory by those who are oppressed.

Deideologizing is a liberation psychology term that has much overlap with the concept of decolonization. Dominant social structures use several sociocultural structures such as school, church, media, and governmental bureaucracies to establish a narrative about the lived experiences of the marginalized individuals. These messages maintain a "cultural stranglehold" on the way these narratives are presented and internalized by society. Thus, supporting a socially just and mentally well context for these populations requires the therapist and client to examine these messages through the lived experiences of those on the margins. Montero (2009) described this process as "the conscious construction and reconstruction of an understanding of the world one lives in, and of one's lived circumstances, as part of a totality" (p. 75). Said another way, deideologizing is creating an understanding of the world around us that is relatively free from the dominant set of beliefs and ideology that distort social phenomena (Montero, 2009).

Furthermore, one of the most important principles of liberation psychology is acknowledgment of the virtues and power of marginalized clients in improving their lived experiences. Chavez et al. (2016) stated that this strength-based approach allows counselors to rely on clients with oppressed social positions to engender the tools and energy that can lead to liberation. Said another way, supporting clients to develop an expanded understanding of their realities and themselves as individuals can facilitate recognition of their wisdom, values, and positive qualities (Chavez et al., 2016). Furthermore, a strength-based approach connects clients with the skills that helped them survive oppression in the first place (Afuape & Hughes, 2016).

In addition to incorporating postmodern frameworks into counselors' theoretical orientation, Singh et al. (2020) created questions that focus on integrating the who and the what related to counseling theories that may promote critical consciousness. These questions could help counselors revise the predominantly individualistic, patriarchal, and Eurocentric thinking typically taught in counseling programs and shift to an explicit focus on greater societal and structural dynamics of injustice:

1. Who is responsible for bringing about societal changes?
2. What values and beliefs do particular counseling theories reflect?
3. What structural changes are needed to reduce harm related to dominance and oppression?
4. What global sociopolitical systems and policies exclude or create barriers to the success of all people?

5. What outside obstacles might someone who is trying to overcome a particular counseling issue face?
6. What could your role as a counselor be to help address the issue?

We the authors encourage fully licensed professional counselors to continue engaging in consultation, peer supervision, and continuing education to integrate and incorporate these questions and theoretical frameworks into their practice.

Case Study

It is our hope that counselors find the summary of cultural responsiveness in the clinical practice of ethics, assessment and diagnosis, the counseling relationship, and counseling theories helpful in integrating a multicultural lens with clients. To assist in further integration of these concepts, we have created a fictional case study for application and synthesis of the material covered in this chapter. Please read through the following client scenario and then answer the reflective questions.

Judy

You are leading a support group for adults with anxiety and/or depression at the community mental health clinic where you work. You notice that Judy, a 40-year-old immigrant ciswoman from the Philippines, has been mostly quiet except for stating why she is coming to this group. You learned at intake during the screening process that Judy reported severe anxiety and panic attacks. Judy currently lives alone with her three cats. Although Judy has a career as a senior manager at a successful tech company, she supports her parents financially who are still in her home country. One day, you gently confront the group and ask for a moment of silence for any members who would like to share their story and haven't yet. To your surprise, Judy chimes in.

Judy starts to talk about how she grew up in an extremely religious household. She went through the entire process of baptism, confirmation, and attended mass each week growing up. In church, the message of honoring one's father and mother was strongly emphasized as an important Christian principle. Judy tearfully states she has become resentful caring for her parents financially as well as emotionally.

At present, Judy says she has a serious boyfriend whom she loves and has been with for a little over five years. Judy's boyfriend Mike has expressed wanting to move into a house with her. Judy would love to build a life with Mike but does not have enough income to support her parents and also become a homeowner. Mike and Judy have also discussed sharing finances and planning for retirement together, but she has virtually no savings as every spare dollar goes back home to her family. In general, Judy has been questioning her faith but is still fearful of Hell. She no longer attends church as she feels conflicted about some of the values she has grown up with. Judy is very distressed when describing her desire to live a full and authentic life but having so much fear and shame holding her back from doing so.

After she is done speaking, several group members verbalize their support. They affirm and reassure her that it is okay to take care of herself and set boundaries with her parents, and that being true to herself is the most important thing. Another member states how Christianity is oppressive and harmful to minorities.

Reflective Questions

1. What salient cultural identities stand out to you, both in regard to Judy and to yourself?
   (a) Using Hays (2001) ADDRESSING model as guide, counselors can fill out the following chart to identify which social identities are an agent (people and groups who have initiative, power, and privilege) and which social identities are a target (people and groups who are oppressed and marginalized). The dimensions explored in the ADDRESSING model (Hays, 2001) include, but are not limited to: age and generational influences, developmental disabilities, disabilities, religion and spiritual orientation, ethnicity, socioeconomic status, sexual orientation, indigeneity, nationality, and gender. We encourage readers to add on other dimensions not listed here (Fig. 5.1).
   (b) After identifying salient agent and target identities, what power dynamics do you notice between yourself and Judy?
2. How do the social positions identified from the first question interact with one another?

Counselor's profile:

	A	D	D	R	E	S	S	I	N	G
Agent										
Target										

Fig. 5.1 Hays (2001) ADDRESSING Model

(a) For example, how might your religious/spiritual background contribute to the here-and-now experience of Judy's dilemma? How might your citizenship status, whether you were born in the United States or emigrated from another country, influence your perspective of Judy's situation with her parents? How do your family of origin experiences impact your group communication styles?

3. Yalom and Leszcz (2020) often describe groups as microcosms of the outside world in that group members replicate experiences and behaviors from the world into the counseling space. What systems and structures do you see playing out in the group dynamics in this scenario?
4. Although the purpose of this exercise is to explore your own awareness of relationship dynamics, what group norms and guidelines would you have implemented at the start of this group to account for the conflict occurring in the scenario, but also in regard to attending to the cultural identities of yourself and each group member?

Conclusion

In culturally responsive counseling, the integration of the therapeutic relationship, ethics, diagnosis and assessment, and theory forms the cornerstone of effective practice. Understanding and respecting the diverse cultural backgrounds of clients is essential for fostering trust and promoting healing. The therapeutic relationship is the heart of counseling and is profoundly influenced by multicultural factors. Building a strong, culturally attuned therapeutic alliance requires empathy, respect, and open communication. Counselors must be aware of their own cultural biases and actively work to create an inclusive and supportive environment where clients feel understood and valued. Part of the therapeutic relationship consists of ethics, which guide counselors in making decisions that honor the dignity and autonomy of clients from all cultural backgrounds. Ethical practice in culturally responsive counseling involves continuous self-reflection, cultural humility, and a commitment to equity and justice. Counselors must navigate ethical dilemmas with a nuanced understanding of cultural norms and values, ensuring that their actions uphold the highest standards of the profession. Furthermore, diagnosis and assessment are critical components of the counseling process that must be approached with cultural sensitivity. Standard diagnostic tools and assessment methods may not fully capture the experiences of clients from diverse backgrounds. Therefore, counselors must modify these tools to be culturally appropriate, considering the client's cultural context, language, and unique experiences. This ensures that assessments are meaningful, paving the way for effective treatment planning. Lastly, counseling theories provide the framework for understanding human behavior and development across different cultural contexts. By adapting theories to accommodate diverse cultures, counselors can better understand the unique experiences and worldviews of their clients, leading to more relevant and impactful interventions.

In conclusion, culturally responsive counseling is an ongoing journey of learning, reflection, and adaptation. By cultivating a strong therapeutic alliance, ethical practices, inclusive diagnostic and assessment methods, and culturally informed theories, counselors can provide more effective and compassionate care. Embracing cultural diversity not only enhances the counseling process but also contributes to the broader goal of social justice and equality in mental health care.

References

Afuape, T., & Hughes, G. (Eds.). (2016). *Liberation practices: Towards emotional wellbeing through dialogue.* Routledge.

Al-khodair, N. A., & Alrawaf, E. A. (2023). Saudi therapists' lived experience of self-awareness. *Counselling & Psychotherapy Research, 23*(2), 487–501. https://doi.org/10.1002/capr.12471

American Psychiatric Association. (1987). *Diagnostic and statistical manual of mental disorders* (3rd ed., rev.). Author.

American Psychiatric Association. (2022). *Diagnostic and statistical manual of mental disorders.* (5th ed., rev.). Author.

American Counseling Association. (2014). 2014 ACA code of ethics. https://www.counseling.org/knowledge-center/ethics.
Astramovich, R. L., & Scott, B. E. (2020). Intersectional advocacy with LGBTQ+ clients in counseling. *Journal of LGBT Issues in Counseling, 14*(4), 307–320. https://doi.org/10.1080/15538605.2020.1827473
Bayne, H. B., & Branco, S. F. (2018). A phenomenological inquiry into counselor of color broaching experiences. *Journal of Counseling & Development, 96*(1), 75–85. https://doi.org/10.1002/jcad.12179
Brown, R. J., & Lewis-Fernández, R. (2011). Culture and conversion disorder: Implications for the DSM-5. *Psychiatry, 74*(3), 187–206. https://doi.org/10.1521/psyc.2011.74.3.187
Campbell, A., Vance, S. R., & Dong, S. (2018). Examining the relationship between mindfulness and multicultural counseling competencies in counselor trainees. *Mindfulness, 9*(1), 79–87. https://doi.org/10.1007/s12671-017-0746-6
Casas, J. M., Suzuki, L. A., Alexander, C. M., & Jackson, M. A. (Eds.). (2016). *Handbook of multicultural counseling*. Sage.
Chavez, T. A., Fernandez, I. T., Hipolito-Delgado, C. P., & Rivera, E. T. (2016). Unifying liberation psychology and humanistic values to promote social justice in counseling. *The Journal of Humanistic Counseling, 55*(3), 166–182. https://doi.org/10.1002/johc.12032
Clark, M., Moe, J., Chan, C. C. D., Best, M. D., & Mallow, L. M. (2022). Social justice outcomes and professional counseling: An 11-year content analysis. *Journal of Counseling & Development, 100*(3), 284–295. https://doi.org/10.1002/jcad.12427
Cochran, S. D., Sullivan, J. G., & Mays, V. M. (2003). Prevalence of mental disorders, psychological distress, and mental health service use among lesbian, gay, and bisexual adults in the United States. *Journal of Consulting and Clinical Psychology, 71*, 53–61.
Day-Vines, N. L., Cluxton-Keller, F., Agorsor, C., Gubara, S., & Otabil, N. A. A. (2020). The multidimensional model of broaching behavior. *Journal of Counseling & Development, 98*(1), 107–118. https://doi.org/10.1002/jcad.12304
Eriksen, K. P., & Kress, V. E. (2005). *Beyond the DSM story: Ethical quandaries, challenges and best practices*. Sage.
Ganz, Z. (2020). Conflicts and challenges faced by ultra-orthodox Jewish social work students: Broaching and a social constructivist approach to supervision as a forum for resolution. *The Clinical Supervisor, 39*(1), 24–44. https://doi.org/10.1080/07325223.2019.1652948
Geller, S. (2021). Cultivating online therapeutic presence: Strengthening therapeutic relationships in teletherapy sessions. *Counselling Psychology Quarterly, 34*(3–4), 687–703. https://doi.org/10.1080/09515070.2020.1787348

Geller, S. M. (2017). *A practical guide to cultivating therapeutic presence*. American Psychological Association.

Geller, S. M., & Porges, S. W. (2014). Therapeutic presence: Neurophysiological mechanisms mediating feeling safe in therapeutic relationships. *Journal of Psychotherapy Integration, 24*(3), 178–192. https://doi.org/10.1037/a0037511

Guindon, M. H., & Sobhany, M. S. (2001). Toward cultural competency in diagnosis. *International Journal for the Advancement of Counselling, 23*(4), 269–282. https://doi.org/10.1023/A:1014443901294

Haskins, N. H., & Appling, B. (2017). Relational-cultural theory and reality therapy: A culturally responsive integrative framework. *Journal of Counseling & Development, 95*(1), 87–99. https://doi.org/10.1002/jcad.12120

Hays, D. G., Prosek, E. A., & McLeod, A. L. (2010). A mixed methodological analysis of the role of culture in the clinical decision-making process. *Journal of Counseling & Development, 88*(1), 114–121. https://doi.org/10.1002/j.1556-6678.2010.tb00158.x

Hays, P. (2001). *Addressing cultural complexities in practice*. American Psychological Association.

Herlihy, B., & Corey, G. (2015). Multicultural and social justice perspectives on boundaries. In B. Herlihy & G. Corey (Eds.), *Boundary issues in counseling: Multiple roles and responsibilities* (pp. 77–107). https://doi.org/10.1002/9781119221586.ch4

Hernández-Wolfe, P. (2011). Decolonization and "mental" health: A Mestiza's journey in the borderlands. *Women & Therapy, 34*(3), 293–306. https://doi.org/10.1080/02703149.2011.580687

Interiano, C. G., & Lim, J. H. (2018). A "Chameleonic" Identity: Foreign-born doctoral students in U.S. Counselor Education. *International Journal for the Advancement of Counselling, 40*(3), 310–325. https://doi.org/10.1007/s10447-018-9328-0

Jack, K., & Miller, E. (2008). Exploring self-awareness in mental health practice. *Mental Health Practice, 12*(3), 31–35. https://doi.org/10.7748/mhp2008.11.12.3.31.c6803

Jensen, M. J., McAuliffe, G. J., & Seay, R. (2015). Developmental level as a predictor of counseling skills. *The Journal of CounselorPreparation and Supervision, 7*(1). https://doi.org/10.7729/71.1065

Keklik, İ. (2023). Internationalization of counseling: Integrating the Western theories and practices into the local ways. *Journal of Multicultural Counseling and Development, 51*(2), 128–135. https://doi.org/10.1002/jmcd.12252

Knox, S., & Hill, C. E. (2016). Introduction to a special issue on disclosure and concealment in psychotherapy [Editorial]. *Counselling Psychology Quarterly, 29*(1), 1–6. https://doi.org/10.1080/09515070.2015.1095156

Kress, V. E., Haiyasoso, M., Zoldan, C. A., Headley, J. A., & Trepal, H. (2018). The use of relational-cultural theory in counseling clients who have traumatic stress disorders. *Journal of Counseling & Development, 96*(1), 106–114. https://doi.org/10.1002/jcad.12182

Ladd, P. D. (2013). Knowledge vs. wisdom in *DSM* diagnosis: A person-centered perspective. In *Ideas and research you can use: VISTAS 2013*. Retrieved from http://www.counselingoutfitters.com/vistas/vistas13/Article_6.pdf

Maddux, J. E. (2002). Stopping the "madness": Positive psychology and the deconstruction of the illness ideology and the DSM. In C. R. Snyder & S. J. Lopez (Eds.), *Handbook of positive psychology* (pp. 13–25). Oxford University Press.

Martín-Baró, I., Aron, A., & Corne, S. (1996). *Writings for a liberation psychology*. Harvard University Press.

Miller, R., & Prosek, E. A. (2013). Trends and implications of proposed changes to the DSM-5 for vulnerable populations. *Journal of Counseling & Development, 91*(3), 359–366. https://doi.org/10.1002/j.1556-6676.2013.00106.x

Mollen, D., & Ridley, C. R. (2021). Rethinking multicultural counseling competence: An introduction to the major contribution. *The Counseling Psychologist, 49*(4), 490–503. https://doi.org/10.1177/0011000020986543

Montero, M. (2009). Methods for liberation: Critical consciousness in action. In M. Montero & C. C. Sonn (Eds.), *Psychology of liberation: Theory and applications* (pp. 73–91). Springer.

Norcross, J. C., & Lambert, M. J. (2018). Psychotherapy relationships that work III. *Psychotherapy, 55*(4), 303–315. https://doi.org/10.1037/pst0000193

Norcross, J. C., & Lambert, M. J. (2019). Evidence-based psychotherapy relationships: The third task force. In J. C. Norcross & M. J. Lambert (Eds.), *Psychotherapy relationships that work: Evidence-based therapist contributions* (3rd ed., pp. 1–23). Oxford University Press. https://doi.org/10.1093/med-psych/9780190843953.003.0001

Paniagua, F. A. (2005). *Assessing and treating culturally diverse clients: A practical guide* (3rd ed.).

Pendse, A., & Inman, A. G. (2017). International student-focused counseling research: A 34-year content analysis. *Counselling Psychology Quarterly, 30*(1), 20–47. https://doi.org/10.1080/09515070.2015.1128395

Pieterse, A. L., Lee, M., Ritmeester, A., & Collins, N. M. (2013). Towards a model of self-awareness development for counselling and psychotherapy training. *Counselling Psychology Quarterly, 26*(2), 190–207. https://doi.org/10.1080/09515070.2013.793451

Pomeroy, E. C., & Anderson, K. (2013). The DSM-5 has arrived. *Social Work, 58*(3), 197–200. https://doi.org/10.1093/sw/swt028

Price, T. A. (2015). *The Black therapist-white client counseling Dyad: The relationship between black racial identity and countertransference*. [Doctoral dissertation, Lehigh University]. https://core.ac.uk/download/pdf/228656504.pdf

Ratts, M., Singh, A., Nassar-McMillan, S., Butler, S. K., & McCullough, J. R. (2016). Multicultural and social justice competencies: Guidelines for the counseling profession. *Journal of Multicultural Counseling and Development, 44*(1), 28–48. https://doi.org/10.1002/jmcd.12035

Rentería, R., Schaefer, A., & Capielo Rosario, C. (2020). Ethical guidelines for working with culturally diverse clients. In L. T. Benuto, F. R. Gonzalez, & J. Singer (Eds.), *Handbook of cultural factors in behavioral health: A guide for the helping professional* (pp. 25–37). Springer.

Richard, K., Koch, J., & Currin, J. (2020). Counseling students' responsibility attributions: Race/ethnicity and trauma narratives. *Current Psychology: A Journal for Diverse Perspectives on Diverse Psychological Issues, 41*(3), 1373–1381. https://doi.org/10.1007/s12144-020-00656-w

Ridley, C. R., Sahu, A., Console, K., Surya, S., Tran, V., Xie, S., & Yin, C. (2021). The Process model of multicultural counseling competence. *The Counseling Psychologist, 49*(4), 534–567. https://doi.org/10.1177/0011000021992339

Sackett & Jenkins. (2019). Utilizing relational cultural theory in addressing sexism in the counseling relationship. *Journal of Creativity in Mental Health, 14*(4), 492–498. https://doi.org/10.1080/15401383.2019.1632768

Sano, K. (2019). *Foreign-born doctoral-level counselor supervisors' use and experience of supervision theories/models* (Publication No.27805292) [Doctoral dissertation, Antioch University]. ProQuest.

Sato, M. (2014). *Experiences and perspectives of clinical supervisors in cross-cultural supervision: The impact of supervisor race and ethnicity.* [Doctoral dissertation, Minnesota State University, Mankato]. https://cornerstone.lib.mnsu.edu/etds/313/

Singh, A. A., Appling, B., & Trepal, H. (2020). Using the multicultural and social justice counseling competencies to decolonize counseling practice: The important roles of theory, power, and action. *Journal of Counseling & Development, 98*(3), 261–271. https://doi.org/10.1002/jcad.12321

Sommers-Flanagan, J., & Sommers-Flanagan, R. (2018). *Counseling and psychotherapy theories in context and practice: Skills, strategies, and techniques.* John Wiley & Sons.

Sue, D. W., & Sue, D. (1977). Barriers to effective cross-cultural counseling. *Journal of Counseling Psychology, 24*(5), 420–429. https://doi.org/10.1037/0022-0167.24.5.420

Sue, D., Sue, D. W., Sue, D., & Sue, S. (2014). *Essentials of understanding abnormal behavior* (2nd ed.). Cengage Learning.

Sue, D. W., Sue, D., Neville, H. A., & Smith, L. (2022). *Counseling the culturally diverse: Theory and practice* (9th ed.). Wiley.

Tao, K. W., Owen, J., Pace, B. T., & Imel, Z. E. (2015). A meta-analysis of multicultural competencies and psychotherapy process and outcome. *Journal of Counseling Psychology, 62*(3), 337–350. https://doi.org/10.1037/cou0000086337

Tittler, M. V., Liu, S., Wei, M., Cheng, D., & Wang, C. (2022). Concerns about counseling racial minority clients: Ethnocultural empathy, insight, and multicultural intervention self-efficacy. *Training and Education in Professional Psychology, 16*(4), 420–428. https://doi.org/10.1037/tep0000333

Tomlinson-Clarke, S. M., & Georges, C. M. (2014). DSM-5: A commentary on integrating multicultural and strength-based considerations into counseling training and practice. *The Professional Counselor, 4*(3), 272–281. https://doi.org/10.15241/stc.4.3.272

Trepal, H., & Duffey, T. (2016). Everything has changed: An interview with Judy Jordan. *Journal of Counseling & Development, 94*(4), 437–441. https://doi.org/10.1002/jcad.12102

Utomo, P., Suherman, M. M., & Tayaban, R. A. (2022). Multicultural counseling: Chance and challenges for the counselors in the 21st Century. *Guidance and Counseling International Conference, 1*, 20–28. https://ejournal.aecindonesia.org/index.php/saicgc/article/view/22

Vasquez, M. J. T., & Johnson, J. D. (2022). Multiculturalism in education, training, and professional development. In M. J. T. Vasquez & J. D. Johnson (Eds.), *Multicultural therapy: A practice imperative* (pp. 125–152). American Psychological Association.

Wampold, B. E. (2001). Contextualizing psychotherapy as a healing practice: Culture, history, and methods. *Applied & Preventive Psychology, 10*(2), 69–86. https://doi.org/10.1017/S0962-1849(02)01001-6

Wampold, B. E. (2021). Healing in a social context: The importance of clinician and patient relationship. *Frontiers in Pain Research, 2*, 684768. https://doi.org/10.3389/fpain.2021.684768

World Health Organization (1992). *The ICD-10 classification of mental health and behavioural disorders: Clinical descriptions and diagnostic guidelines.*

Yalom, I. D., & Leszcz, M. (2020). *The theory and practice of group psychotherapy* (6th ed.). Basic Books.

CHAPTER 6

Cultural Responsiveness in School Counselling

Diana Camilo and Laura Owen

Introduction

Ladson-Billings (1994) defines cultural responsiveness as a pedagogy that empowers students intellectually, socially, emotionally, and politically by using their cultural references to impart knowledge, skills, and attitudes. As a 100-plus year-old profession, school counseling has been shaped by economic, social, and educational policies and individuals. During the Industrial Revolution, the rapid industrial growth was met with social protest and reform as a way to curb the negative social conditions that emerged (Gysbers, 2010). Initially focusing on vocational guidance, school counseling has emerged to focus on the academic, career, and personal-social development of students. Through a comprehensive school counseling

D. Camilo (✉)
College of Education, California State University San Bernardino, San Bernardino, CA, USA
e-mail: Diana.Camilo@csusb.edu

L. Owen
College of Education, San Diego State University, San Diego, CA, USA
e-mail: Lowen@sdsu.edu

S. Sisko (ed.), *Culturally Responsive Psychotherapy, Counselling & Psychology*, Palgrave Texts in Counselling and Psychotherapy,
https://doi.org/10.1007/978-3-031-81831-8_6

program, school counselors deliver curriculum, and collaborate with teachers, parents, and community members (ASCA, 2023). Yet, as schools have become increasingly diverse, school counseling has evolved to focus on systemic change in order to overcome the perpetuation of systemic inequities and the barriers that diverse students and communities face (Holcomb-McCoy, 2022). Moreso, as education has prioritized accountability and evaluation to demonstrate effectiveness (Gysbers, 2010; Safir & Dugan, 2021), school counselors are called to increase their attention to issues related to access, equity, and the success of *every* student (ASCA, 2021a; Eschenauer & Chen-Hayes, 2005). While much has been debated about the role and function of school counselors, the disenfranchisement and harm perpetuated by racist, exclusionary, and outdated policies and practices onto students cannot be ignored or overlooked (Love, 2019; Lee, 2001; ASCA, 2021a). Thus, culturally responsive school counseling addresses the needs of students, while uncovering and responding to systemic issues of bias and barriers (Ladson-Billings, 1994; Khalifa, 2018). Ultimately, culturally responsive school counselors ensure students' lived experiences and cultures are reflected in the programming and services offered.

Attacks on Antiracism and the School Counseling Profession

Racial injustice, assaults on diversity, equity, and inclusion initiatives, and discordant politics not only divide communities, but they further intensify the ongoing harm inflicted on Black and Brown individuals (Holcomb-McCoy, 2022; Kearl & Mayes, 2024; Love, 2019: Mayes & Byrd, 2022). All educators must be willing to call out the policies and systems that sustain racism, give rise to microaggressions, maintain inequitable processes, and silence the voices of those who have been marginalized (Hines et al., 2021). School counselors share in the responsibility to address, eliminate, and prevent actions, decisions, and outcomes that result from racism, white privilege, white rage, and anti-blackness (Hines et al., 2021). Millions of children enter the classroom every day and become witnesses, perpetrators, and/or victims of microaggressions, racelighting, and violence (vicariously and face to face). Each decision to address or ignore these issues in the classroom has lifelong consequences for students and their future.

School counselors have become the target of well-funded parent groups, like "Moms for Liberty" who the Southern Poverty Law Center

(SPLC, n.d.) recently labeled an extremist organization. One of their assertions is that school counselors, along with their professional organization, the American School Counselor Association (ASCA), are responsible for introducing critical race theory into schools through social emotional learning curricula, classroom presentations, and individual counseling sessions (Butler, 2022). They also posit that school counselors are responsible for student "indoctrination" related to issues of sexual identity and race, and they oppose any gender-affirming policies and inclusive curricula believed to reflect "wokeism" (Kearns & Mayes, Forthcoming). In the US, a well-concerted campaign is underway to limit and/or eliminate any interaction between students and the helping professionals trained to support student's developmental journeys. In some states, this goes as far as introducing legislation or school board policies that forbid a child experiencing suicidal ideation or sexual identity questions to connect with their school counselor (Butler, 2022).

Most school counselor training programs prepare their graduates to advocate for the needs of all students, particularly those from marginalized backgrounds. While some trainees readily accept their role at the individual level, others may be less likely to engage in leadership, advocacy, and change at the systems level. However, given the increasing attacks on the profession, the elimination of diversity, equity and inclusion initiatives, and views on perceived "wokeism," school counselors must be prepared to call out harmful and discriminatory acts and assume a leadership role to challenge and dismantle practices, policies, and systems that fail to prioritize the lives of marginalized students deliberately and unapologetically (Shields et al., 2017).

Transformative School Counselor Leadership

Transformative leadership addresses the need for systemic, equitable change (Shields et al., 2017) and is characterized by an activist agenda and a commitment to social justice, equality, and a democratic society (van Oord, 2013). Transformative leaders question justice and democracy, critique inequitable practices, and work towards creating a "better life lived in common with others" (Shields, 2010, p. 559). Transformative school counselor leaders are committed to promoting social justice, implementing initiatives that address issues such as discrimination, bias, and inequitable resource allocation. They lead efforts to create a school culture that values and respects all individuals. Transformative school counselor leaders go beyond traditional school counseling roles by actively engaging in advocacy, policy reform, and systemic change (Shields et al., 2017).

Transformative school counselor leaders address the diverse cultural, social, and emotional needs of students and their leadership helps in developing programs and interventions that are sensitive to and respectful of these differences, fostering a supportive and inclusive school environment. Transformative school counselors lead efforts to incorporate culturally responsive practices into the curriculum and extracurricular activities. This includes integrating diverse perspectives and content into lessons and promoting programs that center cultural diversity in all aspects of planning, execution, and evaluation. They build trusting relationships with students, creating a safe space for them to express their identities and concerns. This trust is crucial for supporting students' social and emotional well-being, which is a foundation for academic success.

They provide or facilitate ongoing professional development for teachers and staff on cultural competence and responsiveness. This ensures that the entire school community is knowledgeable about and committed to meeting the needs of diverse student populations. Transformative school counselor leaders use data to identify opportunity gaps and areas of need within the school population paying close attention to spaces where policies may be contributing to these gaps. They can then lead targeted interventions and monitor progress to ensure that all students receive the support they need to succeed.

Transformative school counselor leaders are skilled in engaging families and communities in the educational process. Their leadership helps in building strong community partnerships that support student learning and well-being, and in creating a culturally responsive school climate. They see parents as allies and welcome them to co-create events, analyze data, and better engage the entire school community.

These school counselor leaders are positioned to identify and challenge systemic barriers that impede student success. Through their leadership, they advocate for policy changes and initiatives that address issues such as discrimination, bias, and inequitable resource allocation. They lead efforts to promote social justice within the school. This includes implementing restorative practices, antiracism initiatives, and programs that foster an inclusive and respectful school culture.

School counselor leadership is crucial for fostering culturally responsive practices, ensuring that all students, especially those from marginalized backgrounds, are supported and empowered to succeed in an equitable and inclusive educational environment.

Principles of Culturally Responsive School Counseling

Although ASCA standards and position statements (ASCA, 2021b, 2022, n.d.-b) establish that school counselors support student development through the appreciation and inclusion of multiculturalism and diversity, we are reminded that school counseling practices are firmly rooted in the values of European American middle-class culture (Lee, 2001). According to Low et al. (2013), "school counselors need a different perspective from which to operate if they are going to ensure students from culturally diverse backgrounds have access to services that promote optimal academic, career, and personal-social development" (pg. 258). In his model, Lee defines a culturally responsive school counseling program as one that functions within a culturally responsive school and the school counselor core role is to enhance the quality of instruction for all students. Within Lee's model, culturally responsive counselors facilitate student development through two premises, 1) all students can *and* want to learn and 2) cultural differences must not be ignored. Thus, school counselors find ways to fundamentally understand the cultural realities of students and how they apply to academic, career, and personal-social development.

School counselors must also advocate for students. Because limited consideration is given to the inequalities and racialized experiences that minoritized students face as a result of systemic racism (Love, 2019), it is important that school counselors develop a heightened awareness of the systemic barrier to education that students face (Atkins & Oglesby, 2018). School counselors must also effectively challenge policies and initiatives that reinforce systemic barriers (Lee, 2001). Lastly, school counselors work to bridge the home and family lives of diverse students and the school. By inviting community members and/or individuals from diverse communities to provide professional development or participate in an advisory board, school counselors mitigate the outcomes of educational practices that invalidate the experiences and customs of culturally diverse home and family life.

Foxx et al. (2020) state that culturally responsive school counselors transform how they think and view their school counseling programs. Through a deep understanding on how prejudice, privilege, and various forms of oppression impact students, school counselors can help to establish a supportive school climate where cultural differences are appreciated. Smith-Adcock et al. (2006) discuss the need for school counselors to advocate for systemic change, outreach into communities, and involvement of families into the students' education. Holcomb-McCoy (2007) defines multicultural [school] counseling as a process where the counselor and student consider their personal and cultural experiences. To highlight the effective use of multicultural counseling, school counseling programs have regularly been referred to as culturally proficient and/or culturally competent. Culturally sustaining programs is the term used to define programs that seek to "perpetuate and foster—to sustain—linguistic, literate, and cultural pluralism as part of the democratic project of schooling" (Paris, 2012, pg. 95).

The following section explores the culturally responsive principles school counselors can embed as they design culturally responsive programs.

School Counselors Empower All Students

According to Ladson-Billings (1995b), beyond focusing on improving students' self-esteem, culturally relevant [educators] demand, reinforce, and produce academic excellence from students. In other words, these [educators] not only attended to the academic needs of their students, but they also influenced students to aim for academic excellence. According to Harley (2009), culturally sensitive school counseling programs can empower students from diverse backgrounds to overcome the negative dominant discourse about their cultural characteristics, thus embracing and utilizing their unique cultural attributes.

When implementing culturally responsive practices, it is important that school counselors communicate high expectations for all students (Ladson-Billings, 1995b). School counselors must also recognize how personal biases often influence the lowering of expectations for students or the types of services and/or resources offered. For example, several scholars have noted that educators often doubt that education is important to students of color and/or families from low-income communities (DeCastro-Ambrosetti, & Cho, 2005). As culture is perceived to encompass factors such as gender, ability, race, ethnicity, sexual orientation, socioeconomic status, and spirituality, it is understandable how biases about expected behaviors, attitudes, beliefs, and values are formed. However, schools cannot ignore the premise that the cultural backgrounds of students are irrelevant to the learning environment (Grothaus et al., 2010; Ladson-Billings, 1995a; Manning & Baruth, 2004). Through a culturally responsive lens, ahe determinants of success are defined by the cultural context of students, their families, and communities instead of Euro-Western standards. School counselors seek to understand ways that all students can be empowered while recognizing their cultural realities and their importance to postsecondary goals.

School Counselors Serve as Facilitators

According to the American School Counseling Association (ASCA), when school counselors seek to establish school-community partnerships, it is essential they work with students, families, school staff, ***and*** community members. As school-based leaders, advocates, and collaborators, school counselors enrich and assess the effect of established partnerships on student success. Culturally responsive school-community partnerships are those that 1) incorporate existing school, family and community strengths, resources and assets, 2) foster resilience through equity-based school-family-community partnerships and parent-family-school agreements founded on empowerment, democracy, collaboration, social justice, and strength-based principles (Bryan et al., 2020), and 3) and work to address and interrupt racism and biases by intentionally collaborating with community leaders, businesses, and organizations that also take an anti-racist stance (ASCA, 2021a; Atkins, & Oglesby, 2018).

School counselors that function as facilitators ensure that the services and programming provided are relevant to and reflect the social, cultural, and linguistic experiences of students (Harley, 2009; Stephens & Lindsey, 2011). According to Stephens and Lindsey (2011), as facilitators, school counselors are well suited to advocate for all students and focus on broader issues of student access and success. As members of school leadership teams, school counselors can lead conversations about existing system disparities and inequities. Specifically, how the shifting in the school's culture and/or organizational structure can address student, family, and community needs.

School Counselors Encourage the Inclusion of Culturally and Linguistically Diverse Students

Students often face a myriad of barriers throughout their academic trajectory, and school counselors are called to understand the barriers that students face to best identify the types of support and resources that students need. Important to consider is students' culture and language when planning school counseling related interventions and activities (Lee, 2001;

Paris, 2012). According to Khalifa (2018), culturally responsive schools must protect and promote practices and interventions that include minoritized students and the spaces in which they exist. Because school environments are often not inclusive of students' cultural identities, culturally inclusive practices should focus on eradicating the lack of belonging and connectedness that students often experience. Khalifa also states that the inclusion of students' cultural identities promotes humanization. Schools can achieve this by establishing and including educational networks beneficial to students, families, communities, and teachers; and by using community-based knowledge to aid school staff to understand, connect to, and appreciate students' identities. Cultural considerations to consider include acculturation phases, external (i.e. food and arts) and internal elements of culture (i.e. values, customs, expectations, social roles, family structure); pull factors (i.e. opportunity, freedom, educational opportunities), or push factors (i.e. poverty, oppression). It is equally important for school counselors to invite parents, guardians, and/or mentors to share about the students' lives and incorporate the shared wisdom within the services provided as part of the school counseling program (Witcht, 2017).

Stephens and Lindsey (2011) identify ***valuing diversity*** as a practice by which schools, through individual behavior and organizational policies and practices, examine how to embrace culture and diversity within the school environment. According to the authors, valuing diversity can be achieved by advocating for all students and school counselors serving as agents for change and equity. School counselors can practice valuing diversity by asking themselves "In what ways do I invite multiple perspectives?" or "To what extent am I able to recognize a value for diversity within instructional strategies, formal and informal curricula, and assessment strategies" (p. 98). School counselors can further reflect on ways that the school environment can ensure the inclusion of diverse perspectives. For example, they can explore ways to include the voices and perspectives of parents, guardians, and other caretakers when making decisions about programming and policies that will impact student learning.

School Counselors Practice Cultural Sensitivity

Students and families hold values and identities deeply rooted in their cultures and communities; values often not recognized or reflected within school-based programming and interventions. Yet, it has been documented that all students, including minoritized students and those from indigenous communities, personally and academically benefit in culturally responsive environments (Gay, 2000; Aronson & Laughter, 2016). Culturally responsive scholars (Ladson-Billings, 1994; Gay, 2000; Whaley & Davis, 2007) argue that well-intended efforts to nurture multicultural school environments *can* fall short when educators do not have a genuine and inquisitive interest in the individuals within diverse environments. At its root, cultural humility [and sensitivity] were proposed by Tervalon and Murray-García (1998) as an alternative to practitioners being multicultural competence. Rather than assuming one has a complete understanding of individuals *because* of cultural traits and or characteristics, practitioners recognize the individuals they work with are different from them. Cultural sensitivity calls for individuals to be seen as more than the cultural boxes they belong to, and practitioners should actively seek to look beyond those boxes.

Cultural sensitivity also requires school counselors to understand how prejudice, privilege, and various forms of oppression affect students (Foxx et al., 2020) and how they relate to various dimensions of students' cultural identity. School counselors must foster a learning environment where students can share about experienced injustices and racialized experiences in school (Francis & Mason, 2022). Using anti-biased language, school counselors help to create an anti-oppressive school environment (Khalifa, 2018), thus fostering a space where students can discuss issues such as academic needs, personal life-issues, and experienced trauma. For school counselors, it is important they approach their work with care and curiosity *about* students and their communities and seek to increase their awareness and sensitivity to the lived experiences of those they serve.

School Counselors Reshape the Delivery of Services

School counselors are trained professionals who support students to succeed academically, personally, and plan their careers (ASCA, n.d.-a.). School counseling services such as guidance lessons, crisis interventions, and consultation and collaboration seek to develop students' cooperation skills, perseverance, study skills, time management, and self-motivation. The increase of school violence, racialized experiences, and exposure to trauma (Holcomb-McCoy, 2022) calls for culturally responsive school counseling to lead the efforts to utilize resources and programming that protects students. As scholars state, school counselors must offer services that invite the wholeness of students' identities, and thus resist dehumanizing and/or excluding them (Mayes & Byrd, 2022). School counselors must take an active role in leading conversations about the restructure of traumatizing and exclusionary practices in schools (Francis & Mason, 2022). As Bryan et al. (2022) state "curriculum and partnership programs and interventions in schools that focus on social-emotional learning, grit, and resilience de-emphasize race and center whiteness and white norms and values, excluding students of color" (p. 135). The reshaping of school counseling programming and services should focus on the experiences, strengths, and needs of students in order to ensure all students succeed and thrive (Bryan et al., 2022). Specifically, cultural forms of resiliency practices by students and their communities.

The reshaping of school counseling programming requires that school counselors analyze how current practices support or exclude minoritized students. As school systems generally adopt a one-size-fits-all or color-blind approach toward policies, curricular content, and other programming, a culturally responsive approach requires that school counselors examine how these approaches in fact harm and exclude students (Bryan et al., 2022). A color-blind approach reinforces the notion that minoritized students must navigate systems in which their identities and unique needs are not considered, and their academic success is in-spite of *rather* than because of. School counselors must also explore the role of race and racism in perpetuating social disparities between dominant and marginalized racial student groups and consider how to address them within the school counseling curriculum. School counselors should also challenge the notion of meritocracy or the "American Dream" as the norm and explore how it may/may not align with the academic goals of students and families.

School Counselors Encourage Student-Controlled Discourse

Genuine care-based counseling calls for school counselors to ask students to share personal feedback (Gay, 2018) regarding the delivery of services, interventions and resources used. School counselors should design school counseling programs based on shared inquiry and dialogue by which students can disclose personal experiences; specifically, those that may influence academic and personal-social outcomes. Student-controlled discourse also minimizes deficit images about students and families and validates their unique experiences and needs. For example, understanding how education and activism are empowerment tools for students and their families.

A format for student-controlled discourse is youth participatory action research (YPAR), a framework that engages students and empowers them to participate in research and social change (Lindquist-Grantz & Abraczinskas, 2020). Through YPAR, students identify programs or issues directly impacting them, and often their communities. Data collection and analysis allows participants to develop solutions and access outcomes (Freire, 2018; Cook & Krueger-Henney, 2017). As Levy et al. (2024) state, YPAR functions as a homeplace for students to be active participants in the creation of environments that nurture and support the growth and development of them as researchers and community members. It is important to note that the power of YPAR is observed in the outcome rather than the selected problem or issue students opt to tackle. As a framework that provides students a platform to share their narratives, express themselves, feel valued, and deepen others' understanding of their cultural assets, YPAR is a powerful tool that supports culturally responsive programming.

Beyond YPAR, school counselors can also engage in student-led discourse in other ways. Mostly, through the intentionality of programming and interventions. According to ASCA, school counseling programs should provide comprehensive services that are delivered to all students systematically and aim to close opportunity gaps (ASCA, 2023). In their book, Atkins and Oglesby (2018) outline ways school counselors can provide social-emotional learning opportunities for students that center their identities and lived experiences. For example, the use of Teaching Tolerance Social Justice standards (2017) allows school counselors to implement anti-bias programming. The four standards of Identity, Diversity, Justice, and Action emphasize the reduction of prejudice and movement toward collective action. School counselors can also establish affinity and leadership groups, which serve as spaces where students from similar backgrounds and/or groups can find solace. Moreso, these groups help to reduce the psychological stress that students have experienced as a result of navigating culturally refuting environments (Atkins and Oglesby, 2018).

School Counselors Incorporate Students' Social Capital

Social capital is the culmination of the network of people and community resources individuals access in order to navigate through society's institutions for the attainment of things such as education, work, or health care (Lad & Braganza, 2013; Yosso, 2005). Students' social capitals can include teachers, coaches, mentors, advisors, peers and friends, alumni, community leaders, and other knowledgeable allies. Students also access nontraditional forms of social capital such as aspirational capital, navigational capital, linguistic capital, familial capital, resistance capital, reflective capital (Yosso, 2005; Clark-Ibañez, 2015), and spiritual capital (Wyttenbach, 2015).

Cultural capital are the skills, knowledge, and language individuals use in order to navigate social institutions, including educational institutions (Bourdieu & Passeron, 1977). Valenzuela (1999) popularized the phrase *authentic care,* which refers to the caring cultures [and spaces] that work to amplify the assets students of color possess. Moreso, these assets are rooted from students' cultural communities and thus, seek to remedy the shortcomings of institutions that have historically underserved them (Curry, 2016). Since the cultural knowledge, skills, and abilities of many students' heritage often go unrecognized or are reflected within the culture of a school, it is critical to understand and embed their *community cultural wealth.*

Defined by Yosso (2005) as the multiple forms of capital that communities of color possess, culturally responsive school counseling practices call for school counselors to establish programming inclusive of the cultural wealth of the communities they serve. Various types of cultural wealth include aspirational, linguistic, social, navigational, familial, resistant, perseverant, and spiritual/faith wealth (Martinez et al., 2020). Important to recognize is the influential power of resistance capital, or the knowledge and skills fostered through oppositional behavior that challenges inequality (Yosso, 2005), as a form of self-empowerment for students and their communities (Clark-Ibañez, 2015). Thus, culturally responsive school counselors advocate for students *and* effectively challenge policies and initiatives that reinforce systemic barriers (Lee, 2001; Holcomb-McCoy, 2022). Education as a source of empowerment serves as a form of aspirational wealth for many communities (Méndez-Pounds, et al., 2018) because the education and knowledge gained from access to educational opportunities will remain with students, regardless of changes to institutional policies or practices. Additionally, education has the transformative potential to prepare students to serve their communities and society through civic engagement (Perez et al., 2010) and by establishing and leading social networks (Clark-Ibañez, 2015; Lukes, 2015).

Because the foundation of education stems from White Eurocentric influence, the knowledge, skills, and experiences from a White perspective are repeatedly centralized and thus, failing minoritized students (Love, 2019; Holcomb-McCoy, 2022). As Ayala and Ramirez (2019) state, relying on the Eurocentric application of cultural capital fails to acknowledge the role of coloniality and its influence on the educational system. According to the authors, school-based staff must develop and work from an awareness of how coloniality reinforces messages that minoritized students do not belong or are the exception whenever they excel. Culturally responsive school counseling extends beyond recognizing and including the social capitals and cultural wealth of students. Thus, culturally responsive school counselors must develop a broader sociopolitical consciousness that leads to the critique and disruption of the school-cultures, biases, policies, and norms that promote and maintain the social inequalities that exclude students and their social and cultural capitals. Given that social capital is central to students successfully navigating their academic career, school counselors should facilitate the inclusion of established support networks; mentors, community organizations and leaders, and allies when designing their programs and planning interventions.

School Counselors Engage in Critical Self-Reflection

To fundamentally implement culturally responsive practices, school counselors must critically reflect on the interventions and practices used within their counseling program. Through critical self-reflection school counselors explore their personal influence, biases held, and the impact of the school counseling program. School counselors should engage in critical self-reflection to examine how oppression and marginalization are manifested within the school environment (Khalifa, 2018; Ladson-Billings, 1994; Atkins & Oglesby, 2018). Specifically, how school-based programming and practices reinforce the oppression and/or exclusion of students. Critical self-reflection should focus on school counselors' personal reactions toward students, parents/guardians, and community partners, and leaders. While the nature of the day-to-day work culture of school counseling can influence counselors to remain neutral about systemic issues, growth requires the magnification of blind spots. While simple in concept, recognizing "flaws" in one's professional work can be difficult and often an emotional process. As Francis and Mason (2022) state, "this work is hard and draining, but the reward is seeing someone else's full humanity, pain, struggles, and potential and using your gifts to help them grow" (p. 76).

Self-reflection implies that culturally responsive school counselors self-reflect, self-evaluate, and self-correct (Atkins & Oglesby, 2018). Thus, feedback from colleagues, annual reviews, attended professional development, or reflections about the daily interactions with students and families can help facilitate what to reflect upon. For example, a school counselor can consider the ways they contribute to the oppression or exclusion of students; perhaps using microinvalidations, biases held, and/or how counseling practices reinforce schoolcentric or meritocratic perspectives. Critical self-reflection is tough work and cannot exist without examining the power and influence school counselors have on the school-environment. School counselors cannot just say they serve all students without harnessing their leadership capacity to advocate for ***and*** with students. Moreso, school counselors that engage in critical self-reflection continuously explore the power and privilege they may or may not have, and how it may influence the extent to which they can be advocates and/or leaders (Francis & Mason, 2022). Strategies to encourage self-reflection include practicing cultural humility, connecting with trusting supervisors and/or colleagues, and seeking feedback from community leaders and partners regarding school counseling programming.

At the program level, school counselors can assess how data, services, structures, policies, and collaborative efforts focus on highlighting students' cultures and lived experiences (Foxx et al., 2020; Francis & Mason, 2022). As school counselors work with a diverse student population, they must consider the extent to which the school counseling program truly serves all students. By engaging in dialogue with parents, families, community members, and leaders, they can understand how to address important issues and how to embed them within the school-wide programming and events (Foxx et al., 2020).

Roadmap for School Counselors

In the following section, we provide a roadmap for personal and professional preparation needed to implement a culturally responsive counseling program. As mentioned throughout this chapter, it is important that school counselors understand the cultural realities of students and how to embed them within the academic, career, and personal-social domains. School counselors must also learn how to navigate the systemic barriers to education that students face in order to challenge the policies and initiatives that reinforce systemic barriers.

System's Advocacy

According to the ASCA Ethical Standards for School Counselors (2022), school counselor advocacy for culturally responsive school counseling programs cannot be ignored as it is continuously reflected throughout standards A-F. For example, the ethical standards call for school counselors to 1) provide all students access to equitable opportunities for all students, 2) advocate for equitable, anti-oppressive, and anti-bias policies and procedures, systems, and practices, 3) provide effective, evidence-based, and culturally sustaining interventions to address student needs, and 4) respect students' and families' values, beliefs, and cultural background; including sexual orientation, gender identity, and gender expression. Thus, the implementation of culturally responsive practices is an ethical responsibility for school counselors. While for some, advocacy is an extension of their counseling approach and program, others are limited by the hurdles presented by the political climate and/or the culture of the school, district, and community. Moreso, operationalizing advocacy competencies into daily practice has been a struggle for the profession (Hilts, 2019).

Accountability within K-12 education is characterized by external monitoring and the emphasis on outcomes and results. According to Smith and Benavot (2019), accountability reforms in education do not achieve their intended impact due to the lack of *structured democratic voice*, or opportunity for the voices and views of those who work, learn, and teach in schools to be included in the process of data review and accountability. The authors suggest that "structured democratic voice in education is most effective when multiple education partners—including parents, teachers, students, and other community members—are able to articulate their views on policy planning and evaluation in ways that their concerns are heard and valued" (pg. 195).

Safir and Dugan (2021) state that although much has been said and acted upon for the purpose of being student-centered, educators have bought into a paradigm that continues to rob students of their voices, marginalizes their gifts, and prioritizes data collection and continuous improvement over transformative learning. Throughout their work, Safir and Dugan focus on shifting data and accountability conversations toward a pedagogy of voice. The following explores how culturally responsive school counselors can lead the groundwork for systems advocacy through the examination of data use and implementation.

Based on the six principles of systemic change by Abercrombie et al. (2015), Atkin and Oglesby (2018) outline in the chapter *Utilizing Data for Systemic Change* various actions and activities school counselors can take to advocate for and lead discussions about systems change.

Under *Principle 1 Understand Needs and Assess*, school counselors examine data gaps and intentionally identify how the voices and perspectives of students, families, and communities have been excluded from the data. Once equity gaps have been identified, school counselors can seek input from students and parents about these gaps. Counselors can engage with parents to better understand the why behind the areas of needs, but most importantly to identify the assets that families and communities access when navigating academic hurdles. Additionally, it is important to include any cultural norms that may unintentionally contribute to gaps in the data measured. *Principle 2: Engage Multiple Actors* calls for school counselors to engage *all* education partners in the process of identifying interventions, and often the policies that will be implemented to address data gaps. School systems are notorious for jumping into action to resolve data gaps. However, the literature continuously reminds us that good outcomes are limited when the voices of teachers, non-certified staff, students, families, communities, local leaders, advocates, and influencers are not included and considered in the process (Atkins & Oglesby, 2018; Smith & Benavot, 2019; Stephens & Lindsey; 2011; Holcomb-McCoy, 2022; Love, 2019). As collaborators and consultants, school counselors can create an advisory group comprising the listed education partners. They can also gather feedback through one-to-one meetings, collaborating with parent liaisons, using informal surveys, and attending grade level meetings.

Atkins and Oglesby (2018) state that *Principle 3: Map the System* relates to the need for school counselors to understand the perspectives of education partners. By seeking to understand the existing assumptions and beliefs education partners hold regarding priorities or needs, school counselors can better understand how individuals relate to each other. School counselors can use climate, teacher, and student/family surveys, community chats or roundtable discussions, professional learning communities, and other activities that gather the voices and narratives of education partners. *Principle 4: Work with Others* focuses on the intentionality of actively working *with* education partners. Culturally responsive school counselors can examine the level to which collaborators are included and supported throughout the implementation process. Questions to consider are, "To what extent do teachers receive modeling and follow-up coaching when utilizing new programming or intervention?" "How are collaborative efforts created to refrain individuals from working in silos?"

Principle 5: Distribute Leadership refers to the distribution of ownership. In other words, school counselors, as leaders and advocates, should distribute ownership over problems and solutions within the school environment. As the success of students is a collaborative effort among all education partners, school counselors can advocate for how they all work together for the good of students. Lastly, *Principle 6: Foster a Learning Culture* is about the ways in which school staff have agency and/or encouraged to solve problems in creative and innovative ways. School counselors can advocate for the use of new ideas, especially those initiated by students, families, and community members. Moreso, an important aspect of principle six is the consideration of space and time for reflection.

School counselors can also host Data Bootcamps to increase the capacity of school staff and other education partners to review and effectively interpret data. The book *Street Data: A Next Generation Model for Equity, Pedagogy, and School Transformation* by Safir and Dugan (2021) provides an equity-focused approach to data review and accountability. Working with district and/or school-based data analysts can also provide opportunities for school counselors to advocate for the use of school-counselor friendly reports and/or platforms. Because accountability priorities can vary by the position a school-staff may hold, it is important that school counselors have access to data and reporting measures that support the continuous growth of a comprehensive school counseling program.

Policies and Procedures

Beyond creating school environments that are inclusive of student, family, and community voices, culturally responsive practices recognize that practitioners and systems must do more than engage in inclusive-only efforts. According to Ladson-Billings (1995a) demonstrating personal accountability by challenging administrative mandates, policies, and practices demonstrates a practitioner's value of doing what is right by students. As school reforms and the restructuring of educational policies have continued to falter in part because of unchanged ideologies and biases about students, particularly minoritized students (Lipman, 1993; Ladson-Billings, 1995a; Love, 2019; Holcomb-McCoy, 2022), schools must continue to move toward policies that disrupt the negative impact of said unchanged ideologies.

School counselors can address the need for policy and practices reform by highlighting the use of exclusionary practices and completing school-wide policy and equity audits.

Exclusionary practices are the actions by school staff that impact students not being engaged in school and/or not being present (Khalifa, 2018). School counselors can examine how exclusionary practices such as high-stakes testing and accountability, in-school suspensions, detention, zero tolerance, pushing-out, counseling toward alternative schooling, grade retention, the hostile treatment of students and families, and emotional and abusive tactics (Khalifa, 2018; Atkins & Oglesby, 2018; Love, 2019) continue to create unwelcoming school environments for students. Thus, culturally responsive school counseling can support movement toward policies and practices that honor students' humanity.

According to Khalifa (2018) equity audits allow for the critical analysis of school policies that negatively impact students. By examining data across multiple areas, school counselors can highlight trends in patterns of and differences in student equity. School counselors can examine how policies directly or indirectly impact school-culture. As members of hiring committees, school counselors can work toward a diverse and inclusive faculty body (Atkins & Oglesby, 2018). Most importantly, equity audits allow for a school-wide reflection about the over-enforcement of school policies against minoritized students. Lastly, school-wide policy audits can support the efforts to move toward the use of restorative and healing practices within counseling programming.

Professional and Personal Development

Developing into a culturally responsive practitioner takes time! While many of the principles and frameworks shared throughout this chapter seem simple in concept, being an all-encompassing culturally responsive school counselor is not easy. To understand the professional development trajectory you should take, it is pertinent to examine what has led to the gaps in the needed knowledge and skills. For the last decade, the profession and school counseling programs have reflected on how to best prepare pre-service counselors to serve the diverse K-12 student population (Hines & Owen, 2022). The standardization of graduate programs and increase in research that focus on multicultural counseling, anti-racist school counseling, and trauma-informed practices, to name a few, have not increased the number of school counselors skilled at developing culturally responsive programming. Moreso, the continuous one-size-fits-all approach to the standardization and professionalization of the school counselor role has created missed opportunities to attend to the uniqueness of students and their communities.

The following are professional development recommendations for how school counselors can develop their culturally responsive practices.

Anti-Racist School Counseling

As racism and exclusionary practices continue to permeate the school counseling profession, school counselors *must* be able to design anti-racist school counseling programming (ASCA, 2021a). As much has been outlined throughout this chapter, it is through the implementation of anti-racist practices that school counselors can move toward cultural responsiveness. Under the *Toolkits, Framework and Resources* page, the American School Counseling Association provides toolkits and resources that focus on developing anti-racist programming. Other helpful resources include the organizations Learning for Justice, the Southern Poverty Law Center, Dr. Betina Love's *Punished for Dreaming* book and study guide, and *Interrupting Racism: Equity and Social Justice in School Counseling* by Atkins and Oglesby (2018).

Data and School-Based Needs Assessment

By developing the skills to review and understand data through an equity lens school counselors are best suited to recognize how oppression and marginalization are manifested within the school environment and the systemic issues that warrant attention (Chen-Hayes, et al., 2013). Equally important is the ability to complete needs assessment to gather the critical perspectives of students, parents, community members, and other education partners (ASCA, 2019). Helpful resources include *Street Data: A Next Generation Model for Equity, Pedagogy, and School Transformation* by Safir and Dugan (2021) and the date-related webinars and tools offered by the American School Counseling Association.

School-Family Community Partnerships

School counselors must also learn how to engage and facilitate the inclusion of the networks students turn to as they are often best informed about the policies and laws, as well as school-level and community issues that impact academic success. Although many school counselors are exposed to consultation and collaboration models, too often, pre-service training focuses on schoolcentric approaches that perpetuate Coloniality and hierarchy in the collaboration process. Bryan et al. (2022) state that school counselors must engage in collaboration that focuses on equity, democratic collaboration, empowerment, social justice, and is strengths based. The authors propose *The Seven-Step Partnership Process Model*, which takes an anti-racist and youth empowerment approach to consultation.

Community Asset Mapping

A community asset map is a comprehensive list of existing community resources that can be used by all education partners (Griffin & Farris, 2010). For school counselors an asset map includes pertinent advocates and allies knowledgeable about the services and laws that relate to students and their communities. Asset maps can also include a list of mental health, after-school and educational programs, community businesses (Chen-Hayes, et al., 2013). The article "School Counselors and Collaboration: Finding Resources Through Community Asset Mapping" provides guidance on creating an asset map.

The following are personal development recommendations for how school counselors can develop their culturally responsive practices.

Critical Self-Reflection

Culturally responsive practices cannot exist without individuals deeply processing and reflecting on 1) how their values, beliefs, and practices have been shaped, and 2) the impact they have on those they serve and work with. According to Khalifa (2018) "critical self-reflection must be personal, but that it cannot *only* be personal" (p. 27). In other words, critical self-reflection is about individuals considering their role, power, and influence across the various systems and individuals they interact with. Moreso, critical self-reflection is about considering how one has been influenced by and how that influence ripples across the various systems navigated. To fundamentally implement culturally responsive practices, school counselors must critically reflect on the interventions and practices used within counseling programs, daily interactions, and the personal reactions they have toward students, parents/guardians, and their networks. School counselors who continuously practice critical self-reflection gain insight and a deeper understanding of social justice perspectives (Atkins & Oglesby, 2018). While simple in concept, recognizing "flaws" in one's professional work can be difficult and often an emotional process. Several strategies that school counselors can practice developing the skill of critical self-reflection include: 1) engaging in supervision with supervisors trained in culturally responsive practices, 2) seeking feedback from community leaders and partners regarding school counseling programming, 3) practicing cultural humility, and 4) establishing a collaborative relationship with partners and education partners. However, it is important to note that these activities must engage in conversations about how school counselors are personally responsible for perpetuating oppressive practices and its impact on students and families.

Self-Care

In addition to the many roles and responsibilities school counselors are required to undertake, developing a culturally responsive program can seem overwhelming and lead to social justice fatigue; the physical, mental, and/or emotional toll incurred through advocating for social change while serving as an agent of an institution (Furr, 2018). It's important school counselors regularly practice self-care to nurture their physical and emotional health. Workplace strategies can include incorporating one culturally responsive strategy at time, practice mindfulness, or centering joy and fun with students and colleagues (Atkins & Oglesby, 2018). Personal strategies include establishing work-life balance or seeking counseling/support to address compassion fatigue or experienced secondary traumatic stress.

Shared Responsibility

Shifting to culturally responsive programming can seem like actions that only a "brave" school counselor can tackle. Because conversations regarding student-focused programming are complex, it's crucial to incorporate the shared wisdom of family, community, and experts (Witcht, 2017). School counselors can invite guest speakers to lead professional development, roundtables, and brown-bag events. They can also attend events hosted within the neighborhood, access virtual resources, or start a culturally responsive affinity group. Lastly, school counselors can invite individuals knowledgeable about culturally responsive practices to serve as coaches and mentors.

Case Study: Implementing Culturally Relevant School Counseling in a Diverse High School

This case study explores the implementation of culturally relevant school counseling at XYZ High School, a diverse public school located in a metropolitan area. The student and community population comprises various cultural, ethnic, and socioeconomic backgrounds. The case study outlines the steps taken to integrate culturally relevant practices, the challenges faced, and the outcomes achieved, guided by Roadmap for School Counselors.

School Background: Jefferson High School serves approximately 1,500 students, with demographics reflecting significant diversity:

- 35% Hispanic/Latino
- 30% African American
- 20% Caucasian
- 10% Asian/Pacific Islander
- 5% Mixed/Other

The school has a history of academic achievement but has struggled with disparities in student performance and engagement across different cultural groups.

System's Advocacy

The counseling team at XYZ High School, led by Head Counselor Ms. Jackson, conducted an initial assessment to identify gaps in their current counseling approach:

1. Cultural Awareness: Limited training and awareness among counselors about the cultural backgrounds and needs of the student body.
2. Student Engagement: Lower engagement and higher dropout rates among minoritized student groups.
3. Parental and Community Involvement: Challenges in engaging parents and education partners from diverse cultural backgrounds.

4. Bias and Stereotyping: Incidents of bias, stereotyping, and exclusionary practices affecting student relationships and trust in counseling services.

Policies and Procedures
The team mapped the existing counseling system and completed an equity audit to identify areas for improvement. This involved:

- Analyzing current counseling practices and their effectiveness.
- Examine data to highlight trends in patterns of and differences in student equity.
- Identifying key actors and resources within the school and community.
- Understanding the interconnectedness of various factors affecting student well-being.

Professional and Personal Development
Anti-Racist School Counseling: The team committed to fostering anti-racist school counseling programming and a learning culture by:

- Encouraging continuous professional development and reflection among counselors.
- Promoting open dialogue about cultural competence and sensitivity.
- Using feedback from students, parents, and staff to refine practices.

School-Family Community Partnerships: To address these issues, the counseling team engaged multiple stakeholders, including students, parents, teachers, community leaders, and cultural organizations. This collaborative approach ensured diverse perspectives and needs were considered in the action plan.

Collaboration was key to implementing the action plan. The team worked closely with teachers to integrate culturally relevant materials into the curriculum, partnered with local cultural organizations for resources, and engaged community leaders in school events and initiatives.

Shared Responsibility: Leadership was distributed among various team members to leverage their strengths and expertise. Ms. Jackson focused on professional development, while other counselors led initiatives on parental engagement, curriculum integration, and community partnerships.

Action Plan

Guided by the Roadmap for School Counselors, the counseling team developed a comprehensive action plan focusing on the following key areas:

1. Professional Development

   - Invite community leaders to conduct ongoing training sessions on cultural competence and sensitivity.
   - Invite guest speakers from different cultural communities to share their experiences and perspectives and help to inform school counseling programming.
   - Encourage school staff and partners to participate in cultural immersion experiences within the community.

2. Counseling Practices

   - Implement individualized counseling plans that consider students' cultural backgrounds and experiences.
   - Use culturally relevant assessment tools and techniques.
   - Create safe spaces for students to discuss cultural identity and experiences of discrimination.

3. Curriculum Integration

   - Integrate culturally relevant materials and discussions into the school's advisory program.
   - Integrate anti-racist practices into school counseling programming.

4. Parental Engagement

   - Provide translation services and culturally appropriate communication strategies.
   - Establish a Parent Advisory Committee representing the diversity of the student body.
   - Organize parent-centered events and workshops to build relationships with parents.

5. Community Partnerships

    - Collaborate with local education partners and cultural organizations to provide resources and support for students and families.
    - Engage community leaders in school events and initiatives to build trust and connection.

6. Self-Reflection

    - School counseling team commits to critically reflect on the interventions and practices used within counseling programs, daily interactions, and the personal reactions they have toward students, parents/guardians, and their networks.

Challenges and Solutions

1. Resistance to Change

    - Some staff members were resistant to altering their counseling practices. This was addressed through continuous professional development and creating opportunities for open dialogue about the importance and benefits of culturally relevant counseling.

2. Limited Resources

    - Budget constraints limit the ability to implement all desired changes at once. The team prioritized actions and sought grants and community partnerships to supplement resources.

3. Building Trust

    - Establishing trust with students and parents from diverse backgrounds took time. Consistent efforts to engage and communicate effectively helped build rapport over the school year.

Outcomes
After one academic year of implementing the action plan, XYZ High School observed several positive outcomes:

- Increased Engagement: There was a noticeable increase in student participation in counseling services.

- Improved Academic Performance: The achievement gap began to close, with improved grades and graduation rates among previously underperforming groups.
- Enhanced Relationships: Stronger relationships between counselors, students, and parents were evident, fostering a more inclusive school environment.
- Cultural Awareness: A more culturally aware and sensitive counseling team capable of addressing the diverse needs of the student population.

The case of XYZ High School demonstrates that culturally relevant school counseling can significantly impact student engagement, performance, and overall school climate. By committing to the principles of understanding needs and assessing, engaging multiple actors, mapping the system, working with others, distributing leadership, and fostering a learning culture, schools can create a supportive and inclusive environment for all students.

Discussion Questions

1. What are some specific strategies you can implement in your school to enhance culturally relevant counseling practices?
2. How can schools overcome resistance to change when implementing culturally relevant practices?
3. What role do community partnerships play in supporting culturally relevant school counseling, and how can schools effectively engage with community organizations?
4. How can schools measure the effectiveness of culturally relevant counseling practices and make necessary adjustments?

This case study illustrates the importance of culturally relevant school counseling and provides a practical framework for implementation in diverse school settings (Banks, 2019; Sue & Sue, 2016; American School Counselor Association, 2019).

Conclusion

As discussed throughout the chapter, culturally responsive pedagogy calls for the use of practices and programming that empowers students intellectually, socially, emotionally, and politically by using their cultural references to impart knowledge, skills, and attitudes (Ladson-Billings, 1994). The ongoing racial injustice and attacks on students and the profession call for school counselors to share in their responsibility to lead the efforts to eliminate and prevent the use of policies and programming that perpetuate racism and inhumane actions. Furthermore, because culturally responsive school counselors transform how they think and view their school counseling programs (Foxx et al., 2020), they are well suited to serve as transformative school leaders who can bridge the implementation of culturally responsive practices by actively engaging in advocacy, policy reform, and systemic change (Shields et al., 2017). Through a deep understanding on how prejudice, privilege, and various forms of oppression impact students, school counselors can help to establish a supportive school climate where cultural differences are appreciated.

Thus, culturally responsive school counseling addresses the needs of students, while uncovering and responding to systemic issues of bias and barriers (Foxx et al., 2020; Khalifa, 2018; Atkins & Oglesby, 2018; Hines & Owen, 2022). Culturally responsive school counselors are intentional about including students' lived experiences and cultures in the programming and services offered. By embedding the culturally responsive principles outlined in this chapter, school counselors can begin to design culturally responsive programs.

References

American School Counselor Association. (2019). *ASCA school counselor professional standards & competencies*. Alexandria, VA: Author. https://www.schoolcounselor.org/asca/media/asca/home/SCCompetencies.pdf

Abercrombie, R., Harries, E., & Wharton, R. (2015, June). *Systems change: A guide to what it is and how to do it*. New Philanthropy Capital. https://www.thinknpc.org/publications/systemschange

American School Counselor Association. (2021a). *The school counselor and anti-racist practices*. Alexandria, VA: Author.

American School Counselor Association. (2021b). *The school counseling and cultural diversity*. Alexandria, VA. Author. https://www.schoolcounselor.org/

Standards-Positions/Position-Statements/ASCA-Position-Statements/The-School-Counselor-and-Cultural-Diversity

American School Counselor Association. (2022). *ASCA ethical standards for school counselors.* Alexandria, VA. Author. https://www.schoolcounselor.org/getmedia/44f30280-ffe8-4b41-9ad8-f15909c3d164/EthicalStandards.pdf

American School Counselor Association. (2023). *The school counselor and school counseling programs.* Alexandria, VA. Author. https://www.schoolcounselor.org/Standards-Positions/Position-Statements/ASCA-Position-Statements/The-School-Counselor-and-School-Counseling-Program

American School Counselor Association. (n.d.-a). *Culturally responsive pedagogy* [Webinar]. https://videos.schoolcounselor.org/culturally-responsive-pedagogy

American School Counselor Association. (n.d.-b). School counselor roles and ratios. https://www.schoolcounselor.org/About-School-Counseling/School-Counselor-Roles-Ratios

Aronson, B., & Laughter, J. (2016). The theory and practice of culturally relevant education A synthesis of research across content areas. *Review of Educational Research, 86*(1), 163–206. https://doi.org/10.3102/0034654315582066

Atkins, R., & Oglesby, A. (2018). *Interrupting racism: Equity and social justice in school counseling.* Routledge.

Ayala, M. I., & Ramirez, C. (2019). Coloniality and Latinx college students' experiences. *Equity & Excellence in Education, 52*(1), 129–144. https://doi.org/10.1080/10665684.2019.1635542.

Banks, J. A. (2019). *An introduction to multicultural education.* Pearson.

Bourdieu, P., & Passeron, J. C. (1977). *Reproduction in education, society, and culture.* Sage.

Bryan, J., Henry, L. M., Daniels, A. D., Edwin, M., & Griffin, D. M. (2022). Infusing an anti-racist framework into school-family-community partnerships. In C. Holcomb-McCoy (Ed.), *Antiracist counseling in schools and communities* (pp. 129–149). American Counseling Association.

Bryan, J., Williams, J., & Griffin, D. (2020). Fostering educational resilience and opportunities in urban schools through equity-focused school-family-community partnerships. *Professional School Counseling., 23.* https://doi.org/10.1177/2156759X19899179

Butler, K. (2022, August 15). Now the far right is going after school counselors. *Mother Jones.* https://www.motherjones.com/politics/2022/08/now-the-far-right-is-going-after-school-counselors/

Chen-Hayes, S. F., Ockerman, M. S., & Mason, E. C. M. (2013). *101 Solutions for school counselors and leaders in challenging times* (1st ed.). Corwin.

Clark-Ibañez, M. (2015). *Undocumented Latino youth: Navigating their worlds.* Lynne Rienner.

Cook, A. L., & Krueger-Henney, P. (2017). Group work that examines systems of power with young people: Youth participatory action research. *Journal for Specialists in Group Work, 2*(2), 176–193. https://doi.org/10.1080/01933922.2017.1282570

Curry, M. W. (2016). Will you stand for me? Authentic cariño and transformative rites of passage in an urban high school. *American Educational Research Journal, 53*(4), 883–918. https://doi.org/10.3102/0002831216660380

DeCastro-Ambrosetti, D., & Cho, G. (2005). Do parents value education? Teachers' perceptions of minority parents. *Multicultural Education, 13*(2), 44–46.

Eschenauer, R., & Chen-Hayes, S. F. (2005). The transformative individual school counseling model: An accountability model for urban school counselors. *Professional school counseling, 8*, 244.

Foxx, S. P., Saunders, R., & Lewis, C. W. (2020). Race, gender, class and achievement: A culturally responsive approach to urban school counseling. *Professional School Counseling*. https://doi.org/10.1177/2156759X19899184

Francis, D., & Mason, E. (2022). Proactively addressing racial incidents in schools: Two perspectives. In C. Holcomb-McCoy (Ed.), *Antiracist counseling in schools and communities* (pp. 57–80). American Counseling Association.

Freire, P. (2018). *Pedagogy of the oppressed* (4th ed.). Bloomsbury Academic & Professional.

Furr, S. C. (2018). *Wellness interventions for social justice fatigue among student affairs professionals* (Publication No. 10748341). [Doctoral dissertation, Loyola University Chicago]. ProQuest Dissertations & Theses. https://ecommons.luc.edu/luc_diss/2803

Gay, G. (2000). *Culturally responsive teaching: Theory, research, and practice.* Teachers College Press.

Gay, G. (2018). *Culturally Responsive Teaching: Theory, Research, and Practice.* Teachers College Press.

Grothaus, T., Crum, K. S., & James, A. B. (2010). Effective leadership in a culturally diverse learning environment. *International Journal of Urban Educational Leadership, 4*(1), 111–125.

Griffin, D., & Farris, A. (2010). School counselors and school-familycommunity collaboration: Finding resources through community asset mapping. *Professional School Counseling, 13*, 248–256. https://doi.org/10.1177/2F2156759X1001300501

Gysbers, N. C. (2010). *School counseling principles: Remembering the past, shaping the future. A history of school counseling.* American School Counseling Association.

Harley, D. A. (2009). Multicultural counseling as a process of empowerment. In C. C. Lee, D. A. Burnhill, A. L. Butler, C. P. Hipolito-Delgado, M. Humphrey, O. Munoz, et al. (Eds.), *Elements of culture in counseling* (pp. 127–147). Pearson.

Hilts, D. (2019). School counselors perceptions of barriers to implementing a RAMP-designated school counseling program. *Professional School Counseling, 23*, 1.
Hines, E., Harris, P., Mayes, R., & Owen, L. (2021). College and career readiness for students of color: Using an antiracist ecological framework. In C. Holcomb-McCoy (Ed.), *Antiracist counseling in schools and communities.* American Counseling Association.
Hines, E., & Owen, L. (Eds.). (2022). *Equity-based career development and post-secondary transitions: An American imperative.* Information Age Publishing.
Holcomb-McCoy C. (2007). *School counseling to close the achievement gap: A social justice framework for success.* Corwin Press.
Holcomb-McCoy, C. (2022). *Antiracist counseling in schools and communities.* American Counseling Association.
Kearl, B. & Mayes, R. D. (2024). Moms for Liberty and the *dispositifs* of white motherhood: Toward a Black whiteness study of maternal educational politics. *International Journal of Qualitative Studies in Education.*
Khalifa, M. (2018). *Culturally responsive school leadership.* Harvard Education Press.
Lad, K., & Braganza, D. (2013). Increasing knowledge related to the experiences of undocumented immigrants in public schools. *Educational Leadership and Administration: Teaching and Program Development, 24*, 15.
Ladson-Billings, G. (1994). *The dreamkeepers: Successful teachers of African American children.* Jossey-Bass Publishers.
Ladson-Billings, G. (1995a). Toward a theory of culturally relevant pedagogy. *American Educational Research Journal, 32*(3), 465–491. https://www.jstor.org/stable/1163320
Ladson-Billings, G. (1995b). But that's just good teaching! The case for culturally relevant pedagogy. *Theory Into Practice, 34*(3), 159. https://doi.org/10.1080/00405849509543675
Ladson-Billings, G. (2014). Culturally relevant pedagogy 2.0: a.k.a. the Remix. *Harvard Educational Review, 84*(1), 74–84.
Lee, C. C. (2001). Culturally responsive school counselors and programs: Addressing the needs of all students. *Professional School Counseling, 4*(4), 257–261. https://www.jstor.org/stable/42732264
Levy, I. P., Edirmanasinghe, N., & Ieva, K. (2024). The intersection of hip hop and Youth Participatory Action Research (YPAR) in school counseling to create and sustain homeplace. *Theory into Practice, 63*(1), 38–48. https://doi.org/10.1080/00405841.2023.2287762
Lindquist-Grantz, R., & Abraczinskas, M. (2020). Using youth participatory action research as a health intervention in community settings. *Health Promotion Practice, 21*(4), 573–581. https://doi.org/10.1177/1524839918818831

Low, S. K., Kok, J. K., & Lee, M. N. (2013). A holistic approach to school-based counselling and guidance services in Malaysia. *School Psychology International, 34*(2), 190–201. https://doi.org/10.1177/0143034312453398

Lipman, P. (1993). *The influence of restructuring on teachers' beliefs about and practices with African American students.* Unpublished doctoral dissertation, University of Wisconsin, Madison

Love, B. (2019). *We want to do more than survive: Abolitionist teaching in the pursuit of educational freedom.* Beacon Press.

Lukes, M. (2015). *Latino immigrant youth and interrupted schooling: Dropouts, dreamers, and alternative pathways to college.* Channel View Publications.

Manning, M. L., & Baruth, L. G. (2004). *Multicultural education of children and adolescents* (4th ed.). Pearson.

Martinez, R. R., Akos, P., & Kurz, M. (2020). Utilizing Latinx cultural wealth to create a college-going culture in high school. *Journal of Multicultural Counseling and Development, 48*(4), 210–230. https://doi.org/10.1002/jmcd.12195

Mayes, R. D., & Byrd, J. A. (2022). An antiracist framework for evidence-informed school counseling practice. *Professional School Counseling, 26*(1a). https://doi.org/10.1177/2156759X221086740

Méndez-Pounds, J., Nicholas, D. A., Gonzalez, N., & Whiting, J. B. (2018). "I am just like everyone else, except for a nine-digit number": A thematic analysis of the experiences of DREAMers. *The Qualitative Report, 23*(2), 442–455. https://nsuworks.nova.edu/tqr/vol23/iss2/12

Paris, D. (2012). Culturally sustaining pedagogy: A needed change in stance, terminology, and practice. *Educational Researcher, 41*(3), 93–97.

Perez, W., Cortez, R. D., Ramos, K. & Coronado, H. (2010). "Cursed and blessed": Examining the socioemotional and academic experiences of undocumented Latina and Latino college students. *New Directions for Student Services, 2010*(131), 35–51. https://doi.org/10.1002/ss.366

Safir, S., & Dugan, J. (2021). *Street data: A next generation model for equity, pedagogy, and school transformation.* Corwin.

Shields, C. M. (2010). Transformative leadership:Working for equity in diverse contexts. *Educational Administration Quarterly, 46*, 558–589. https://doi.org/10.1177/0013161X10375609

Shields, C. M., Dollarhide, C. T., & Young, A. A. (2017). Transformative leadership in school counseling: An Emerging paradigm for equity and excellence. *Professional School Counseling, 21*(1b). https://doi.org/10.1177/2156759X18773581

Smith-Adcock, S., Daniels, M. H., Min Lee, S., Arley Villalba, J., & Arce Indelicato, N. (2006). Culturally responsive school counseling for Hispanic/Latino students and families: The need for bilingual school counselors. *Professional School Counseling, 10*(1), 92–101. https://doi.org/10.1177/2156759X0601000104

Smith, W. C., & Benavot, A. (2019). Improving accountability in education: The importance of structured democratic voice. *Asia Pacific Education Review, 193–205.* https://doi.org/10.1007/s12564-019-09599-9

Southern Poverty Law Center. (n.d.). *Moms for liberty.* https://www.splcenter.org/fighting-hate/extremist-files/group/moms-liberty

Stephens, D. L., & Lindsey, R. B. (2011). *Culturally proficient collaboration: Use and misuse of school counselors.* Corwin.

Sue, D. W., & Sue, D. (2016). *Counseling the culturally diverse: Theory and practice.* Wiley.

Tervalon, M., & Murray-García, J. (1998). Cultural humility versus cultural competence: A critical distinction in defining physician training outcomes in multicultural education. *Journal of Health Care for the Poor and Underserved, 9*(2), 117–125. https://doi.org/10.1353/hpu.2010.0233

Valenzuela, A. (1999). *Subtractive schooling: U.S.-Mexican youth and the politics of caring.* SUNY Press.

van Oord, L. (2013). Towards transformative leadership in education. *International Journal of Leadership in Education, 16*(4), 419–434. https://doi-org.libproxy.sdsu.edu/10.1080/13603124.2013.776116

Whaley, A. L., & Davis, K. E. (2007). Cultural competence and evidence-based practice in mental health services: A complementary perspective. *American Psychologist, 62*(6), 563–574. https://doi.org/10.1037/0003-066X.62.6.563

Witcht, S. (2017). *Culturally responsive pedagogy* [Webinar]. American School Counseling Association. https://videos.schoolcounselor.org/culturally-responsive-pedagogy

Wyttenbach, M. M. (2015). *The educational experience of DACAmented students: Utilizing capitals to confront barriers and navigate the American educational experience* (Publication No. 3723200) [Doctoral dissertation, University of Wisconsin-Madison]. ProQuest Dissertations & Theses Global.school counselors. Corwin

Yosso, T. (2005). Whose culture has capital? A critical race theory discussion of Community cultural wealth. *Race Ethnicity and Education, 8*(1), 69–91.

CHAPTER 7

Cultural Responsiveness in Rehabilitation Counseling

Debra A. Harley, Keisha G. Rogers, and Andrea Hampton Hall

Introduction

The goal of rehabilitation counseling (RC) is to work collaboratively with clients with chronic illnesses and disabilities (CID) to achieve maximum function possible through counseling and a variety of services and advocacy. RC is a field of practice that is predicated on a foundation of social justice in which persons with CID are to be respected and treated with dignity. Practitioners are ethically obligated to work to facilitate an obtainable quality of life for persons with CID, researchers to develop evidence-based practices, and educators to train counselors to engage with cultural

D. A. Harley (✉)
College of Education, University of Kentucky, Lexington, KY, USA
e-mail: dharl00@uky.edu; debra.harley@uky.edu

K. G. Rogers • A. H. Hall
Rehabilitation Counseling, Winston Salem State University, Winston-Salem, NC, USA
e-mail: rogerslg@wssu.edu; aha440@uky.edu

S. Sisko (ed.), *Culturally Responsive Psychotherapy, Counselling & Psychology*, Palgrave Texts in Counselling and Psychotherapy,
https://doi.org/10.1007/978-3-031-81831-8_7

responsiveness in working with diverse populations. Often, the way persons with CID are perceived is through bias lens that compartmentalize their identities because of their disabilities rather than through an intersectional perspective. Individually and collectively, persons with CID are intersectional beings with varied experiences and identities who have been relegated to the margins of society. Persons with CID are recognized as diverse and as members of a multicultural society not only because of their (dis)ability but also of their culture, race, ethnicity, age, gender, gender identity, sexual orientation, socioeconomic class, religion, geography, immigrant and refugee status, indigenous history, dimensions of personal identity and individual differences, and their intersecting identities.

An intersectional perspective reveals the restriction of diversities which can lead to intensification of inequalities and multiple discriminations (e.g., being a woman with a disability who is a member of a racial or sexual minority group, Dungs et al., 2020). That is, "diversity categories transport fixed ideas about a group that can promote the maintenance of an unquestioned form that distinguishes itself from the 'others' as well as the perpetuation of stereotypes and prejudices about groups" (Dungs et al., 2020, p. 2). Diversity categories mainly address only one aspect of categorization while ignoring the other. For example, the category of race mainly speaks to minorities, not the majority; age to older persons, not younger; sexual orientation to lesbian, gay, bisexual, transgender, and queer or questioning (LGBTQ+), not heterosexual; gender to women, not men; and ability to limits of functional capacity, not capacity. Clearly, concentrating on one category while neglecting other categories can lead to exclusion and dichotomy which is opposite of the focal point of cultural responsiveness which is the intersection and interdependence of multiple categories or identities (Crenshaw, 1991).

Culturally diverse persons with CID are challenged from multiple and intersectional perspectives, including functional limitations related to the disability and stereotypes attached to their multiple identities, which can both privilege and disadvantage them depending on positionalities. Because "each group of culturally diverse populations that receive vocational rehabilitation services has unique qualities and expectations, as well as different perceptions of disability…it is critical that people involved in service delivery be aware of how mores and attitudes of each culture is likely to affect how services are offered" (Thomas et al., 2002, p. 2). The purpose of this chapter is to explore the educational, supervision and clinical challenges and implications in rehabilitation counseling for inclusivity of culturally diverse persons with CID through an intersectional perspective and cultural tailoring. Cultural tailoring refers to the adaptation of research design, materials, and other components of the intervention to reflect cultural needs and preferences of the target population (Joo & Liu, 2020). Information is presented on the influence of colonialism in the history of the United States, the role of race, discrimination, and privilege in establishing vocational rehabilitation (VR) and contributing to outcome disparities for culturally diverse persons with CID, and the impact of cultural responsiveness in the field of VR counseling. Specific attention is given to implications for counselor supervision and strategies to be culturally responsive.

The intent of this chapter is to assist in counseling supervision to understand majority world view (i.e., non-Eurocentric) about disability and the influence of power and oppression that impacts individuals with CID who have membership in multiply marginalized groups. Majority world refers to individuals who are not of European descent. The Council for Accreditation of Counseling and Related Educational Programs (CACREP) standards require that "graduates demonstrate both knowledge and skill across the curriculum as wells as professional dispositions first with respect to universal counselor functions and secondly with respect to their CACREP specialized practice areas" (CACREP, 2024, p.1). The standards address current issues and seek to apply them to future societal, academic, and professional context. One such requirement is that all entry-level programs (i.e. master's level) meet 11 standards on social and cultural identities and experiences. In addition, the rehabilitation counseling specialization must address effects of sigma and attitudinal barriers as they relate to disability (CACREP, 2024). The 2017 Commission on Rehabilitation Counselor Certification (CRCC) Code of Ethics incorporated diversity within 12 main sections of professional practice, however, the 2023 Code added a section specific to multicultural considerations. The new section is intended to reduce bias, minimize discrimination, and prevent harm in practice. Moreover, cultural competencies are introduced as more than just aspirational directives but also as enforceable tenets of conduct (Henry et al., 2023).

The term Black, Indigenous, and other People of Color (BIPOC) is used throughout this chapter to refer to people of non-European orientation of identity. The reader is encouraged to consider intersectionality as central to culturally diverse people with CID as well as the influence of a lifespan perspective on perceptions about disability.

Historical Background in the United States

The country that became United States was initially settled with "the first people" (indigenous cultures), Paleo-Indians, and other indigenous cultures (Native Americans). European colonization transformed Native American culture through destruction of custom, beliefs, and cultural practices as well as the introduction of disease, the taking of land, and the concentration of first people on reservations. European Colonization began in the late fifteenth century, with the greatest settlement occurring after the 1600th and establishment of 13 British colonies by the 1760s. The U.S. proclaimed independence from Britain in 1776. Slavery was established throughout colonization in the Americas. Although slavery in the U.S. was abolished around 1805 in northern states, southern states maintained the practice until 1865. Subsequently other forms of pro-slavery practices were continued for decades in the form of indentured servitude and Jim Crow laws.

Colonization is recognized as the direct cause of replacement and eradication of cultures of various indigenous people in the Americas (Mark, 2020). At the core of colonial practices is the "us" and "them" racial dichotomy of white supremacy in which white people are believed to be superior to nonwhite people. That is, people of European (white) origin were deemed better than non-European, and white dominant people and practices, beliefs, and culture have been normalized over time and are now considered standard in the United States (i.e., white privilege, McIntosh, 1989). In similar ways, ability status became the norm for assigning value to people and defining quality of life, thus, assigning advantage to people without CID and disadvantage to those with CID. Internalized dominance (members of the dominant, privileged, or powerful identity group) has been used to not only justify colonialism, slavery, and race, gender, and sexual orientation oppression, exclusion, and marginalization throughout history but also disability discrimination (Harley, 2019. These racial, gender, and ability dominant cultures possess self-imposed privileges that permit them to leave the *other* out. BIPOC with CID are the most marginalized in life because categorically and intersectionally they have been the most disadvantaged (United Nations, 2012). The privilege that is imbedded in colonialism and ableism that gives members of these groups advantages is one that they embrace and, at the same time, the disadvantage and marginalization assigned to the *other* is difficult for them to acknowledge because "the defensiveness, denial, and resistance are deep" (DiAngelo, 2018).

Establishment of Rehabilitation Counseling

RC has existed for more than 100 years in one form or another (Hartley & Tarvydas, 2022). The first federal VR program, the *Smith-Sears Veterans Rehabilitation Act* of 1918 (also known as the *Soldier's Rehabilitation Act*), was established to provide VR services to veterans who acquired a disability during World War I (WWI). Two years later the *Smith-Fess Act* (also known as the *National Civilian Vocational Rehabilitation Act*) established the civilian VR program to assist civilians with disabilities to provide services such as vocational guidance, training, occupational adjustment, prosthetics, and job placement services. In 1935, the Social Security Act established the federal-state VR program as a permanent program that could be terminated only by an Act of Congress.

VR services historically have been disproportionately inaccessible to and successful for BIPOC (Giles, 1992). The way in which the federal government attempted to rehabilitate African American veterans with disabilities after WWI is one of the earliest forms of documentation of the lack of cultural responsiveness in the RC system which led to "new forms of racial knowledge and racial labor in postwar America" (Lawrie, 2016, p. 109). The Federal Board of Vocational Education (FBVE) was charged with rehabilitation efforts of transitioning the citizen-solider into the citizen-worker. The FBVE not only exhibited paternalism but racism toward and exclusion of Black veterans through the rehabilitation process. Specifically, the officials at the FBVE, consistent with the country at large, perceived Black people as inferior and took two approaches toward Black veterans: (1) they "struggled to determine whether they could, even should, mend broken black bodies often seen as 'defective by definition'" and (2) they "often accused Black veterans of trying to 'unjustly profit from their innate inferiority'" (Lawrie, 2016, p. 109). Lawrie (2016) likened the perceptions and practices of the FBVE to that of "salvaging the Negro" for work in the postwar employment sector in which "the FBVE sought to frame social policy along biological lines, and to rationalize racial labor hierarchies as a constituent part of the republican body politic" (p. 109). These efforts remained part of the RC system for a long period as evident by low acceptance rates of Black clients for service in the federal-state VR civilian system (see Wilson et al., 2001a, 2001b).

Subsequent legislation resulted in the evolution of the modern system of RC, including two key pieces of legislations considered as the disability civil rights laws (i.e., The *Rehabilitation Act of 1973* and the *Americans with Disabilities Act of 1990*). In addition to mandating access and accommodations, prohibition of discrimination based on disability in employment and education, both Acts empowered persons with CID to have equal partnership status in decisions and informed choice about their employment outcomes, specific VR services, and who and how service would be provided.

In its infancy the field of RC had prescribed power in the form of paternalism for counselors who had the ability, even the authority, to decide what is best for clients and to which resources they should have access. Paternalism is the notion that people in positions of power make "benevolent" decisions that remove the decision making and choice of individuals (Hartley et al. 2021). Although the RC system moved eventually from paternalism to empowerment for persons with CID, "professional power was rooted in a system, that in order to maintain itself, depends on clients who are powerless" (Sales, 2007, p. 3). For BIPOC clients much of their experience with various service systems in the U.S. has been a relationship in which they were powerless, being told what to do, given less choices, and perceived as not being qualified to make decisions on their own behalf. Also, when working with culturally diverse clients, attention should be given to hierarchical structure in the counselor-client relations. For example, Western approaches to counseling is to build an egalitarian relationship with the client, however, many Asian American clients, for example, feel more comfortable with a hierarchical counselor-client relationship. The counselor must also be aware that their age, level of education, and professional standing are important aspects in the hierarchal structure of Asian American culture (Kim-Goh et al., 2014). Therefore, it is important to consider how these types of experiences might affect the counseling process.

The professional practice of RC evolved as a unique counseling specialty out of counseling into a beacon of civil rights, advocacy, and accommodations to empower people with CID (Hartley & Tarvydas, 2022). In 1999 at the National Multicultural Conference and Summit in California a consensus was reached that the inclusion of marginalized groups beyond race and ethnic groups as part of multiculturalism must include a broad range of significant differences (e.g., race, gender, sexual orientation disability, etc.). This is a contribution of RC to the development of the field of multicultural counseling (Kim et al., 2023). Yet, RC professionals and practices continue to struggle in efforts to be culturally responsive to clients from diverse groups. Similarly, education training programs, counselor supervision, and clinical services experience the same challenges. The field of RC is multidisciplinary. Rehabilitation counselors work in a variety of settings, including but not limited to state rehabilitation programs, private practice, college disability resources centers, forensics, hospitals and medical settings, employee intervention programs, and social service agencies.

Overwhelmingly rehabilitation services in the United Kingdom (UK) were for physical disabilities (medical) and known as intermediate care. The term rehabilitation was first used in the UK parliament in a health context in 1940. Rehabilitation services in the UK were developed in a piecemeal way, focused on specific problems such as spinal cord injury, polio, back pain, equipment and adaptations, heart disease, and so forth. Each service was developed in isolation rather than interdisciplinarity (Wade, 2021). Healthcare recognized rehabilitation as a crucial addition to services for ill people in 1916. The Great War ushered in the publications using the term rehabilitation. In the UK, rehabilitation for 'shell shock' (psychological) was recognized in 1916. Major John Todd from the Board of Pension Commissioners for Canada published *The Meaning of Rehabilitation* which stresses that civilians should have access, the person must be active in the process, free access for service personnel needed to extend to civilians different interventions, including training, treatment, job placement, and follow-up (Wade, n.d.). Modern interest in rehabilitation started in the mid-nineteenth century. The theoretical foundation for rehabilitation emerged in 1977 with the introduction of the biopsychosocial model of illness which used expert multidisciplinary teams (Wade, 2021). In addition, the UK seems to separate physical and sensory disabilities from addiction and mental disabilities. After "the 1959 Mental Health Act and the 1962 Hospital Plan presaged the rundown of the asylums and the assimilation of psychiatric care into the wider hospital system," mental health services were developed and reorganized. However, it was not until 1990 National Health and Community Care Act that community-based mental health care became the responsibility of local authorities (Turner et al., 2015, p. 602).

The reader is cautioned to be aware that discussion of RC (or vocational rehabilitation) policies and practices in the UK has shifted over time since the UK's departure from the European Union in 2016. For modern

RC service delivery "the VR professional is required to gain and maintain knowledge, education and professional experience for compliance with the Disability Discrimination Act (DDA) and specifically with reasonable adjustments" (Vocational Rehabilitation Association UK, 2007, p. 12). The DDA prohibits discrimination against people with disabilities in education, employment, provision of goods, services, and facilities (Sayce & Boardman, 2003). Government initiatives in the UK consists of similar legislation to their U.S. counterpart, for example, the Employment and Support Allowance (like SSI/SSDI in the U.S.) and the New Deal for Disabled People (NDDP, like Ticket-to-Work in the U.S.). The medical model of rehabilitation remains the dominant course in the UK, whereas in the U.S. the psychosocial model is prevalent (Harley et al., 2018).

Vocational rehabilitation in Australia has a history of 70+ years and strongly parallels that of the U.S. in service delivery and education preparation of RCs. Development of community-based counseling in Australia began with the establishment of the National Marriage Guidance Council in 1948 to address marriage and relationship issues following WWII. Subsequently, other forms of specialized professional counseling were developed (Schofield, 2013). The RC professional associations in Australia have developed Codes of Ethics applicable to the RC environment (McLennan et al., 2021). Contemporary VR government policy in Australia recognizes VR as a key strategy to increase employment rates of people with disabilities. Since 2006 the notion of "mutual responsibility," in which any person with a capacity to work is required to seek work and, in return, the government provides employment assistance. People with disabilities applying for income support are referred for a job capacity assessment and referral to VR. In 2010 disability employment services were redesigned into two types of services; one for people not requiring long-term support (disability management services) and the other, for people with a permanent disability requiring regular, ongoing support to maintain employment (essential support services, like supported employment in the U.S., Buys et al., 2014).

Although the development of counseling in Australia drew from major theoretical trends in the UK and the U.S., several unique theoretical approaches have been developed by Australian therapists and have been impactful in Austrian counseling practice. These include *narrative therapy* (White & Epston, 1990), the *conversational model* (Hobson, 1985), and *no bullshit therapy* (Young, 2011). From a culturally responsive perspective, each of these approaches takes into consideration diversity issues, especially given Australia's geographic character whose population is concentrated in a small number of metropolitan areas and then large portions of sparsely populated regions, the high number of immigrants and the diverse ethnic mix of the population, and the complex history of its Indigenous population (Schofield, 2013).

Early Multicultural Counseling in Rehabilitation

For much of its history rehabilitation counseling was predicated on the theoretical constructs of Eurocentricity. The beginning of the multicultural counseling movement in the 1950s was focused on assimilating minorities into the majority. Historically, professional organizations in RC segregated RC issues related to multicultural counseling, diversity, equity, inclusion and accessibility (DEIA), and social justice from the mainstream (Levine, et al., 2022). It was not until the National Association of Non-White Rehabilitation Workers (NANWRA), now known as the National Association of Multicultural Rehabilitation Concerns (NAMRC), was established in 1969 that an organized group was dedicated to advocating for diversity issues within the profession.

Early forms of cultural responsiveness (known now as multicultural counseling competence, MCC) emerged in the helping and human service profession in the 1970s. A shift in the conceptual framework from psychodynamic, behavioral, and humanistic to culture-centered counseling and psychotherapy occurred in the 1990s in which Paul Pedersen (1997) conceived "cultured-centered counseling" as the core of culturally informed and sensitive interventions (Tanaka-Matsumi, 2022). The intent was to use a culture-centered perspective of these traditional theories to adapt and enhance their usefulness with diverse populations. However, work remained to be done because of how multiculturalism was sometimes used. For example, in South Africa multiculturalism was used to rationalize oppression, and the American version was grounded in the individualistic values and needed to be adapted to fit a collectivist context (Pedersen, 2002). Pedersen (2002) contends, to effect positive consequences, the solution must be framed in the client's cultural context. In addition, counselors who employ multicultural empathy are more likely to embrace cultural diversity and scored high on emotional intelligence (Miville et al., 2006). To disregard multicultural context is equivalent to unethical practice (Arredondo & Toporek, 2004).

Stebnicki et al. (1999) proposed a holistic approach to multicultural rehabilitation counseling (HMC) in which RC recognizes and appreciates both the individual uniqueness and human commonalities among persons with CID. This approach emphasizes the appreciation of each person by simultaneously considering many different relevant client characteristics including racial/ethnic identity, religious affiliation, gender identity/expression, socioeconomic status, geographic location, national identity, and lifestyle. The authors identify a core supposition of the HMC approach is that effective counseling is individualized, and an emphasis should be on understanding what is meaningful to the client as a person, rather than viewing the person as a representative of a certain racial/ethnic/cultural group. A key component of the HMC requires counselors to resist the urge to see experiences as a monolith, as everyone makes meaning in unique and nuanced ways.

Impact in the Counseling Profession

Over two decades ago, Lee and Ramirez (2000) asserted, "the future of multicultural therapy rest upon multicultural therapists and clients to be co-intentional social engineers of the future, to be active participants in the lives of culturally different people who are striving to live effectively and efficiently in a pluralistic society" (p. 279). Counselors must work with clients that are often from cultures other than their own. The need for training in cultural responsiveness is anticipated to accelerate in the age of rapid globalization (Tanaka-Matsumi, 2022). There are differences in cultures regarding views of health and CID, help-seeking patterns, stigma, and historical and current issues of discrimination (Gopalkrishnan, 2018). Cultural responsiveness impacts the working alliance between counselor and client. The counselor brings their own professional and personal cultural beliefs as does the client bring personal experiences and cultural perceptions that can create a cultural gap in the therapeutic relationship. In instances where the counselor and client come from different cultures, counselors may make assessments without "linguistic, conceptual and normative equivalence" which could lead to errors in service provision decision, overdiagnosis, or misdiagnosis (Marsella, 2011, p.6). Marsella (2011) emphasizes that not all problems are internal to the client and that the client's well-being is influenced by the external environment. Thus, it is the counselor who works across cultures who must be a social activist and challenges some of the societal contexts that impact their clients as steps are taken to decolonize the RC profession and recognize the value of indigenous knowledge and non-Eurocentric orientation.

Cultural responsiveness has significantly impacted rehabilitation counseling with a call to the profession to not only advocate on behalf of diverse and marginalized groups but to value clients from these groups as partners in the development of the counseling and treatment process, as well as promote empowerment and full engagement. In essence, "multicultural competency is critical for accurate clinical assessment and diagnosis and for effectively serving a diverse population of clients" (Smith, 2021, p. 295). Counselors with the best intentions are capable of negatively impacting the psychological safety needed to facilitate building the rapport that is necessary for effective counseling by committing microaggressions with clients who are BIPOC. "Perpetrators of microaggressions are often unaware that they engage in such communications when they interact with racial/ethnic minorities" (Sue et al., 2007, p.271). Racial microaggressions are defined as "brie and commonplace daily verbal, behavioral, and environmental indignities whether intentional or unintentional, that communicate hostile, derogatory, or negative racial slights and insults to the target person or group" (Sue et al., 2007, p. 273). Edmondson and Bransby (2023) define psychological safety as a state in which a person feels safe to take risk that consists of interpersonal components like sharing ideas, questions, and concerns without fear of negative consequences or judgment. A White counselor who consistently exhibits racial microaggressions effects the mental health of their clients. Subtle forms of racism manifest in everyday interactions. Edmondson and Bransby's study (2023) emphasized the importance of cultural competence in counseling to effectively support individuals from different backgrounds.

Gopalkrishnan (2018, 2019) asserts the necessity to go beyond *cultural competence* frameworks and practice toward developing *culturally dynamic partnerships* (CDP). The perception is that cultural competence (i.e., awareness, knowledge, skills, and action) was sufficient as a starting point in working across cultures but others have identified several flaws. First, the value neutral position ignores the differences in power and the nature of historical and present-day oppression experienced by cultural groups (Pon, 2009). Second, the competence approach focuses on the providers and their institutions and their capabilities to provide culturally appropriate services and disregard the participation of the clients and their communities (U.S. Department of Health and Human Services, 2001). Finally, cultural competence draws on static notions of cultures rather than the reality of cultures being dynamic and transformative (Chen, 2015; Pon, 2009). In addition to the four dimensions of cultural competence, the new multicultural and social justice competence (MSJCCs) calls for "understanding the complexities of diversity and multiculturalism on the counseling relationship, recognizing the negative influence of oppression on mental health and well-being, understanding individuals in the context of their social environment, and integrating social justice advocacy into various modalities of counseling" (Ratts et al., 2016, pp. 30–31). CDP rejects the notions of developing competencies to do something to the *other* and focuses on people working with each other (Gopalkrishnan, 2018, 2019).

Grimmett et al. (2024) examined the intent and impact of multicultural counseling and training on the experiences of community clients using the Community Counseling, Education, and Research Center (CCERC) model. The model's social justice approach focuses on enhancing the accessibility (in-person and online) and affordability (sliding fee scale), as well as centering the multicultural and social justice counseling competencies (the impact of oppression that client have experienced and a focus on intersectionality of privilege and marginalization experienced by clients and counselors alike) at a counselor education program-based counseling center or training clinic. The CCERC is a multicultural and social justice-based model based on developing a relationship with clients as full and equal partners in counselor education, counseling, research, scholarship, and advocacy. The study focused on how clients experienced five components of the identity foundation of the model: (1) a love ethic grounded in treating all people with respect and dignity, (2) a wellness focus that attends to the physical, psychosocial, social, cultural, emotional, relational, political, and spiritual development needs, rather than solely on mental illness, (3) trauma informed and account for traumatic experiences in assessment, conceptualization, counseling, and consultation processes, (4) center faculty and coordinators teach multiculturalism through carefully selected readings, trainings, supervision, and community experiences focused on putting into practice cultural humility, and (5) research and scholarship efforts intentionally include clients as active, informed, and consenting partners in studies and dissemination of findings. The participants who received counseling services were 20% African America/Black presenting with family issues, 3% Hispanic/Latino with mental health history, 7% multiracial/multiethnic with previous counseling experience, and 66% White Americans presenting with hospital admission for mental health issues, 70% females presenting with safety issues, and 23% males who thought seriously about hurting themselves or others. A thematic analysis of client responses about their experiences revealed that counseling was validating, positive, meaningful, and helpful. Clients reported a sense of safety, comfort, and competence communicated through the actions and skills of the counselors.

Counselor training and research in a sociocultural context (Casas et al., 2016; Middleton et al., 2000; Sue et al., 1992) have become and remain a requisite in the rapid age of globalization (Tanaka-Matsumi, 2022). Although not initially nor easily endorsed, professional organizations, accreditation and licensing bodies, counseling educational training and preparation programs, and government entities now consider cultural inclusivity and cultural responsiveness as paramount to promoting positive outcomes for BIPOC and marginalized persons with CID.

Supervision

Clinical supervision has a critical role and function in the education of RCs, and inclusion of multicultural supervision competencies within RC preparation programs is essential for quality service to clients of VR services (Boston et al., 2011). Boston et al. stress that in training programs, supervision occurs typically at three interwoven simultaneous levels: university faculty supervisor/doctoral student supervisee, doctoral supervisor/master's degree supervisee, and master's degree counselor/client. Each of these levels offers opportunity for developing multicultural competencies, however, less attention has been given to cultural differences among the supervisor, supervisee, and client. Addressing cultural differences among supervision participants is increasingly important because of diversity on a global scale. Thus, supervisors should acquire competencies not only in universal supervisor techniques but culturally normative techniques as well (Boston et al., 2011). In addition, it is important to recognize that we live in a global society in which people move about and communicate freely and bring with them their worldview. Counselor supervision should involve an understanding of how worldviews not only influence responses but may also create conflict between all parties involved because of power and oppression. Implicit in the interplay between power and oppression is not the lack of power *plus* privilege by the *other*, rather the way it is used by those with possession of power to marginalize and oppress the *other* (Troop & Harley, 2019).

Inherent in supervision is an unequal power dynamic in which supervisors hold the power. When working with supervisees of one's own culture or different culture, supervisors should work to improve cultural responsivity in clinical supervision. In addition, if a supervisor has less multicultural knowledge than the supervisee, the supervisory relationship could be adversely impacted. Harris and O'Donoghue (2020) recommend culturally focused supervision training program supporting both same-culture and different culture supervisors to provide cross-cultural supervision for cultural-specific staff within mainstream and their own community and human service organizations. Vekaria et al. (2023a) found five themes from supervisees' perceptions about improving cultural responsivity in supervision: integrating race/ethnicity into the profession, attending to the supervisory relationship, increasing cultural competence, addressing the power dynamic, and promoting cultural humility. In addition, supervisees felt that supervisors need to take responsibility to develop their personal and professional cultural identity due to the existing power dynamics inherent within the supervisory relationship. In an exploration of supervisees' perspectives on the supervisory relationship in the context of culturally responsive supervision, supervisees were from racially or ethnically minoritized backgrounds with White supervisors perceived their supervision as significantly less culturally responsive, with significantly lower quality supervisory relationships. Conversely, greater perceived cultural responsivity in supervision significantly predicted better supervisory relationships regardless of supervisee cultural background (Vekaria et al., 2023b). In addition, supervisees report many supervisors lack the necessary awareness, conceptualizations, skills, or multicultural complexity to promote supervisees' needed multicultural development and professional identity, especially for students with non-privileged identities (Seward, 2014). Moreover, training programs and professional organizations should take responsibility of integrating cultural responsivity into clinical training on a wider level.

In a study of supervisor cultural responsiveness and unresponsiveness in cross-cultural supervision, 13 BIPOC supervisees and 13 European American supervisees were studied using qualitative research (Burkard et al., 2006). In culturally responsive supervision, all supervisees felt supported for exploring cultural issues which positively affected the supervisee, the supervision relationship, and client outcomes. In culturally unresponsive supervision, cultural issues were ignored, actively discounted, or dismissed by supervisors which negatively impacted the supervisee, the relationship/or client outcomes. European American supervisees and BIPOC supervisees' experiences diverged significantly, with BIPOC supervisees experiencing unresponsiveness more frequently and with more negative effects than European American supervisees.

Peters (2017) suggests multiculturalism (and diversity) in clinical supervision requires a commitment to understanding and exploring narratives and experiences of identity, community, and culture. A continual process and intention of integrating social location and cultural factors is required. Conceptual frameworks for supervisors and counselors within supervision and counseling (i.e., Chun and Singh, 2010; Ratts & Pedersen, 2014) offer ways to approach social locations and intersectionality. Training and supervision must divest from the Eurocentric theories as foundational to counseling and develop training and practices from the margins due to the sociopolitical and sociohistorical foundations of counseling, counselor education, psychology, and other mental health professions (Peters, 2017, p.178).

The literature suggests several things incumbent of supervisors to demonstrate cultural responsiveness in working with supervisees. One, supervisors must develop a comprehensive understanding of intersectionality because intersections are foundational to human beings and their experiences and assigning meaning in the world, as well as to the stigma and oppression they face (May, 2015). Two, supervisors must go beyond exploring just intersecting locations and address stigma, oppression, and marginalization through an intersection lens, as well as privilege (Quinn & Dickson-Gomez, 2016). Three, adopt cultural humility and model and teach it through interpersonal interactions in supervision, and teach cultural humility through outside activities and experiences. When engaging in cultural humility, supervisors adopt an initiate-invite-instill approach. A critical part of this process is for supervisees to do a self-assessment of their strengths and challenges (an assess-build-connect [ABC] approach) in counseling culturally diverse clients (Hook et al., 2018).

Approaches to Cultural Responsiveness in Counseling

Various models and techniques have emerged for cultural responsiveness in counseling (e.g., multicultural and social justice counseling competencies [MSJCC], Ratts et al. (2016); multicultural competencies [MCC], Sue et al., 1992; and feminist theory (hooks, 1984)). P. A. Hays's 2022 book, *Addressing Complexities of Counseling and Clinical Practice: An*

Intersectional Approach, offers an overview of counseling techniques that can help counselors achieve a better understanding of a client's unique cultural contexts, as well as cultural influences as a multidimensional combination of positionalities. Of note is Hays's focus on ADDRESSING framework. This acronym stands for age, disability, religion, ethnicity, social status, sexual orientation, indigenous heritage, national origin, and gender. While these categories do not fully explain and expand on culture, it is a useful tool that counselors can use as a starting point to begin to understand cultural context and intersection. Hays considers these cultural characteristics from a power perspective (e.g., power vs. less power). Other dimensions often influenced by culture including trauma, people living in poverty, rurality, communication style, and language can also be considered within the ADDRESSING framework.

While rehabilitation counseling engages counseling techniques from psychology and counseling in general, it is important to consider the context in which these techniques are used with culturally diverse clients. Other considerations include the demand placed on the counselor and the clients, the specialized knowledge of disabilities, and environmental, social, cultural, and intersectional factors that interact with disabilities and culture. In other words, culturally responsive RC services must be delivered in a way that aligns with a client's cultural background. RC do not diagnose disability or psychopathology, rather they create an atmosphere in which clients feel accepted to address barriers to vocational success, community integration, and independence, of which part is the client's worldview. At the core of RC practice is an emphasis on individualized services and a philosophy of holistic counseling, full inclusion, and empowerment (Kim et al., 2023). The culturally responsive task of RC in the application of counseling approaches is to respond competently to the ways in which social others perceive the category of disabilities and the influence on access of resources which may result in more restrictions to participation for some more than others (Mpofu et al., 2012). Mpofu and colleagues emphasized concepts rooted in a human rights perspective monitor assumptions on which opportunities are configured and distributed to accommodate the full range of human (cultural) attributes, thus making it likely for inclusive sociocultural systems.

Multicultural Training

Developing culturally responsive counseling skills is a complex process which requires multidimensional or multifaceted models (Dickson & Shumway, 2011). That is, multicultural learning experiences should be developmental and build upon sequential experiences to provide a foundation for more comprehensive approaches of cultural competency-based training. In addition, multiple formats of training such as didactic instruction and internships with applied experiences (Killian & Floren, 2020) provide for higher skills efficacy. Learning experiences should be in transformative multicultural learning environments that challenge one's assumptions and beliefs about self within the socio-political context of culturally diverse others (Clarke & Tomlinson-Clarke, 2009).

Hall and Theriot (2016) evaluated undergraduate and master's level social work students to assess the effectiveness of more diversity training at different locations, course instruction, and assignments on multicultural awareness, knowledge, and skills. Participants in the study were enrolled in required cultural diversity social work courses. A pre-post-test was used in a longitudinal design. The results indicate that previous diversity training at different sites consistently predicts higher pre-post scores while previous diversity training sites and pre-post scores predict post-test scores. Participants who had trained in two more settings scored higher than students with less training sites. The authors concluded that diversity content should be integrated across the curriculum, providing multiple locations and opportunities for students to gain multicultural awareness, knowledge, and skills. Arguably, a multidimensional model may propel movement beyond cultural competence and to cultural proficiency in which the counselor actively obtains training of new counseling approaches for working with culturally diverse clients as well as become an advocate for cultural responsiveness. Culturally responsive education programs should facilitate integration of cultural competency across the curriculum, profession specific rather than generic training, integration of multidisciplinary case studies for analysis of cultural factors, and access to training materials for instructors (Lee & Matteliano, 2009).

Equally important to acquisition of cultural competency for students in training is for educators to be able to effectively measure cultural competence and cultural humility considering professional guidelines, accreditation standards, and universities call to improve cultural competence (Rodriguez et al., 2022). Although a plethora of trainings are designed to expose counselors to different cultures and to understand belief, values, and behaviors to achieve competence (Lekas et al., 2020), measuring cultural competence and cultural humility has yet to receive substantial attention. Researchers and counselor educators must develop uniformity and rigor of such measures. According to Kumas-Tan et al. (2007), several concerns persist regarding cultural competence measures. The first is about reliability of existing instruments that were normed on predominately white, middle-class, highly educated populations. Second is the question of utility, whereas many instruments are lengthy and cumbersome, and may not be relevant to trainees, as well as concerns about validity. Finally, measures are based on the awareness, knowledge, and skill model of cultural competence, however, there is ongoing dispute about the meaning of and components of cultural competence (Kumas-Tan et al., 2007).

Integrating Intersectionality and Multiculturalism

Intersectionality (Crenshaw, 1989) is a framework for understanding how social identities (race, ethnicity, gender, sexual orientation, ability, gender identity, etc.) overlap with one another and with systems of power that advantage people in the workplace and broader society; it is how people with overlapping identities experience systems of power (Kraus et al., 2017). Operationally, intersectionality is "the study and critique of how multiple social systems intersect to produce and sustain complex inequities" (Grzanka et al., 2017, p. 453). As important as it is to understand what intersectionality is, it is equally as important to understand what it is not. According to Bumb et al. (2020), intersectionality is not a replacement for diversity or other perspectives that promote DEIA, nor is it an add on of one identity to another, and it is not solely an American phenomenon. Although intersectionality is not a scientific theory, in counseling and psychology "it has proven to be a powerful tool for conceptualizing oppression and privilege, as well as for challenging systemic inequality through research, teaching, practice, and advocacy" (Grzanka et al., 2020, p. 306).

The integration of intersectionality and multiculturalism is a commonsense approach to counseling, teaching, research, and advocacy. Imagine if you will, the function of the human body as an integrated system in which each part is unique, yet contributes to the overall function of the body where each part is affected by the other part. If there is pain or dysfunction in one part of the body that is being treated, the impact of the pain or treatment on rest of the body is not to be ignored. If our physical well-being is a function of our whole self, so too is our rehabilitation. The medication we use for one illness must consider the effects on other parts of the body (helping one body part while adversely affecting another). While each body system performs its own function, the overlap of one on the other may make us feel better or worse. So, if we can see how one body system can benefit from treatment (advantaged) while the other may not (marginalized), it becomes clear how our overall well-being is compromised (intersectional). Thus, the benefit of treatment must be weighed against our individual predisposition and characteristics, as well as what influence them (external power).

Issues/Concerns

Although education training programs, counselors, and professional organizations acknowledge the need for cultural responsiveness, there is a persistent challenge of knowing how to move beyond Sue et al.'s (1982) tripartite model of cultural competence: (1) the awareness of one's own personal beliefs, values, biases, and attitudes, (2) awareness and knowledge of the worldview of culturally diverse individuals and groups, and (3) utilization of culturally appropriate intervention and skills. One challenge is client outcomes. Discrepancies in RC services, access, employment outcomes, and earnings persist categorically and individually for persons with CID from culturally diverse groups (Yin et al., 2021). Similar disparities in mental health care for culturally diverse groups include inequities in access, symptom severity, diagnosis, and treatment, and treatment outcomes (Medlock et al., 2017). A second challenge is significant political backlash against teaching Critical Race Theory (CRT; Delgado, 1995) in classrooms. CRT maintains that racism and microaggressions are everyday occurrence, and as a result have become normalized and ultimately invisible (Delgado & Stefancic, 2017). This political backlash speaks to the maintenance of colonialism and white privilege as well as denial of the existence of systemic racism (Settles-Tidwell et al., 2021) that persists in the U.S. and pervades all segments of society. Third, concurrent with the backlash against CRT is the continued request for DEIA training and measures of cultural competency efficacy in counseling and other human services disciplines and healthcare (Rodriguez et al., 2022). Although the discipline of RC has demonstrated a more proactive investment in DEIA and cultural responsiveness, the ability of many RCs to effectively implement their knowledge and skills in ways to maximize benefit to their clients continues to raise concerns (Cartwright et al., 2018). Concerns related to several of these diverse populations—race/ethnicity, sexual orientation, and age—are discussed next.

Race/Ethnicity

Early research identified racial disparities between BIPOC and White clients in types of services and amount of funds spent by state VR agencies, with BIPOC being accepted for services at lower rates, receiving less paid services, and closed unsuccessfully at higher rates (Harley et al., 2001; Wilson et al., 2001a, 2001b). Despite legislative acts and policy efforts, these trends persist, particularly for African Americans (Vryhof & Balcazar, 2020). Although White individuals with CID were less likely to apply for VR services than their non-White counterparts, White clients had higher eligibility rates, service rates, and employment (Yin et al., 2021). These trends are further disturbing because in the U.S., BIPOC are more likely to have CID than those who are White, to experience increased severity in their disability, and experience multiple barriers to accessing services (Vryhof & Balcazar, 2020). Among all the VR services, job placement assistance (JPA) was the strongest predictor of successful employment for American Indian and Alaska Native (AI/AN), and for those who received JPA, the second most important service predicting successful employment was maintenance (Salimi et al., 2023). The implication is that both quality of service and time in service are key when working with AI/AN with CID. Cultural responsiveness would suggest that cultural partnership in the counseling alliance is increasingly important.

Smith (2015) underscores these trends are further complicated by professions which provide counseling services that are profoundly influenced and created by and for Western European male individuals which are predicated on historical adversity and race-based exclusion. In addition, a historical legacy of mistreatment and racism toward BIPOC continue to reemerge and present current challenges of mistrust in the system of care for counseling and rehabilitation (Vryhof & Balcazar, 2020). The result is a fractured alliance with those clients who already have experienced microaggressions and the impact of colonialization which are reinforced using non-culturally responsive techniques.

Bellini (2003) conducted an exploration of the relationship between RCs' multicultural competency and VR outcomes in the context of counselor-client racial similarity and difference for clients with CID. The results demonstrated significant main effects as well as complex interaction effects among client race, counselor race, and counselor multicultural competency in relation to rehabilitation rate and vocational training rate. That is, clients from different racial groups experienced different outcomes in the VR process in the agency in this study as a function of the counselor's race and multicultural competency.

Sexual Orientation

The discipline of RC has a long history of exclusion of LGBTQ+ persons in the literature and service provisions. Harley et al. (1996) in a content analysis of RC journals on cultural diversity from 1984 to 1994 found that of the 1,601 articles reviewed only 128 addressed cultural diversity, of which only 3 were on sexual orientation. Current RC literature on LGBTQ+ persons remains sparse. Most of research on CID among this population are the healthcare literature and issue about substance use disorders and other mental health issues. The forefront of diversity works is focused on racial issues with exceedingly limited availability regarding the experiences of LGBTQ+ persons (Levine et al., 2022), yet LGBTQ+ persons report disparate rates of CID (Dispenza et al. 2017a). In a study of mental health practitioners (MHP) working with LGBTQ+ persons with CID to determine the most helpful clinical counseling practices with this population, MHP identified maintaining competence in intersectionality, utilizing affirmative consciousness, utilizing social justice practice ideologies, and upholding professional ethical values and behaviors (Dispenza et al., 2017a). In an examination of the educational experiences and practices that contribute to the development of certified RC working with LGBTQ+ persons living with CID, Dispenza et al. (2017b) found five major categories: formal didactic education, affirmative supervision and consultation during practice/internship, extracurricular-related training, identification, and family of origin. Pebdani and Johnson (2014) found less than half of RC students reported receiving graduate-level training on sexuality.

Of LGBTQ+ persons living with CID and receiving VR services, sexual minority women and bisexual-identified persons were more likely to report dissatisfaction with service than gay men (Dispenza & Hunter, 2015). The authors concluded that more consideration of LGBTQ+ issues in RC is necessary. Concerns for LGBTQ+ clients are attitudes of counselor toward them, issues of safety and disclosure, discrimination, stigma, heterosexism, and intersectional marginalization. Considering the erosion of equal rights of sexual minorities these negative attitudes are of concern for LGBT clients and further highlight the need for counselors to not only be aware of their own attitudes and beliefs but to understand the impact of their own biases and the dynamics of discrimination, stereotypes, power, privilege, intersectionality, and oppression when working with LGBTQ+ individuals (Ginicola et al., 2017). Esteban et al. (2023) found a significant positive association between satisfaction with counseling and LGB clients' perception that their counselor demonstrated knowledge and positive attitudes. In general, research on LGBTQ+ clients with CID are not a priority, nor is research conducted with authentic participation of LGBTQ+ people with disability in the services and research that is about them (O'Shea et al., 2020).

Age

Disability prevalence in older adults is increasing. As people age, they are at risk of incurring age-related disability. In addition, older adults are staying longer in the workforce, thus, increasing risk of work-related injury. Moreover, an increase in life expectancy contributes to increases in people with CID who are growing older with a disability. Brown and Johnson (2014) found people aging with a disability, who could benefit from VR services, are not being served, and those who are served, are getting neither comprehensive services nor high-quality outcomes. The type of disability and benefits received also impact older adults' participation in VR services and outcomes. Certain VR services and work disincentives interact to predict the likelihood of employment outcomes among this population (Miller et al., 2016). Over the course of their lifetime, older adults represent one of the most diverse groups because of societal changes they have experienced. Their intersectional identities comingle with time to create multiple categories of marginalization for them in profound ways.

CID in young people offer complexities and intersectionalities. For example, LGBTQ+ young people are more likely to report MH concerns compared to heterosexual and cisgender peers (Johns et al., 2020), to experience minority stress and discrimination (Rich et al., 2020), and different demographic groups of LGBTQ+ report varying rates of disability identification (The Trevor Project, 2023). In addition, adverse experiences of LGBTQ+ young people with CID have long-term effects that carry over into adulthood and across the lifespan which impact their health.

Application of Postmodernism

According to Henry et al. (2023), "to better understand the role of power and privilege in this society, and at play within our profession, critical disability theory (Schalk, 2017) and CRT both provide a framework to challenge, dismantle, and eradicate systems of oppression" (p. 278). Furthermore, application of a critical disability lens at organizational (service providers), educational (training), and research and policy levels to illuminate exclusionary diversity, systems will be accountable to reconceptualizing what it means to be considered disabled, BIPOC, and marginalized from the perspective of people who live this experience as participatory agents of change in the process of DEIA in rehabilitation counseling (Reaume, 2014). Cultural humility has also been discussed widely in the multicultural counseling literature and found consequential. Both cultural humility and cultural competence share conceptual alignment, emphasize on different aspects of counselor characteristics and behaviors in cultural contexts, and play an integral, but slightly varied role during the counseling process (Zhu et al., 2023). Approaches of cultural responsiveness in counseling are shifting away from cultural competence as "the baseline benchmark—the bare minimum standard to ethically practice with clients—to frameworks such as cultural humility, intersectionality, and decolonizing disability/mental health to ensure we reach all the people who have disability/mental health needs in ways that align with their cultural identities and reduce the impact oppression has on them" (Hargons, 2021, p.1).

Cultural competence and cultural humility address the importance of cultural learning but have a clear line of distinction. On the one hand cultural competence implies that learning is a destination or has an end and is top-down (training is provided in the field for workers of organizations) approach that may lead to stereotyping. On the other hand, cultural humility considers cultural learning as a life-long endeavor and includes one's own identity within the social construct (Tervalon & Murry-Garcia, 1998). The either/or argument of competence versus humility is challenged by Greene-Moton and Minkler (2019) in favor of both approaches as beneficial which are complementary rather than competitive.

Decolonizing employs cultural humility and intersectionality, permitting counselors to reconnect to the humanization (to bring down from pedestals) of counseling, to include systems and oppression into the counseling practice and analysis, as well as to center the person and their cultural and political identities back into the work (Mullen, 2023). Mullan asserts that decolonizing requires counselors to examine and reflect on how they have been part of oppressive cultures and systems. Broadly stated, decolonizing counseling is about questioning and unlearning beliefs and standards of practice that are based on the dominant Eurocentric perspective.

Case Study of Culturally Responsive Counseling

Counselor

The counselor is a 31-year-old Caucasian female with a master's degree in rehabilitation counseling. She uses cognitive-behavioral theory (CBT). She has worked as an RC for three years. Her previous work experience was in a faith-based organization with women in an offender work release program. The counselor is deeply rooted in her religious beliefs and denominational doctrine.

Client

Tess is 23-year-old, first-generation Arab American women who identifies as bisexual. She has a limited work history and was employed as a stocker at a warehouse for the past seven months, earning minimum wage. Her work history is limited because of several convictions and prison time for forgery and robbery. She lives in a rural community with no public transportation. Her house is located five miles from the town limit. Tess has no previous mental health history. She acquired an injury in a car accident resulting in a spinal cord injury leaving her unable to use her legs. As a result, she lost her job. The employer did not have another job position that Tess could apply. She has no other source of income and has applied for social security disability insurance (SSDI) and public assistance. Tess presents with symptoms of depression, anxiety, stress, and paranoia. She attributes her symptoms to concerns of financial insecurity, prospects of reincarceration, and her family finding out about her sexual orientation.

Counseling Session

During the initial counseling session, the counselor focused on establishing rapport and her understanding of Arab/Arab American culture. However, prior to the initial meeting with Tess the counselor did some research on Arab/Arab American culture. The counselor also did some reflection about her personal views and beliefs about Arab culture. Given the counselor's work experience and personal religious beliefs and practices, she also did a self-inventory about her perceptions of working with a client who is bisexual. During her meeting with the client, the counselor shared that she had limited experience working with Arab American clients. She assured the client that she was there to work with her and wanted to understand Tess's worldview. The counselor indicated to Tess that she may ask her specific cultural questions to help her to be better informed. The counselor asked Tess to share how she can balance her multiple identities and if she faces any challenges because of them.

Case Discussion

In this case study, the counselor made cultural responsiveness part of the counseling process. The counselor did a self-inventory of her own awareness, self-education, and reflection. The counselor recognized her own concerns and lack of knowledge about Arab culture. The counselor used cultural humility in several ways. First, she put culture up front and acknowledged the importance of the client's unique culture. Second, the counselor stepped outside of her comfort zone to explore the unknown, as well as educate herself about the client's culture. The counselor recognized that she could not rely solely on the client to educate her about the client's culture. Third, the counselor understood that her views may be different from that of the client, and it was not a matter of one or the other being wrong, rather the client's values are important because they guide the client's decision making. Finally, the counselor was aware that Tess had multiple marginalized identities and incorporated that intersectionality of the client should be addressed.

Conclusion

Culturally responsive training, education, and supervision of counselor trainees tend to demonstrate an important role in developing cultural competence and cultural humility and positively impacted client outcomes. As we continue to struggle to meet the professional, ethical, and humanitarian responsibility to embrace DEIA, we all have in common diversity and intersectionality that may impact us across the lifespan. For people with CID, their intersection between disability and marginalization and other social positionalities echoes the importance of counselors having a sophistication beyond cultural competence.

References

Arredondo, P., & Toporek, R. (2004). Multicultural counseling competencies equals ethical practice. *Journal of Mental Health Counseling, 26*(1), 44–55. https://doi.org/10.17744/mehc.26.1.hw2enjqve2p2tj6q

Bellini, J. (2003). Counselors' multicultral competencies and vocational rehabilitation outcomes in the context of counselors—client racial similarity and differences. *Rehabilitation Counseling Bulletin, 46*, 164–173.

Boston, Q., Vaughn, M., Pitt, J., Soldner, J. L., Turner-Whittaker, T., & Robertson, S. (2011). Promoting multicultural competencies in early career rehabilitation counselor supervision. *Australian Journal of Rehabilitation Counseling, 17*(1), 36–45. https://www.academic.edu/906721/Promoting_Multicultural_Competencies_in_Early_Caree_Rehabilitation_Counsellor_Supervisiors

Brown, P., & Johnson, K. (2014). Aging with a disability and state vocational rehabilitation services. *Work, 48*(3), 441–451. https://doi.org/10.3233/WOR-131781

Bumb, N., Carlson, C., & Iyer, L. (2020). Change the world – for whom? Why addressing racism must be a top corporate priority. *Fortune*. https://fortune.com/2020/09/21-change-the-world-companies-must-tackle-racism

Burkard, A. W., Johnson, A. J., Madson, M. B., Pruitt, N., Contreras-Tasych, D., Kozlowski, J. M., Hess, S. A., & Knox, S. (2006). Supervisor cultural responsiveness and unresponsiveness in cross-cultural supervision. *Journal of Counseling Psychology, 53*(3), 288–301. https://doi.org/10.1037/0022-0167.53.3.288

Buys, N., Matthews, L. R., & Randall, C. (2014). Contemporary vocational rehabilitation in Australia. *Disability and Rehabilitation*, [online]. https://doi.org/10.3109/09638288.2014.942001

Cartwright, B. Y., Harley, D. A., & Rogers, K. G. (2018). Cultural competence and social justice. In V. M. Tarvydas & M. T. Hartley (Eds.), *The professional practice of rehabilitation counseling* (2nd ed., pp. 343–358). Springer.

Casas, J. M., Suzuki, L. A., Alexander, C. M., & Jackson, M. A. (Eds.). (2016). *Handbook of multicultural counseling* (4th ed.) SAGE.

Chen, G. M. (2015). Theorizing global community as cultural home in the new century. *International Journal of Intercultural Relations, 46*, 73–81. https://doi.org/10.1016/j.ijintrel.2015.03.024

Chun, K. Y. S., & Singh, A. A. (2010). The bisexual youth of color intersecting identities development model: A contextual approach to understanding multiple marginalization experiences. *Journal of Bisexuality, 10*(4), 429–451. https://doi.org/10.1080/15299716.2010.521059

Clarke, D., & Tomlinson-Clarke, S. (2009). Creating non-traditional multicultural learning environments through cultural exchange. *International Journal of Learning, 16*, 481–487.

Council for Accreditation of Counseling and Related Educational Programs. (2024). *2024 CACREP Standards.* https://www.cacrep.org/wp-content/uploads/2023/06/2024-Standards-Combined-Version-6.27.23.pdf

Crenshaw, K. W. (1989). Demarginalizing the intersection of race and sex: A Black feminist critique of antidiscrimination doctrine, feminist theory and antiracist politics. *University of Chicago Legal Forum, 1.* http://chicagounbound.uchicago.edu/uclf/vol1989/iss1/8

Crenshaw, K. W. (1991). Mapping the margins: Intersectionality, identity politics, and violence against women of color. *Stanford Law Review, 43*, 1241–1199. https://doi.org/10.2307/1229039

Delgado, R. (Ed.). (1995). *Critical race theory: The cutting edge.* Temple University Press.

Delgado, R., & Stefancic, J. (2017). *Critical race theory: An introduction.* University Press.

DiAngelo, R. (2018). *White fragility: Why it's so hard for white people to talk about racism.* Beacon Press.

Dickson, G. L., & Shumway, B. A. (2011). *A framework of multi-faceted approaches to multicultural training.* https://counselingoutfitters.com/vista/vista11?Article_69pdf

Dispenza, F., Elston, N. C., Huffstead, M. E., Suttles, M. G., & Golubovic, N. (2017a). Rehabilitation counselor preparation to work with LGBTQ persons living with chronic illness/disability: A qualitative content analysis. *Rehabilitation Research, Policy, and Education, 31*(1), 27–39. https://doi.org/10.1891/2168-6653.31.1.27

Dispenza, F., & Hunter, T. (2015). Reported use of and satisfaction with vocational rehabilitation services among lesbian, gay, bisexual, and transgender persons. *Rehabilitation Research, Policy, and Education, 29*(4), 421–424. https://doi.org/10.1891/2168-6653.29.4.421

Dispenza, F., Varney, M., & Golubovic, N. (2017b). Counseling and psychological practices with sexual and gender minority persons living with chronic illnesses/disabilities (CID). *Psychology of Sexual Orientation and Gender Diversity, 4*(1), 137–142. https://doi.org/10.1037/sgd0000212

Dungs, S., Pichler, C., & Reiche, R. (2020). Disability & diversity studies as a professional basis for diversity-aware education and training in medicine. *GMS Journal for. Medical Education, 37*(2). https://doi.org/10.3205/zma001316

Edmondson, A. C., & Bransby, D. P. (2023). Psychological safety comes of age: Observed themes in an established literature. *Annual Review of Organizational Psychology and Organizational Behavior, 10*, 55–78. https://doi.org/10.1146/annurev-orgpsych-120920-055217

Esteban, C., Francia-Martinez, M., Vazquez-Rivera, M., Crespo, F., Bruno-Ortiz, T., Santiago-Ortiz, A. M., & Martinez-Taboas-A. (2023). Sexual orientation knowledge and attitudes and its association with therapy satisfaction among lesbian, gay, and bisexual + Hispanic Puerto Ricans. *BMC Public Health, 23*, 857. https://doi.org/10.1186/s12889-023-15811-8

Giles, F. L. (1992). *The vocational rehabilitation of minorities [and] reactions.* https://eric.ed.gov/?id=ED358592

Ginicola, M. M., Filmore, J. M., & Cheri, S. (2017). Developing competency in working with LGBTQI+ communities' awareness, knowledge, skills and action. In M. M. Ginicola & J. M. Filmore (Eds.), *Affirmative counseling with LGBTQI+ people* (pp. 3–20). American Counseling Association.

Gopalkrishnan, N. (2018). Cultural diversity and mental health: Considerations for policy and practice. *Front Public Health, 6.* https://doi.org/10.3389/fpuph.2018.00179

Gopalkrishnan, N. (2019). Cultural competence and beyond: Working across cultures in culturally dynamic partnerships. *The International Journal of Community and Social Development, 1*(1), 28–41. https://doi.org/10.1177/2516602619826712

Greene-Moton, E., & Minkler, M. (2019). Cultural competence or cultural humility? Moving beyond debate. *Health Promotion Practice, 21*(1), 142–145. https://doi.org/10.1177/1524839919884912

Grimmett, M. A., Lupton-Smith, H., Beckwith, A., Messinger, E., Edwards, M., Moody, B., Clark, C., Mohamed, R., Englert, M., & Bates, D. (2024). Intent and impact: Connecting multicultural and social justice counselor training to community client experiences. *Journal of Multicultural Counseling and Development, 52*, 107–121. https://doi.org/10.1002/jmcd.12292

Grzanka, P. R., Flores, M. J., VanDaalen, R. A., & Velez, G. (2020). Intersectionality in psychology: Translational science for social justice. *Translational Issues in Psychological Science, 6*(4), 304–313. https://doi.org/10.1037/tps0000276

Grzanka, P. R., Santos, C. E., & Moradi, B. (2017). Intersectionality research in counseling psychology. *Journal of Counseling Psychology, 64*(5), 453–457. https://doi.org/10.1037/cou0000237

Hall, J. M., & Theriot, M. T. (2016). Developing multicultural awareness, knowledge, and skills: Diversity training makes a difference? *Multicultural Perspectives, 18*(1), 35–41. https://doi.org/10.1080/15210960.2016.1125742

Hargons, C. (2021). Cited in Yellin, C. *Moving beyond mere cultural competence in counseling: What to know.* https://www.counselingschools.com/blog/expanding-cultural-competence

Harley, D. A. (2019). *Cultural diversity in mental health and disability counseling for marginalized groups*. Linus Learning.

Harley, D. A., Feist-Price, S., & Harley, R. J. (1996). Cultural diversity: A content analysis of the rehabilitation literature. *Journal of Applied Rehabilitation Counseling, 27*(2), 59–62. https://doi.org/10.1891/0047-2220.27.2.59

Harley, D. A., Fleming, A. R., Greer, S. L., & Mundt, P. (2018). Disability policies and practices in the rural United Kingdom. In D. A. Harley, N. A. Ysasi, M. L. Bishop, & A. R. Fleming (Eds.), *Disability and vocational rehabilitation in rural settings: Challenges to service delivery* (pp. 437–454). Springer International Publisher.

Harley, D. A., Wilson, K. B., & DeShea, L. (2001). The exploration of social security disability insurance, race, and work status at closure on successfully rehabilitated customers in the United States. *Journal of Rehabilitation Administration, 25*(3), 137–143. https://www.researchgate.net/publication/289991817_The_explorartion_of__Social_Security_Disability_Insurance_race_and_work_status_at_closure_on_successfully_rerhabilitated_customers_in_the_United_States

Harris, T., & O'Donoghue, K. (2020). Developing culturally responsive supervision through yard up time and the CASE supervision model. *Australian Social Work, 73*(1), 64–76. https://doi.org/10.1080/0312407X.2019.1658796

Hartley, M. T., & Tarvydas, V. M. (2022). Rehabilitation counseling: A specialty practice of the counseling profession. In M. Hartley & V. M. Tarvydas (Eds.), *The professional practice of rehabilitation counseling* (3rd ed., pp. 1–20). Springer.

Hartley, M. T., Tarvydas, V. M., & Saia, T. A. (2021). Rehabilitation counseling. In C. C. Cottone, V. M. Tarvdas, & M. T. Hartley (Eds.), *Ethics and decision making in counseling and psychotherapy* (5th ed., pp. 209–234). Springer.

Hays, P. A. (2022). *Addressing cultural complexities in counseling and clinical practice: An intersectional approach*. American Psychological Association.

Henry, J. S., Kulesza, E. T., Awodeha, N. F. W., Hicks, S. B., Middleton, R. A., & Robinson, M. (2023). A way forward with multicultural considerations, advocacy, and accessibility across the 2023 revised Code of Professional Ethics for Rehabilitation counselor educators and practitioners. *Rehabilitation Counseling Bulletin, 66*(4), 274–282. https://doi.org/10.1177/00343552221146164

Hobson, R. F. (1985). *Forms of feeling: The heart of psychotherapy*. Tavistock Publishing.

Hook, J. N., Watkins, C. E., Davis, D. E., Owen, J., van Tongeren, D. R., & Ramos, M. J. (2018). Cultural humility in psychotherapy supervision. *The American Journal of Psychotherapy, 70*(2), 149–166. https://doi.org/10.1176/appi.psychotherapy.2016.70.2.149

hooks, b. (1984). *Feminist theory: From margin to center*. Routledge.

Johns, M. M., Lowry, R. R., Haderxhanaj, L. T., Rasberry, C., Robin, L., Scales, L., Stone, D., Suarez, N., & Underwood, J. M. (2020). Trends in violence victimization and suicide risk by sexual identity among high school students – youth risk behavior survey, United States, 2015–2019. *MMWR Morbidity Mortality Weekly Report, 69*(Suppl-1), 19–27. https://doi.org/10.15585/mmwr.su6901a3external

Joo, J. Y., & Liu, M. F. (2020). Culturally tailored interventions for ethnic minorities: A scoping review. *Journal of Advanced Nursing, 8*(5), 2078–2090. https://doi.org/10.1002/nop2.733

Killian, T., & Floren, M. (2020). Exploring the relationship between pedagogy and counselor trainees' multicultural and social justice competence. *Journal of Counseling & Development, 98*(3), 295–307. https://doi.org/10.1002/jcad.12324

Kim, J. H., Ntinda, K., Townsend, C., Thomas, K., Lee, D. H., Ortega, C., & Yu, H. J. (2023). Multicultural and social justice counseling within the scope of rehabilitation counseling. *Journal of Rehabilitation, 89*(2), 30–40.

Kim-Goh, M., Choi, H., & Yoon, M. S. (2014). Culturally responsive counseling for Asian Americans: Clinician perspectives. *International Journal for the Advancement of Counseling, 37*, 63–76. https://doi.org/10.1007/s10447-014-9226-z

Kraus, M. W., Park, J. W., & Tan, J. J. X. (2017). Signs of social class: The experience of economic inequality in everyday life. *Perspectives on Psychological Science, 12*(3), 422–435. https://doi.org/10.1177/1745691616673192

Kumas-Tan, Z., Beagan, B., Loppie, C., MacLeod, A., & Frank, B. (2007). Measures of cultural competence: examining hidden assumptions. *Academic Medicine, 82*(6), 548–557. https://doi.org/10.1097/AMC.0b013e3180555a2d

Lawrie, P. R. D. (2016). Salvaging the Negro: Vocational rehabilitation and African American veterans, 1917–1924. In *Forging a labor race: The African American worker in the progressive imagination* (pp. 109–134). NYU Press.

Lee, G. K., & Matteliano, M. A. (2009). *A guide to cultural competence in the curriculum: Rehabilitation counseling.* https://cirrie-sphhp.webapps.buffalo.edu/culture/curriculum/guides/rc.pdf

Lee, R. M., & Ramirez, M. (2000). The history, current status and future of multicultural psychotherapy. In I. Cuellar & F. A. Paniagus (Eds.), *Handbook of multicultural mental health: Assessment and treatment of diverse populations* (pp. 279–309). Academic Press.

Lekas, H. M., Pahl, K., & Lewis, C. F. (2020). Rethinking cultural competence: Shifting to cultural humility. *Health Service Insights, 13.* https://doi.org/10.1177/1178632920970580

Levine, A., Ruiz, D., Becton, A. B., Barnes, E., & Harley, D. A. (2022). Diversity and equity in rehabilitation counseling professional associations: An evaluation of current perspectives and future directions. *Rehabilitation Counselors and Educators Journal, 11*(2). https://doi.org/10.52017/001c.38190

Mark, J. J. (2020). European colonization if the Americas. *World History Encyclopedia.* https://www.worldhistory.org/European_Colonization_of_the_Americas

Marsella, A. J. (2011). Twelve critical issues for mental health professionals working with ethno-culturally diverse populations. *Psychology International, 22*, 6–9. https://www.indigenouspsych.org/Members/Marsella,Anthony/MarsellaTwelveConsiderations.pdf

May, V. M. (2015). *Pursuing intersectionality, unsettling dominant imaginaries.* Routledge, Taylor & Francis Group.

McIntosh, P. (1989). *White privilege: Unpacking the invisible knapsack.* https://www.nationalseedproject.org/images/decuments/Knapsack_plus_Notes_Peggy_McIntoshpdf

McLennan, V., Buys, N., Martthews, L., Randall, C., Millington, M., & Crocker, R. (2021). *Advancing rehabilitation counseling professional identity in Australia.* http://hdl.handle.net/10072/415088

Medlock, M., Weissman, A., Wong, S. S., et al. (2017). Racism as a unique social determinant of mental health: Development of a didactic curriculum for psychiatry residents. *MedEdPORTAL.* https://doi.org/10.15766/mep_2374-8265.10618

Middleton, R. A., Rollins, C. W., Sanderson, P. L., Leung, O., Harley, D. A., Ebener, D., & Leal-Idrogo, A. (2000). Endorsement of professional multicultural rehabilitation competencies and standards: A call to action. *Rehabilitation Counseling Bulletin, 43*(3), 219–240. https://doi.org/10.1177/003435520004300407

Miller, E., Gonzalez, R., & Kim, J. H. (2016). Vocational rehabilitation outcomes among older adults with diabetes. *Journal of Vocational Rehabilitation, 44*(1), 109–121. https://doi.org/10.3233/JVR-150784

Miville, M. L., Carlozzi, A. F., Gushue, G. V., Schara, S. L., & Ueda, M. (2006). Mental health counselor qualities for a diverse clientele: Linking empathy, universal-diverse orientation, and emotional intelligence. *Journal of mental health Counseling, 28*, 151–165. https://doi.org/10.17744/mehc.28.2.6khc06t87c2fr7y3

Mpofu, E., Chronister, J., Johnson, E. T., & Denham, G. (2012). Aspects of culture influencing rehabilitation and persons with disabilities. In P. Kennedy (Ed.), *The Oxford handbook of rehabilitation psychology* (pp. 543–553). https://doi.org/10.1093/oxfordhb/9780199733989.013.0030

Mullen, J. (2023). *Decolonizing therapy: Oppression, historical trauma, and politicizing your practice.* W. W. Norton & Company.

O'Shea, A., Latham, J. R., McNair, R., Despott, N., Rose, M., Mountford, R., & Frawley, P. (2020). Experiences of LGBTIQA+ people with disability in healthcare and community services: Towards embracing multiple identities. *International Journal of Environmental Research and Public Health, 17*(21). https://doi.org/10.3390/ijerph17218080

Pebdani, R. N., & Johnson, K. L. (2014). Rehabilitation counseling students report on training and sexuality. *Rehabilitation Counseling Bulletin, 53*(3), 173–175. https://doi.org/10.1177/0034355214553308
Pedersen, P. (1997). *Culture-centered counseling interventions: Striving for accuracy*. SAGE.
Pedersen, P. (2002). The making of a culturally competent counselor. *Online readings in Psychology and Culture, 10*(3). https://doi.org/10.9707/2307-0919.1093
Peters, H. C. (2017). Multicultural complexity: An intersectional lens for clinical supervision. *International Journal of Advance Counseling, 39*, 176–187. https://doi.org/10.1007/s10447-017-9290-2
Pon, G. (2009). Cultural competency as new racism: An ontology of forgetting. *Journal of Progressive Human Services, 20*(1), 59–71. https://doi.org/10.1080/10428230902871173
Quinn, K., & Dickson-Gomez, J. (2016). Homonegativity, religiosity, and the intersecting identities of young black men who have sex with men. *AIDS and Behavior, 20*(1), 51–64. https://doi.org/10.1007/s10461-015-1200-1
Ratts, M. J., & Pedersen, P. (2014). *Counseling for multiculturalism and social justice: Integration, theory, and application* (4th ed.). American Counseling Association.
Ratts, M. J., Singh, A. A., Nassar-McMillan, S., Butler, S. K., & McCullough, J. T. (2016). Multicultural and social justice counseling competencies: Guidelines for the counseling profession. *Journal of Multicultural Counseling and Development, 44*(1), 28–48. https://doi.org/10.1002/jmcd.12035
Reaume, G. (2014). Understanding critical disability studies. *CMAJ, 186*(16), 1248–1249. https://doi.org/10.1503/camj.141236
Rich, A. J., Salway, T., Scheim, A., & Poteat, T. (2020). Sexual minority stress theory: Remembering and honoring the work of Virginia Brooks. *LGBT Health, 7*(3), 124–127. https://doi.org/10.1089/lgbt.2019.0223
Rodriguez, M. M. D., Reveles, A. K., Litson, K., Patterson, C. A., & Vazquez, A. L. (2022). Development of the awareness, skills, knowledge: General (ASK-G) scale for measuring cultural competence in the general population. *PLoS One, 17*(9), e0274505. https://doi.org/10.1371/journal.pone.0274505
Sales, A. (2007). *Rehabilitation counseling: An empowerment perspective*. Pro-Ed.
Salimi, N., Gere, B., & Shahab, A. (2023). State-Federal vocational rehabilitation services, demographic characteristics and employment outcomes for Native Americans with mental illnesses. *Community Mental Health Journal, 60*(3). https://doi.org/10.1007/s10597-023-01191-1
Sayce, L., & Boardman, J. (2003). The Disability Discrimination Act 1995: Implications for psychiatrists. *Advances in Psychiatric Treatment, 9*(6), 397–404.
Schofield, M. J. (2013). *Counseling in Australia*. https://doi.org/10.1002/9781119222736.ch35

Schalk, S. (2017). Critical disability studies as methodology. *Lateral, 6*(1). https://doi.org/10.25158/L6.1.1.13

Settles-Tidwell, M., Dolid, A., Ingram, S., Watters, R., Vogel, K., et al. (2021). Commentary –An anti-American ban on critique: A critical policy commentary. *Journal of Leadership, Equity, and Research, 7*(1), 1–8. https://doi.org/10.13140/RC.2.2.30030.43841

Seward, D. X. (2014). Multicultural course pedagogy: Experiences of master'-level students of color. *Counselor Education and Supervision, 53*(1), 62–79. https://doi.org/10.1002/j.1556-6978.2014.00049.x

Smith, J. R. (2015). Mental health care services for African Americans: Parity or disparity? *The Journal of Pan African Studies (Online), 7*(9), 55–63. https://www.jpanafrican.org/docs/vol7no9/7.9-7-Jacksoj-Smith.pdf

Smith, T. J. (2021). Multicultural ethics in rehabilitation services. *Journal of Vocational Rehabilitation, 54*(3), 295–304. https://doi.org/10.3233/JVR-211140

Stebnicki, M. A., Rubin, S. E., Rollins, C., & Turner, T. (1999). A holistic approach to multicultural rehabilitation counseling. *Journal of Applied Rehabilitation Counseling, 30*(2), 3–6. https://psycnet.apa.org/record/1999-12000-001

Sue, D. W., Arredondo, P., & McDavis, R. J. (1992). Multicultural counseling competencies and standards: A call to the profession. *Journal of Counseling & Development, 70*(4), 477–486. https://doi.org/10.1002/j.1556-6676.1992.tb01642.x

Sue, D. W., Bernier, J. E., Durran, A., Feinberg, L., Pedersen, P., Smith, E. J., & Vasquez-Nuttall, E. (1982). Position paper: Cross-cultural counseling competencies. *The Counseling Psychologist, 10*(2), 45–52. https://doi.org/10.1177/0011000082102008

Sue, D. W., Capodilupo, C. M., Torino, G. C., Bucceri, J. M., Holder, A., Nadal, K. L., & Esquilin, M. (2007). Racial microaggressions in everyday life: Implications for clinical practice. *American Psychologist, 62*(4), 271. https://doi.org/10.1037/0003-066X.62.4.271

Tanaka-Matsumi, J. (2022). Counseling across cultures: A half century assessment. *Journal of Cross-Cultural Psychology, 53*(7–8). https://doi.org/10.1177/00220221221111810

Tervalon, M., & Murry-Garcia, J. (1998). Cultural humility versus cultural competence: A critical distinction in defining physician training outcomes in multicultural education. *Journal of Health Care for the Poor and Underserved, 9*, 117–125. https://doi.org/10.1353/hpu.2010.0233

The Trevor Project. (2023). *The mental health of LGBTQ+ young people with disabilities.* https://www.thetrevorproject.org/reseqrch-briefs/the0mental-health-of-lgbtq-young-people-with-disabilities

Thomas, D. F., Rosenthal, D. A., Banks, M. E., & Schroeder, M. (2002). Diversity in vocational rehabilitation: People, practice, and outcomes. https://www.academia.edu/100538001/Diversity_in_Vocational_Rehabilitation_People_Practice_and_Outcomes

Troop, C., & Harley, D. A. (2019). Understanding power and privilege. In D. A. Harley (Ed.), *Cultural diversity in mental health and disability counseling for marginalized groups* (pp. 107–129). Linus Learning.

Turner, J., Hayward, R., Angel, K., Fulford, B., Hall, J., Millard, C., & Thomas, M. (2015). The history of mental health service in modern England: Practitioner memories and the direction of future research. *Medical History, 59*(4), 599–624. https://doi.org/10.1017/mdh.2015.48

U.S. Department of health and Human Services. (2001). *Mental health: Culture, race, and ethnicity: A supplement to mental health: A report of the surgeon.* https://pubmed.ncbi.nlm.nih.gov/20669516

United Nations. (2012). *Realizing the future we want for all. Report to the Secretary General.* https://www.u.n.org/millenniumgoals/pdf/Post_2015_INTTreport.pdf

Vekaria, B., Harrydwar, L., Thomas, T., & Ononaiye, M. (2023a). Supervisee perspectives on improving cultural responsivity in clinical supervision. *Clinical Psychology Forum, 1*(371), 66–76. https://doi.org/10.53841/bpscpf.2023.1.371.66

Vekaria, B., Thomas, T., Ohiri, P., & Ononaiye, M. (2023b). Exploring the supervisory relationship in the context of culturally responsive supervision: A supervisee's perspective. *The Cognitive Behavior Therapist, 16*, e22. https://doi.org/10.1017/S1754470X23000168

Vocational Rehabilitation Association-UK. (2007*). Vocational rehabilitation standards of practice.* http://voca-vr.co.uk/pdf?VRA_standards_of_practice.pdf

Vryhof, J., & Balcazar, F. E. (2020). African Americans and the vocational rehabilitation service system in the United States: The impact on mental health. In R. Majors, K. Carberry, & T. S. Ransaw (Eds.), *The international handbook of Black community mental health* (pp. 275–292). Emerald Publishing Limited. https://doi.org/10.1108/978-1-83909-964-9202020118

Wade, D. T. (2021). The future of rehabilitation in the United Kingdom National Health Service: Using the COVID-19 crisis to promote change, increasing efficiency and effectiveness. *Clinical Rehabilitation, 35*(4), 471–480. https://doi.org/10.1177/0269215520971145

Wade, D. T. (n.d.). *Evolution of rehabilitation.* https://rehabilitationmatters.com/what-is-rehabilitation-2/context-of-rehabilitation/evolution-of-rehabilitation

White, M., & Epston, D. (1990). *Narrative means to therapeutic ends.* Norton Publishers.

Wilson, K. B., Harley, D. A., & Alston, R. J. (2001a). Race as a correlate of vocational rehabilitation acceptance: Revisited. *Journal of Rehabilitation, 67*(3), 35–41.

Wilson, K. B., Harley, D. A., McCormick, K., Jolivette, K., & Jackson, R. L. (2001b). A literature review of vocational rehabilitation acceptance and explaining bias in the rehabilitation process. *Journal of Applied Rehabilitation Counseling, 32*(1), 24–35. https://doi.org/10.1891/0047-2220.32.1.24

Yin, M., Pathak, A., Lin, D., & Dizdari, N. (2021). Identifying racial differences in vocational rehabilitation services. *Rehabilitation Counseling Bulletin, 66*(1). https://doi.org/10.1177/00343552211048218

Young, J. (2011). *A "no bullshit" approach to counseling in drought-affected rural communities.* Unpublished doctoral dissertation, La Trobe University, Melbourne, Australia.

Zhu, P., Luke, M. M., Liu, Y., & Wang, Q. (2023). Cultural humility and cultural competence in counseling: An exploratory mixed method investigation. *Journal of Counseling & Development, 101*(3), 264–276. https://doi.org/10.1002/jcad.12469

CHAPTER 8

Cultural Responsiveness in Relationship Counseling

Yun Shi and Lindsay Vik

Introduction

Relationship counseling has a unique history and professional identity that both parallel and diverge from the counseling field in general. As a result, cultural responsiveness in relationship counseling both resembles and differs from individual counseling. In relationship counseling, the counselor needs to attune to each party's cultural background and needs, which can be especially challenging when clients' cultural beliefs and practices clash with each other, not to mention with the counselors. How can the counselor join with one set of cultural beliefs without invalidating the other? What's more, a relationship counselor must work with not just two individual clients, but their relationship, with its unique history and dynamics. And a counselor needs to establish an alliance with each and all of them. How, then, can a relationship counselor respond with cultural understanding and sensitivity to all the relevant parties at the same time? These tasks add layers of complexity to counseling.

Y. Shi (✉) • L. Vik
Portland State University, Portland, OR, USA
e-mail: yun4@pdx.edu; lvik@pdx.edu

S. Sisko (ed.), *Culturally Responsive Psychotherapy, Counselling & Psychology*, Palgrave Texts in Counselling and Psychotherapy,
https://doi.org/10.1007/978-3-031-81831-8_8

Relationship counseling, and its closely related cousin, family counseling, have a rich history of addressing these complexities. However, they also possess obvious gaps since much of the relationship and family counseling theories have been developed in the Western world, particularly in the United States in the twentieth century, with its distinctive sociocultural and political context (Doherty, 2020). Therefore, one cannot adequately discuss cultural responsiveness in relationship counseling without acknowledging the context in which it was developed, the societal concerns it aimed to address, and its theoretical limitations.

Informed by the contemporary multicultural, diversity, and social justice theories, this chapter aims to help relationship-oriented or relationship-serving counselors and therapists (called "relationship counselors" in this chapter) develop awareness, attitudes, knowledge, and skills to serve clients in a culturally responsive manner. It starts by reviewing the multistage development of culturally responsive practice in relationship counseling, highlighting the paradigm shift in multiculturalism that has moved beyond gaining cultural knowledge and skills to serve diverse populations who are fundamentally regarded as "others" (Hutton & Sisko, 2020). Decolonizing relationship counseling requires counselors to examine the lens through which they view themselves and others, as well as the colonial mindset inherent in the dominant counseling theories and practices (Singh, et al., 2020). In doing so, counselors learn to see the world from clients' perspectives, recognize the power, privilege, and oppression issues embedded in our society, clients' lives, and clinical work, and appreciate the need for advocacy and social change.

The focus of this chapter, however, is on clinical practice. The Common Concerns section utilizes a case example to illustrate common concerns expressed by relationship counselors working with clients from different cultural backgrounds. At the end of the chapter, another case example is provided with reflection questions to help readers practice culturally responsive relationship counseling.

Another main component of this chapter is application of the postmodern critique. In this section, we integrate the Multicultural Social Justice Counseling Competencies (MSJCC; Ratts et al., 2016) with the six key principles for multicultural perspectives and responsiveness in counseling and psychology identified by Sisko (2020). Again, the focus here is on application. With each key principle, we introduce specific approaches, life and clinical experiences, application guidelines, and experiential exercises to guide the development of awareness, knowledge, and skills for relationship counselors. Throughout the chapter, we infuse case examples, clinical experiences, and exercises based on our clinical and training experiences with diverse client populations and relationship systems. These are designed to assist readers in developing culturally responsive counseling skills essential to providing relationship counseling to clients.

Historical and Theoretical Background

Relationship Counseling: Seeing from the Systems Lens

Relationship counseling has a unique developmental history that both parallels and diverges from the general counseling field, but always reflects the larger sociocultural political environment it is rooted in. Scholars described its start as marriage counseling in the United States in the 1930s, in the middle of the Great Depression. At a time of significant social change, economic and psychological stress, low birth rate, with desertions and divorce threatening the stability of marriage, the marriage counseling movement was launched. Rather than counseling, though, the emphasis of the time was on public education and outreach in places such as college campuses and faith communities (Doherty, 2020). In the 1940s and 50s, pioneers of this rapidly expanding field pushed counseling in radical new directions, focusing not just on solving relationship problems of couples, but also on birth control, mutual sexual satisfaction, and more modern gender roles (Nichols & Davis, 2017).

Then in the 1960s, the feminist movement began to challenge traditional gender roles, raise awareness of violence and sexual abuse in relationships and families, and highlight the unequal distribution of power in families and society (Corey, 2017). Meanwhile, the gay liberation movement prompted a reexamination of human sexuality and intimate relationships (Doherty, 2020). These movements had a profound impact on relationship counseling, in which counselors help clients explore and negotiate relationship dynamics, mutual satisfaction, and individual happiness.

Also arising in the 1960s, another group of pioneers—family therapists—developed systems theory, which fundamentally changed how relationship counseling views individuals, relationships, and families. A systems perspective views families and relationships as systems. Each system has its set of rules and routines, often unspoken but understood by its members. Behaviors and issues are best understood through the interactions of members of a system and by the way they serve the system. The systems perspective marked "a concept shift from evaluating individuals to focusing on system dynamics, or how individuals within a system react to one another" (Corey, 2017, p. 404). Rather than focusing on symptom reduction, a "first order change" that tinkers with but ultimately maintains the existing system, systems-oriented counselors aim to make a "second order change"—changing the structure or rules of the system itself (Davey et al., 2011). The systemic perspective is fundamental to the training and practice of relationship and family counseling.

The Multicultural Movement

The past few decades saw large-scale global migration, rising racial and ethnic diversity in Western societies, and increasing cultural clashes. The multicultural movement responded to these global and local events by calling for respect towards others and embracing cultural diversity (Rober & Haene, 2014; Singh et al., 2020). In 1992, the publication of Multicultural Counseling Competencies (MCC; Sue et al., 1992) addressed the concern that counseling training and practices often represented European and white American perspectives with little room for other cultural worldviews. MCC challenged the idea that counseling is "culture-free," and asked the counseling field to meet the needs of culturally diverse clients. To achieve this goal, the MCC required the counselors to (a) examine their assumptions, values, and biases; (b) understand the worldview of culturally diverse clients; and (c) develop appropriate intervention strategies and techniques.

MCC initially addressed only race and ethnicity, which later expanded to include other social identities such as gender and socioeconomic status. The principles of MCC laid the foundation of culturally responsive counseling. However, its application was difficult. Understanding the worldviews of culturally different clients presented unique challenges. There have been ongoing experiments and debates on the best or most appropriate ways to see from diverse clients' perspectives. Some earlier attempts introduced counselors to different cultural groups by summarizing their cultural characteristics and offering a checklist of interventions that address these characteristics. This inevitably led to stereotyping a large group of individuals via a limited number of character traits. Where is the individual in this characterization? Also, a more mechanical application of MCC tacitly accepts the assumption that mainstream (white, Western) counselors are the standard, and that they simply need to add an overlay of cultural knowledge and skills in serving diverse populations to work with those who are fundamentally regarded as "others" (Sisko, 2020).

To address these issues, later multicultural theories expanded the definition and scope of "culture." For example, the Multicultural Relational Perspective (MRP; Hardy, 2016) views culture as "a broad-based multidimensional concept that is comprised of, but not limited to, race, class, religion, sexual orientation, gender, family or origin, ethnicity, age, regionality, and so forth" (Hardy, 2016, p. 4). According to MRP, every one of us is embedded in culture, in an intersectionality of different cultural identities, and every encounter between the counselor and client is a cross-cultural encounter. Inherent in this perspective is the paradigm shift, from helping "mainstream" counselors expand their Euro-centered viewpoint through gaining knowledge on how to serve diverse "others," to focusing on counselors' inherent assumptions and bias and promoting intercultural dialogue.

From Diversity to Social Justice

MCC and traditional multiculturalism are also critiqued for their failure to address the inequality of power and privilege in societies, groups, and relationships. As Hardy, a leading family counselor, described,

> ... we as a discipline need to tease out a bit some of the nuances and distinctions that exist between diversity and social justice. I think that they're first cousins, but they have different emphases. With diversity, it means acknowledging and finding ways to appreciate differences. How do we include it? How can we be more inclusive?
>
> Social justice has more to do with critiques around power and the inequitable distribution of power. The more diversity-oriented orientation would be one that would embrace some piece of the ideology, "I'm okay, you're okay." This presupposes that we're all situated equally. I think a social justice perspective, while it appreciates differences, also attempts to look at the ways in which we are situated differently and the ways in which everyone possesses power but not everyone possesses it equally. Social justice is about, in one sense, rectifying fractures and ills that may be attributable to the inequitable distribution of power. Social justice is about recognizing that some voices are louder than others, that some people have greater access to power than others, and then what do you do about that? What is your resolve to alter that? (Wyatt, 2008)

Moving forward, Multicultural Social Justice Counseling Competencies (MSJCC; Ratts et al., 2016) integrated the developments in multiculturalism and social justice movements. MSJCC reflects a much broader understanding of social and cultural identities that goes beyond race and ethnicity, also emphasizing the intersectionality of an individual's multiple identities. It brought attention to the negative impact of oppression on mental health, and highlighted the importance of power, privilege, and oppression in understanding client issues. It called for balancing individual counseling and social justice advocacy, claiming that "certain situations will call for individual counseling. Other situations may require interventions that take place in the community" (Ratts et al., 2016, p. 34).

Divergence and Convergence between Relationship and Individual Counseling

Relationship counselors have faced the same challenges that gave rise to multiculturalism and social justice movements in recent decades. Rober and Haene (2014) observed that being culturally competent is highly valued in the field and promoted as "a correction to the ethnocentric ideas and practices that have ruled the Western intellectual world" (p. 10). A considerable number of relationship and family counselors examined issues such as gender inequality and power differences, gender and sexual discrimination, underprivileged and "hard to reach" families, institutional discrimination, political oppression, racism and anti-racist practices, racial and ethnic minority groups, immigrant families, and so on (Teh & Winley, 2021).

Despite their foundation in systems thinking, in the past few decades, scholars have observed a trend for relationship and family counselors to narrowly focus on the nuclear family or the individuals in the relationship, rather than focusing on larger sociopolitical systems (Lebow, 2021). Recent studies, however, began to pay attention to the larger social, cultural, economic, and political systems and their impact on relationship counseling. McDowell et al. (2019), for example, expanded the traditional systems model and promoted "third-order thinking," which includes a heightened awareness of "the impact of societal systems and power dynamics as well as collective meaning making and culture" when working with clients.

Setting the Stage: Culturally Responsive Relational Counseling

With the gradual paradigm shifts in counseling, and more specifically within relational counseling, it is vital to recognize how a more inclusive and expansive view of relationships and systems plays out within our sessions. To begin framing a culturally responsive practice, the authors want to encourage readers to actively reflect on and engage with their own experiences and identities while reading this chapter. Our hope is that these questions help you process how this may connect to your current (or approaching) clinical practice. To understand and begin looking at the impact on the counseling profession, we want readers to consider how cultural responsiveness relates to relational counseling and their initial reactions to relational work.

Reflection Questions:

When you consider doing relational counseling, what assumptions come up for you regarding the types of clients or client concerns you may work with? How could these biases or assumptions shape what you focus on or pursue in session?

What identities and experiences do you hold that inform how you feel and think about relationships and families?

Enacting culturally responsive counseling with relationships requires ongoing work, both in our research, text, and selves as inherently cultural, relational beings. As discussed, recognizing how the counselor is positioned is an essential first component of the MSJCC framework (Ratts et al., 2016, Singh et al., 2020) and we encourage readers to practice identifying how they are positioned in relation to their clients across the many facets of identity and culture. Outlining the beginnings of this process, the authors recognize and encourage readers to view this chapter and the inherent work it proposes as a steppingstone in building a culturally responsive practice.

As clinicians, recognizing the nuanced position you hold requires consistent consideration as it varies given the families or relationships you are working with. As recommended by Estrada (2018), this examination increases counselor self-awareness and recognizes how we are positioned within the lived context of our clients' lives. By engaging in this critical self-exploration, we can understand our positionality and how this interacts with our clients' identities and experiences. Here one of the authors shares a bit about her positionality to demonstrate how this can be applied for clinicians seeking to implement the MSJCC framework and begin to integrate a responsive practice.

LV, a first-generation college graduate, holds numerous privileged positions as a white cisgender, bisexual woman in a long-term monogamous relationship. She is currently able-bodied and navigates the world with some chronic health issues that impact her work, relationships, and mental health. Raised in the United States, LV's worldview is deeply informed by a colonized, Western view of mental health and relational processes. While recognizing these layers of influence is an important first step, ongoing considerations and critical exploration are fundamental to her work when seeking to practice culturally responsive counseling. When considering work with a relationship client, LV often explores initial assumptions and values that are present in relation to the clients. While this step may seem obvious, we have found that the *active* practice while doing relational work is particularly vital as the needs, assumptions, values, roles, and make-up of various relational systems are deeply unique to each client, and client system.

To further explore this, counselors must recognize that the positions they hold in relation to their clients may vary across the clients you are working with. Even within the families and relationships you see! Exploring the unique perspectives of each person is a crucial component that distinguishes relational work from individual counseling. Gaining experience and practice assessing intrapersonally, in addition to interpersonally, creates a more responsive environment. As noted by McDowell (2015), the roots of family and relational counseling are embedded in Western perspectives and even when integrating critical social theory into practice, we leave out many ways of knowing and being. By broadening our conceptualization to not only understanding the unique factors for each member of the relational system, but also through the lens of "third-order thinking" (McDowell et al., 2019), we are more prepared to effectively and ethically support relational clients.

When considering interventions and how to engage relationships, counselors are often straddling the knowledge they possess already and learning more about their clients specific, nuanced experiences. Inviting clients to share their knowledge, beliefs, and wants allows the client to assume the position of "expert" in their own lives. Similarly, shifting our conceptualization to incorporate the broader social systems allows for a critical examination of oppressive structures that inform and impact how families and relationships move through the world. With this consideration, relational counselors shift from only focusing on the inner workings of the relational system to the potentially corrosive, oppressive systems informing them (McDowell, 2015; Martín-Baró, 1994). This provides needed content to understanding and assessing power and roles within family or relationship systems and allows for curious exploration into patterns, needs, and assumptions present.

In this section, we hope to "set the stage" for readers to begin implementing a more culturally responsive approach when working with relational systems and why it is important given the shifts we have experienced in this field. We see this as a major impact on the counseling field; by more actively and critically exploring how we interact with, contribute too, and then challenge and deconstruct systems impacting us and our clients, we are better prepared to support their mental health work.

Common Concerns Illustrated with a Case Example

In this section, we use a vignette based on a composite of our clients to address many of the common concerns in providing culturally responsive relationship counseling. As demonstrated, the principles of decolonization, intersectionality, cultural humility, self-awareness, engagement and connection, and activism are utilized throughout the counseling process.

Case Example: A Chinese Mother-daughter Relationship

A mother and daughter seek counseling from you about their relationship issues. They are both immigrants to the United States from China. The daughter came to the U.S. in her early 20s and the mother in her 60s. The daughter reported that she was not close to her mother growing up as she was raised by maternal grandparents. The mother explained that having children raised by family members is a common cultural practice where she came from, and the mother herself was raised by a maternal aunt as a child. A few years ago, the daughter sponsored the mother to immigrate to the United States because the mother was getting old and lived alone. Since arriving in the United States, the mother has been living with her daughter, her daughter's husband, and their young children. The mother helps with childcare and house chores. As an only child, the daughter feels a sense of responsibility to care for her aging mother, but she is also troubled by their different ways of thinking, interacting, and behaviors. Feeling stuck and helpless, she decided to seek counseling with her mother.

The following are some of the common concerns expressed by relationship counselors.

A. What are my immediate thoughts and feelings when I hear about getting this referral? How would I feel if I am from the clients' cultural background? What if the clients' background is new to me?

It is not uncommon for counselors to be concerned about working with clients from different cultural backgrounds. Counselors may feel that they do not know anything, or enough, about the client population, or doubt their ability to work with diverse populations. In my (author YS) experience supporting immigrants, refugees, and minority clients in the United States in the past 20 years, I have seen a wide range of counselor successes with clients from different cultural backgrounds. The most successful counselors are self-aware, empathic, open to learning clients' perspectives, withholding judgment based on the counselor's own values and expectations, and meeting clients where they are. These counselors exemplify the principles of counselor self-awareness, decolonization, and cultural humility.

Client factors also contribute to counseling success. Some clients are more open to working with counselors from different cultural backgrounds than others. Sometimes clients intentionally seek out counselors from outside their community (especially if it is a small, closely knit community) to maintain confidentiality and get fresh perspectives. It is YS's experience that many clients are open to sharing their cultural backgrounds with an interested listener, and in fact along the way may learn to recognize their own assumptions and the values formed by their culture. In this case, by asking the daughter and mother to explain to the counselor their cultural values and assumptions, the counselor could help them to examine these often unspoken values and cultural norms in the open and have an opportunity to consciously and jointly decide whether or not they want to follow them.

Counselors who work with clients from a similar cultural background can also experience a wide range of reactions based on shared cultural norms, within-group stereotypes, or their own personal or family backgrounds. In this case, the counselor' own values regarding adult children's responsibility towards their aging parents could influence their thoughts and feelings. The daughter could be viewed as a martyr of cultural responsibility and earn the counselor's sympathy for being sandwiched between the older and younger generation before counseling starts. A counselor's own experience and unprocessed trauma of abandonment or attachment wounds could trigger strong countertransference that potentially impacts how they view the daughter, the mother, and their relationship. Therefore, whether or not the counselor is from the same cultural background, they might feel themselves aligning more with one or the other side of the relationship, and thus having more empathy towards one and more judgment towards the other.

B. What information and assumptions do I have about these clients? How do I navigate between holding information about the clients' culture and keeping stereotypes at bay?

Many counselors have learned about diverse cultures through books or training that summarize an entire culture with a few bullet points. When YS was attending multicultural counseling class 20 years ago in the United States, she was surprised and dismayed to find her culture and people being taught as exhibiting "deference to authority figures," "conformity to family and social norms and expectations," "respect for elders and ancestors," and so on (Kim et al., 2001). She felt reduced to a list which did not always match her experience and identity and obscured her individuality and humanity. Many years later, she recognized the utility of providing a basic understanding of the core values of a culture to people who are not familiar with it, if appropriately presented as a starting point to understand clients' unique experiences. However, the feeling of unease remains.

In this case, counselors who have no awareness of the value placed on family and the cultural expectation for adult children to take care of their aging parents would miss the foundational context of their clients' relationship. However, counselors who understand clients only through these principles are not seeing the whole person navigating and negotiating with their environment. The daughter, feeling called by the cultural norm to care for her mother, is experimenting with ways to meet both cultural expectations and personal needs. By asking her mother to help with house chores and childcare duties, she initially maintained a psychological balance to fulfill her responsibilities as a daughter and her needs as a working mother. As the mother-daughter value clashes and conflicts increase, she is considering a variety of options, including asking her mother to move out if counseling fails to help. She could benefit from a counselor who doesn't hold rigid values, one who can walk in her shoes and explore best options with her.

The daughter has lived in the United States for many years. As a result, she may have more shared cultural beliefs and values with the counselor. The mother, on the other hand, may match more of the Asian stereotypes the counselor was exposed to and may be less likely to be seen as an individual with unique experiences, thoughts, and feelings. The counselor must take special care to look at the world through the mother's perspective and validate the mother's thoughts and feelings. Through intentional empathy with the mother, the counselor could see the confusion, hurt, and fear underlying the mother's presentation as someone who left behind everything, she was familiar with to live in a vastly different environment, relying on her children and feeling alienated and powerless. The mother is seen to possess the nuances of a specific person with her own identity, not merely a representation of a label.

C. What do I do when the values presented by the clients clash with my own? How am I going to be authentic and supportive of clients at the same time?

Much of counselors' work on self-awareness, decolonization, and cultural humanity will be tested when their client's values clash with their own. As argued by Rober and Haene (2014), counselors cannot fully brush aside their values, especially the ones central to their personal and professional identity. The counselors can, however, try to withhold their judgment, at least temporarily, about these conflicted values. Thus, the values are not perceived as good or bad, right or wrong, but as beliefs arising from specific sociocultural, political environments. This way the values can be examined and evaluated as to how they are serving the client and the counseling relationship.

To illustrate the point, let's assume one of the values held by the clients in our vignette is respecting and yielding power to authority figures. The clients insist on calling the counselor "Doctor," and expect clear directions from the counselor on how to resolve their challenges. This clashes with the person-centered approach of the counselor, who views the counseling relationship as a power-sharing, collaborative one. Should the counselor bracket their own professional values and follow the clients' lead? Should counselors confront their clients' expectations and share with them their own values, perhaps convincing them to adopt the counselor's (more enlightened) view? Or should the counselor invite the clients to discuss the expectations and underlying values and together examine whether these expectations and values serve them? In practice and in theoretical arguments, counselors have chosen each of the above routes at various times. Which one would you choose, and for what reasons?

D. How do I talk about cultural differences with clients?

One of the first things to do when working with clients from different backgrounds, in our opinion, is to address the "elephant in the room." Since both counselors and clients are aware of their difference in cultural backgrounds, talking about it in an open and respectful manner can be both liberating and empowering. Because of the power difference in counseling, we believe that it is the counselor's responsibility to provide a clear structure and safe space for such discussions.

Day-Vines et al. (2020) proposed a multidimensional model of broaching behavior to guide counselors' discussion of sociocultural differences with clients. Broaching is defined as "the counselor's deliberate and intentional efforts to discuss those racial, ethnic, and cultural (REC) concerns that may impact the client's presenting concerns" (p. 107). The intra-counseling dimension breaks the ice by opening up the discussion of REC concerns and acknowledging the counselor's limitations in understanding the client's perspectives at times. Using our vignette, the counselor may say, "We are from different cultural backgrounds. What is it like for you to work with me? What are your questions or concerns?" "If it seems that I'm not getting what you're telling me or if I misunderstand you, could you let me know?"

The intraindividual dimension explores the various sociocultural identities clients have, as well as their intersectionality, highlighting power, oppression, and privilege when appropriate. Going beyond the individual level, the counselor should address the power dynamics in the clients' relationships. For example, the counselors can help the mother and daughter to examine the changing power and status in the relationship since the daughter is taking on more of the breadwinner and decision maker role as the one who is more familiar with the U.S. society. The counselor could address power differentials in the counseling relationship, not only between the counselor and clients, but also potentially between the mother and daughter due to their level of familiarity and comfort with the counseling process.

The intra-REC dimension addresses members' differences within the same REC group and the inter-REC dimension examines shared experiences by members of the REC group. The daughter and mother are both Asian immigrant women, yet they differ considerably in how they think, feel, and behave, how they raise children, how they would run the household, and so on. The mother could have judged the daughter based on her divergence from traditional Asian role expectations, while the daughter may be frustrated with the mother's more Asian perspective now that they are living in the United States. Yet their shared identity as Asian immigrant women could profoundly impact their sense of safety and belongingness.

E. I am having an easier time connecting with one party in the relationship because of the shared experience and identity and finding myself struggling to connect with the other.

The split alliance has long been acknowledged as an important and challenging issue in relationship counseling. In the case example, the daughter may be the one initiating relationship counseling and therefore may be far more invested in it. Since the daughter is educated and working in the United States, she and the counselor may share more in their cultural background and communication style. The mother, on the other hand, comes from a drastically different culture later in her life, has limited contact with U.S. society, and still abides by Chinese cultural norms. In this instance, the counselor could easily find themselves developing a different alliance with daughter and mother.

To make counseling work, relationship counselors must develop an alliance with each member of the relationship, and the relationship itself. Yet it is common for members of the relationship to have different, or even conflicting, levels of motivation, styles, and goals for counseling. Sprenkle et al. (2009) pointed to "the parallel needs to maintain a strong alliance with the person who brought the couple or family to therapy and to the simultaneous need to ensure that alliances are balanced by paying special attention to building the alliance with the less involved family member" (p. 103).

Research has shown the importance of counselors forming an alliance with the member holding more power in the relationship (to keep the clients coming), the one with less power in the relationship (so as not to replicate the unequal relationship that exists outside counseling), and the relationship itself (each member could form an alliance with the counselor and still feel that the counselor is not a good fit for the relationship) (McDowell et al., 2022; Sprenkle et al., 2009).

Adding to the complexity of the split alliance, in this case, the counselor may feel that they share less common ground with the mother and are less familiar with ways of engagement with her. A common strategy to work with split alliances is through direct discussion of the alliance problem.

The counselor, however, may be concerned with the mother's indirect communication style, and worry that such direct discussion may cause discomfort for the mother.

Still, literature and the authors' own clinical experience highlight the importance of addressing alliance issues directly and early on. But how to address these issues is the key. Sprenkle et al. (2009) emphasize a curious, nonjudgmental attitude, and for relationship counseling, more active engagement with the clients as compared to individual counseling. McDowell et al. (2022) propose a socioculturally attuned approach that focuses on attuning to, naming, and valuing client experiences, among other steps. And the authors have learned that in order to fully attune with clients' perspectives, counselors need to critically evaluate and put aside their own lens through which they view and judge clients' thoughts and actions.

Another way to connect with clients is through shared human experiences. Rober and Haene (2014) remind the field that while it is important to bring into awareness cultural differences, counselors should also remember their shared humanity with their clients. For example, like the daughter, the counselor is someone's child and has navigated relationship issues such as attachment and differentiation with their parents or primary attachment figures. Like the mother, the counselor (hopefully) has shared experiences of being in a new environment, trying to learn a different set of rules and behavioral codes in order to fit in. With the mother-daughter relationship, the counselor could tap into their own experience with significant relationships in life, with its full range of human emotions and societal expectations.

Application of Postmodern Framework

Extensive studies have been devoted to cultural responsiveness in action. Building on decades of scholarship and practice, the Multicultural Social Justice Counseling Competencies (MSJCC; Ratts et al., 2016) suggest four developmental domains to guide counselors in developing a culturally responsive mindset, knowledge, skills, and interventions. The four domains are: (1) counselor self-awareness ("Therapist, Know Thyself"), (2) the client worldview, (3) the counseling relationship, and (4) counseling and advocacy interventions. To illustrate how counselors develop competencies in these domains, we will highlight the six key principles for multicultural perspectives and responsiveness in counseling and psychology identified by Susan Sisko (2020): decolonization, intersectionality, cultural humility, self-awareness, engagement and connection, and activism. Some of the key principles, such as counselor self-awareness, intersectionality, decolonization, and cultural humility, lie at the foundation of each developmental stage as they influence how counselors view themselves, understand their clients, form a therapeutic alliance with them, and collaborate with them to develop culturally responsive actions. Each principle is operationalized using contributions from leading systemic scholars, life and clinical experiences, application guidelines, and experiential exercises to guide the development of awareness, knowledge, and skills for relationship counselors.

Counselor Self-awareness

From the beginning of counseling and psychology, counselors' self-understanding has been regarded as essential to their professional effectiveness (Sisko, 2020). Cultural responsiveness further requires counselors to be aware of their own cultural beliefs, social identities, and biases. Multicultural and Social Justice Counseling Competencies (MSJCC) situate counselor self-awareness as the first step and the foundation of the MSJCC developmental tasks (Ratts et al., 2016). Counselor self-awareness is a complex concept and an ongoing process. Using Multicultural Relational Perspective (MRP) and Watts Jones (2016) location of self (LOS), we suggest the following steps for relationship counselors to deepen their self-awareness.

Many Selves

To help counselors become more aware of their cultural and social identities, Hardy (2016) suggests that each of us is composed of many *selves*—a racial self, a gendered self, a sexual orientation self, an ethnic self, a country-of-origin self, a family of origin self, a religious/spirituality self, a (dis)ability self, and so forth. Some of our selves are more privileged while others are more marginalized or underprivileged. For example, one of the authors (YS) is middle-aged, heterosexual, middle-class, immigrant, Asian, and female. The heterosexual and middle-class selves may experience the world differently than the immigrant, Asian, and female selves as the former selves tend to carry more privilege than the latter ones. The age factor could possess privileged or marginalized positions depending on the context, as will be demonstrated below. By developing a multidimensional view of the self, counselors build the skills to see themselves and their clients in a more layered and nuanced way.

Critical Reflection and Interrogation

After gaining a comprehensive understanding of their many social and cultural identities, counselors are encouraged to engage in "critical self-reflection and self-interrogation" (CSR/SI; Hardy, 2016) to actively question one's developing sense of self-awareness. Critical self-reflection involves "looking within" to identify one's "realities, biases, assumptions, and wounds," while self-interrogation requires one to "critically examine one's deeply held internalized views about race, gender, ethnicity, and sexual differences" (Hardy, 2016, p. 12). These steps are ongoing processes and take courage and commitment in their application. It is our experience that engaging critical self-reflection and self-interrogation is like peeling an onion. Every time we thought we were done with an issue, we discovered more hidden layers of assumptions and beliefs, some functioning at the emotional or unconscious level. This continued process of self-examination forms the core of self-awareness.

Self in Context

The next step in the self-awareness development is to take the self-understanding and examination to the larger relational and social context. Hardy uses the phrase "Self in Relationship to Other" (SIRO) to argue that the self-identity is socially constructed and not set in stone. Instead, it is fluid and changeable, affecting and being affected through our interaction with other people's selves. To address this complexity of mutually influencing interactions, Hardy and Bobes (2016) suggests using self-reflection during intense conversations, "to have an unrelenting commitment to remain curious—not just about 'the other' but also about one's own perceptions, feelings, and reactions" (p. 12). The counselors' ability to hold both one's own and others' identities, observe how these identities impact interactions, and keep in mind that these identities and interactive dynamics could change with different contexts, are essential skills in understanding cultural nuances in interpersonal interactions.

We will use a personal example to demonstrate the Self in Relationship to Other concept. As YS ages, she experiences more respect and social power when traveling in East Asia, which has a cultural tradition of requiring young people to yield more power and respect to older ones. She has followed the cultural norm, allowing younger acquaintances to call her Ms. Shi, Teacher Shi, Big Sister Shi, or Aunty Shi while she instead addressed them by their full or first name. Reflecting on this, YS realized that social positioning, power, and privilege are conveyed by the ways people address each other in a culturally defined manner. Back in the United States, YS has a considerably different experience, in which most people address each other in the same manner, unaffected by age. Furthermore, her age intersects with her gender (female) and immigration status (immigrant and nonnative speaker) to form a subtle self and societal expectation that sometimes hinders her from taking social space and getting heard. An ongoing practice for YS to develop self-awareness is to see the interactions in context, observing how she perceives and is being perceived by others via intersectionality of identities, how her own feelings, thoughts, and actions are influencing and being influenced by others, and how social space is negotiated. In these ways, the self-concept is defined in its immediate social context while being influenced by the larger social, cultural, and political environment.

Self as the Counselor/Location or Use of Self

Hardy (2016) suggests another layer of counselor self-awareness, in which counselors draw on their self-knowledge and reflection as an interpersonal tool to promote connection. For example, counselors can self-disclose based on their self-awareness to provide valuable information to the client in a here-and-now manner. To provide valid feedback to clients, the counselors have to be clear about their own values, assumptions, and reactions, so that the feedback is about the clients rather than the counselors' unresolved issues. Hardy (2016) calls this Location or Use of "Self."

Watts Jones (2016) expands the location of self (LOS) concept to address "issues of oppression and social location" in clinical work and supervision (p. 17). In this approach, the counselor or supervisor (usually the ones holding more power in the relationship) shares their sociocultural identities and thus initiates a conversation with clients or supervisees about how their identities impact not only themselves but also the counseling or supervisory relationship. This approach highlights the importance of counselors' and clients' sociocultural identities and brings questions of power, privilege, and oppression right into the center of counseling and supervision, thus breaking the silence that often surrounds these issues.

My many selves	*How do i identify?*	*What are my realities, biases, assumptions, and wounds related to this identity?*	*Name 2–3 contexts where i experience this identity. are my experiences similar or different?*	*How does this identity influence my self as a counselor? my relationship with clients?*
Age and generation				
Disability and/or physical health status				
Religion and spiritual orientation				
Ethnicity and race				
socioeconomic status				
Sexual orientation				
Indigenous heritage				
National origin				
Gender				
Other identity important to me				

Using the ADDRESSING (Hays, 2008) model for Counselor Self-awareness

Intersectionality

An individual's many selves do not function parallel to each other. Instead, they interact with each other to form complex, multifaceted cultural and social identities. The concept of intersectionality emphasizes "the critical insight that race, class, gender, sexuality, ethnicity, nation, ability, and age operate not as unitary, mutually exclusive entities, but as reciprocally constructing phenomena that in turn shape social inequalities" (Collins, 2015, p. 2).

Experiential Activity

Using the case example, the counselor can ask mother and daughter to reflect on how their experiences change with the intersection of different identities. This exercise aims to help mother and daughter see their similar and different experiences and understand each other's different perspectives based on their social locations. Mother and daughter can take turns answering these questions, or they can try to answer each other's questions.

(To mother and daughter) What is your experience as a woman?
(To mother) As an older woman?
(To daughter) As a younger woman?
(To mother) As an older immigrant woman who speaks limited English?
(To daughter) As a younger immigrant woman who speaks fluent English and is educated in the United States?
(To mother) As an older immigrant woman who speaks limited English and has little income?
(To daughter) As a younger immigrant woman who speaks fluent English, is educated in the United States, and earns a middle-class salary but has to support parent and child?

Counselors can adjust questions to achieve maximum impact. Afterwards, counselors should guide the mother/daughter through a reflection process on their experience of the exercise and its impact on them.

Decolonization

In counseling and psychology, diverse perspectives are often seen as deviations while Western, colonial knowledge is viewed as the core foundation (Sisko, 2020). This biased belief about whose knowledge matters has been embedded in mental health systems throughout counselors' training and practice. The dominant group (i.e. colonizer) ideologies and cultural practices are often taken for granted as the universal truth, without examination or even awareness by counselors and clients. Inherent in this belief is the power hierarchy that privileges colonial knowledge and those who possess it (Goodman & Gorski, 2015). Such power difference then results in long term, intergenerational inequities in the distribution of wealth and opportunities (McDowell & Hernández, 2010).

Decolonization, therefore, is concerned not just with cultural differences or group identities but, more importantly, with differences in power and access to opportunity (Hernández-Wolfe, 2011). It asks, "who sets standards, who evaluates, who is on top of the hierarchy" (Duan, 2012)? To demonstrate how deeply rooted the colonial knowledge is in counseling and psychology, Duan, a Chinese born and U.S. trained psychologist, reflected on her decade of experience training counselors in China (2012):

> The first day I went to China, I told them, "you know what I am telling you is gonna be rooted in the Western culture and we need to think about Chinese culture. We need to think about adapting. We need to think about reconstructing" … Now that I look back, it was no more than lip service because I really didn't understand how … significant a role the culture has played when you move something from one cultural environment to an ecologically, culturally entirely different environment.

Duan (2012) gave an example of teaching a Chinese counselor in training to restrain from giving clients directions for action, since it was viewed as being too directive and hindering clients' independent thinking and growth, from the Western counseling theoretical framework Dr. Duan was trained in. Later she found the student losing effectiveness in serving her Chinese clients. She further observed that Chinese "counselors-in-training often try hard to suppress the urge to give directives in sessions and hide the fact from their supervisors if they use too many directives. Trainees and counselors do not want to appear to be directive because this would be viewed as non-professional" (Duan et al., 2015, p.59). Here being "professional" is clearly linked to the Western definition of counseling and given status and power over the native Chinese way of helping, which often includes expectations that a counselor will be more directive.

Duan then conducted a series of studies to understand the role of counselors giving directions ("directives") in Chinese culture and found that directives are indeed regarded as necessary and appropriate by both Chinese clients and counselors. Counselors use directives to enhance the therapeutic relationship by giving clients what they seek, and to keep clients engaged in the counseling process beyond sessions (Duan et al., 2012, 2015).

In family and relationship counseling, McDowell and Hernández (2010) observed that students from marginalized communities are frequently asked to demonstrate knowledge and skills of the dominant culture, with their own cultural heritage often questioned and devalued. The authors suggest that decolonization requires a fundamental reexamination of knowledge that has been taken for granted as valid or universal in the field for many years, and for multiple, formerly marginalized voices to be heard and valued. All voices need to be given a space to participate and collaborate with each other, without privilege, access, and power being monopolized by one voice. To achieve this, mere academic discussions and organizational changes are not enough. Every counselor must engage in self-awareness to reflect on their own assumptions and values and explore how they can truly meet their clients where they are. In addition, McDowell (2015) explores the use of critical social theories to decolonize family therapy. The aim with this work is to better understand the ways in which systems of power, privilege, and colonizer perspectives have been rooted across the foundations of relational work and unwind them from more contemporary work.

Experiential Activity

Reflection through journaling: Can you identify an instance when a non-dominant concept was considered wrong, inferior, or unprofessional? What was your judgment at that time? What did you base your judgment on? How would you view that concept differently with a decolonization perspective? What action can you take to challenge colonial knowledge?

Cultural Humility

Cultural humility goes beyond developing knowledge and skills to work with diverse clients. It includes both intrapersonal (an accurate view of self) and interpersonal components (an interpersonal stance that is other-oriented rather than self-focused, characterized by respect for others and a lack of superiority) (Hook et al., 2013). Tervalon and Murray-Garcia (1998) distinguish it from cultural competence by remaining tentative about applying cultural knowledge they have previously acquired so that they do not perpetuate the power imbalance in counseling. They describe it as a lifeline process of self-reflection and self-critique.

Zhu et al. (2021) examined how counselors develop and enact cultural humility in counseling and counselor education. Based on interviews with 14 experienced counselor educators, the authors developed a grounded theory to describe how participants developed or enacted cultural humility through a multilayered process. To summarize, cultural humility is rooted in the context of multicultural counseling, in which cultural humility is regarded as a way of being, learning about culture as a lifelong commitment, and all culture and cultural beings viewed as having both value and limitations. Most participants in this study experienced cultural encounters that created tension and discomfort, knocking them out of their comfort zone. Participants reacted by leaning into the discomfort and addressing the cultural dynamics that hindered relationships. They could admit mistakes, become transparent about their own limitations, or seek assistance from others.

In this process, the participants realized that cultural humility involves "bringing one's authentic self, although flawed and imperfect, into cultural encounters," that it is not about "being nice, agreeable, overcompensating, or trying very hard to avoid conflict" (p. 82). Sometimes they need to confront others, but the confrontation should be done in a nonthreatening, gentle manner. As a result of these meaningful cultural humility moments, participants experienced significant learning and growth, deepening of relationships, and a more open mindset.

This grounded theory further identifies several conditions that impact one's development or enactment of cultural humility. For example, having exposure to diverse cultural frameworks, being able to engage in introspection without falling into defensiveness, and feeling safe and trusting in the relationships all contribute to the development or enhancement of cultural humility.

Experiential Activity

Use the grounded theory study of Zhu et al. (2021) to design an activity to further develop your cultural humility. What elements of the participants' experiences strike you as particularly interesting, helpful, or relevant? What could you learn from the multilayered process to enhance your cultural humility?

Engagement and Connection

Comstock et al. (2008) point out that cultural oppression and social injustice often lead to feelings of isolation, shame, and humiliation among people from marginalized groups. Sisko (2020) suggests that relationships help to break down barriers like power and hierarchy and reduce isolation and shame. It is the authors' experience that to effectively engage and connect with clients, counselors must strive to see the clients' world from their perspectives and meet clients where they are. In this process, power and hierarchy based on colonialism are broken down and clients receive the understanding and acceptance they deserve.

In working with immigrant and refugee clients, YS has encountered many instances in which clients seek help to meet their case management needs before they are ready to address their mental health needs. Many counselors are not comfortable with this. They want to focus their work on mental health and are frustrated that clients do not seem engaged. Seeing from clients' perspectives, counselors would understand that many clients face daily living challenges such as inadequate financial support, lack of housing, needing childcare, or feeling overwhelmed dealing with social services or school systems. According to Maslow's hierarchy of needs, physiological and safety needs need to be taken care of before higher levels of needs such as love, belonging, esteem, and self-actualization, which often fall into the traditional domain of counseling and psychology. But how can an overwhelmed immigrant mother who does not speak English and is losing food stamps and Medicaid for failing to submit the required paperwork be engaged to talk only about their feelings and relational needs when their family's subsistence is being threatened? How can such a mother feel connected with a counselor who only wants to talk about mental health issues? In this case, counselors who see their clients' most urgent needs and act to provide help will gain clients' trust and connection.

Experiential Activity

Please reflect on your past experiences engaging and connecting with clients. What successes and challenges stood out to you? What elements contribute to the successes and challenges? How can you use the culturally responsive engagement and connection principle to improve client engagement and connection?

Activism

Culturally responsive counselors empower clients through sharing power, raising consciousness, co-constructing solutions, and engaging in advocacy (Brown, 2010). Here we apply socioculturally attuned therapy guidelines—Attune, name, value, interrupt, envision, transform (ANVIET)—to demonstrate how relationship counselors can promote culturally responsive and social justice oriented activism in clinical practice with the mother and daughter in Case Example 1 (McDowell et al., 2019).

First, counselors seek to **attune** to "the emotional, experiential, and relational impact of societal systems on individuals and relationships" (p. 17). One of the core conflicts between the mother and daughter is the fact that the daughter was raised by nonparental family members growing up. The daughter feels abandoned by her mother and holds a deep sense of resentment. The counselor invites them to explore the mother's decision to have her daughter raised by other family members at individual, relationship, and larger sociocultural economic and political systems levels. When the daughter begins to understand how cultural norms, economic pressure, and political ideology shaped the mother's decision, she no longer sees the decision as personal and intentional and the mother as someone who abandoned her daughter.

In **Naming** these underlying systems, the mother and daughter recognize unfair circumstances and stop blaming each other for the attachment wounds and relational pain they suffer. **Valuing** "includes listening carefully and helping clients put into words what has been previously silenced, dismissed, or marginalized" (p. 17). For the first time, the mother gets to reflect on the cultural norms and economic struggles that had her separated from her own parents when she was growing up and the pain she has been suppressing all these years. She then becomes much more open to listen to and hold her daughter's pain.

Going beyond understanding what is unjust, the ANVIET model encourages counselors to "actively **interrupt** unequal power dynamics," help clients "**envision** solutions," and support clients to "**transform** their relationships into what they have envisioned" (p. 17). In the case example, the mother and daughter express a strong desire to develop a loving relationship and open communication. They envision talking and laughing together without the bitterness of the past and a feeling that they are not seeing "eye to eye." To achieve these goals, the daughter reflects on her assumptions of a good mother based on her internalized U.S.-dominant cultural expectations and recognizes that she overtly and covertly devalues her mother's cultural practice. The mother examines her belief system in which the child has to yield to their parent's authority and decision making and realizes that this belief system no longer serves her relationship with the daughter, who is the one more connected with the outside world.

By recognizing and interrupting the maladaptive beliefs and assumptions, the mother and daughter can transform their relationship into their vision.

Experiential Activity

Apply the ANVIET model to a relationship you are seeing, particularly one that has been challenging for you. What difference does it make in your case conceptualization? client's response? treatment outcome?

Case Study: An Evolving Relationship

Our earlier case example walks you through factors impacting a family system and reflects on the domains of the MSJCC framework (MSJCC; Ratts et al., 2016) and six key principles for responsive counseling by Sisko (2020). The authors want to provide readers with an additional opportunity to begin framing their own exploration and continued learning. As discussed earlier in this chapter, this is but a launching point for your [the readers] continued growth and we hope that the following case study and prompts can serve as an opportunity to apply the principles and seek information to inform your understanding of the clients. The case study below provides a look into culturally responsive romantic relationship counseling and seeking to support a partner's navigating transition, growth, and challenges.

Setting the Stage

Throughout this chapter, we deliberately used the word "relationship" to bring attention to the assumptions behind relationship counseling. Relationship counseling as a field has used/experimented with a variety of names, each reflecting the unique sociocultural and political environments relationship counselors work in and their ever-changing professional identity. From "Marriage and Family Therapy/Counseling" to "Couple and Family Therapy/Counseling" to "Counselor specializing in couples and family counseling" to just "relationship counseling," relationship counselors have been expanding traditional definitions of what a relationship means in counseling (Kleist, 2024; Wampler, 2018). For today's relationship counselors, relationships can include more "traditional" relational units such as marriage, couples, nuclear families, to more inclusive relationships such as polyamorous or multi-partner relationships, blended families, friendship groups, business partners, and so on. Being culturally responsive means developing necessary awareness, knowledge, skills, and advocacy actions to serve diverse populations of our contemporary society.

Relational counseling has evolved significantly over the years and more recently, we have seen a shift to be more inclusive and expansive (McDowell, 2015). A component of this shift is to challenge the belief you will only ever work with heterosexual, monogamous couples in counseling. Rooted in challenging the limiting, harmful, Westernized perspectives of love, culturally responsive counselors are expanding their understanding of what constitutes "functional" romantic relationships to include diverse relational dynamics and types (Fern, 2020). This case study explores supporting a primary partnership looking to expand their relationship to include another partner. They seek counseling with you to explore potential challenges and issues that arise from this change and to increase their ability to communicate and express emotions. As you complete the activity, approach it as a clinician having just completed an intake session and preparing to engage in long-term relational counseling.

Clients:

Primary Client A: E, 32-year-old cisgender white woman, is a software engineer.

Primary Client B: A, 34-year-old non-binary white person, is a freelance artist.

Secondary Client: S, 30-year-old cisgender, biracial man, is a teacher. S is biracial; his mother is white and father is Black.

Presenting Issues: E and A have been in a committed polyamorous relationship for six years. They have recently been discussing the possibility of inviting a new partner, S, into their relationship. However, they are facing significant communication challenges and struggling to establish clear boundaries regarding S's role and integration into their dynamic.

Background: E and A met in graduate school and bonded over shared interests in technology and art. They decided early in their relationship to explore polyamory as both felt it aligned with their personal beliefs about love and relationships. S, a mutual friend, has known E and A for several years and recently expressed interest in exploring a romantic connection with both of them.

Counseling Goals (as articulated by the clients):

Improving Communication: E and A want to enhance their ability to communicate openly and honestly with each other about their feelings, desires, and concerns regarding adding S to their relationship.

Establishing Boundaries: They seek support in defining clear boundaries with S to ensure all parties feel respected, valued, and understood within the evolving relationship structure.

Navigating Emotions: Addressing feelings of jealousy, insecurity, and fear that may arise as they navigate the complexities of adding a new partner while maintaining their existing connection.

Experiential Activity: complete the following chart to explore ways in which the six key principles for culturally responsive relational counseling can be applied.

6 Principles	*What assumptions, biases, experiences, and values impact your understanding of these clients?*	*What power structures and oppressive systems may be impacting these clients?*	*What resources might support your ongoing development and learning to support these clients?*
Decolonization			
Intersectionality			
Cultural humility			
Self-awareness			
Engagement and connection			
Activism			

Conclusion

As you conclude this chapter, the authors hope there are a variety of emotions, thoughts, and considerations floating through your mind. Perhaps, you find you are craving more definitive information or more examples of clinical applications. If so, that means we have done our job in igniting your curiosity and championing the idea that you, as a counselor, will always be challenged to push yourself to grow. We also hope that you feel empowered to explore how you can be more responsive to your clients' deeply unique needs, particularly within the relational units you work with. We offer a broad question to prompt some reflection following your reading. What are your initial thoughts and feelings after reading this chapter and what is an element of culturally responsive relational counseling that you want to better understand? Why?

We hope this discussion of the history and evolution of relational counseling, and the importance of relational practice and its impact on the field, along with the provided case examples, help give insight into the critical need for culturally responsive relational counseling. The authors want to acknowledge that becoming culturally responsive is a lifelong process and that no one can claim to be the expert in this ongoing exploration and examination. We are honored to share with you some of the lessons we have learned through our clinical work. We hope that this is just a starting point in your journey to embrace a reflective and engaged learning perspective needed in counseling to adapt, grow, and learn with and from your clients.

References

Brown, L. S. (2010). *Feminist therapy* (1st ed.). American Psychological Association.

Collins, P. H. (2015). Intersectionality's definitional dilemmas. *Annual Review of Sociology, 41*(1), 1–20. https://doi.org/10.1146/annurev-soc-073014-112142

Comstock, D. L., Hammer, T. R., Strentzsch, J. L., Cannon, K., Parsons, J., & Salazar, G., II. (2008). Relational-cultural theory: A framework for bridging relational, multicultural, and social justice competencies. *Journal of Counseling and Development, 86*(3), 279–287.

Corey, G. (2017). *Theory and practice of counseling and psychotherapy* (10th ed.). Cengage Learning.

Davey, M., Duncan, T., Kissil, K., Davey, A., & Fish, L. S. (2011). Second-order change in marriage and family therapy: A web-based modified Delphi study. *The American Journal of Family Therapy, 39*(2), 100–111.

Day-Vines, N. L., Cluxton-Keller, F., Agorsor, C., Gubara, S., & Otabil, N. A. A. (2020). The multidimensional model of broaching behavior. *Journal of Counseling and Development., 98*(1), 107–118. https://doi.org/10.1002/jcad.12304

Doherty, W. J. (2020). The evolution and current status of systemic family therapy. In *The handbook of systemic family therapy* (Vol. 1, pp. 33–49). Wiley Blackwell. https://doi.org/10.1002/9781119438519.ch2

Duan, C. (2012). *Lessons learned: Understanding the meaning of internationalization of counseling*. Microtraining Associates.

Duan, C., Hill, C., Jiang, G., Hu, B., Chui, H., Hui, K., Liu, J., & Yu, L. (2012). Therapist directives: Use and outcomes in China. *Psychotherapy Research, 22*(4), 442–457.

Duan, C., Hill, C. E., Jiang, G., Hu, B., Lei, Y., Chen, J., & Yu, L. (2015). The counselor perspective on the use of directives in counseling in China: Are directives different in China as in the United States? *Counselling Psychology Quarterly, 28*(1), 57–77. https://doi.org/10.1080/09515070.2014.965659

Estrada, D. (2018). Training and supervision across disciplines to engage in cross-cultural competence and responsiveness: Counseling and family therapy. In S. Singh-Poulsen & R. Allen (Eds.), *Cross-cultural responsiveness & systemic therapy: Focused issues in family therapy*. Springer. https://doi.org/10.1007/978-3-319-71395-3_7

Fern, J. (2020). *Polysecure: Attachment, trauma, and consensual nonmonogamy*. Thorntree Press. https://doi.org/10.1007/s10508-018-1286-4

Goodman, R. D., & Gorski, P. C. (Eds.). (2015). *Decolonizing "multicultural" counseling through social justice*. Springer.

Hardy, K. V. (2016). Toward the development of a multicultural relational perspective in training and supervision. In K. V. Hardy & T. Bobes (Eds.), *Culturally sensitive supervision and training* (pp. 3–10). Routledge.

Hardy, K. V., & Bobes, T. (2016). Core competencies for executing culturally sensitive supervision and training. In K. V. Hardy & T. Bobes (Eds.), *Culturally sensitive supervision and training* (pp. 11–15). Routledge.

Hays, P. A. (2008). *Addressing cultural complexities in practice: Assessment, diagnosis, and therapy* (2nd ed.). American Psychological Association.

Hernández-Wolfe, P. (2011). Decolonization and "mental" health: A Mestiza's journey in the borderlands. *Women & Therapy, 34*(3), 293–306.

Hook, J. N., Davis, D. E., Owen, J., Worthington, E. L., Jr., & Utsey, S. O. (2013). Cultural humility: Measuring openness to culturally diverse clients. *Journal of counseling psychology, 60*(3), 353.

Kim, B. S., Atkinson, D. R., & Umemoto, D. (2001). Asian cultural values and the counseling process: Current knowledge and directions for future research. *The Counseling Psychologist, 29*(4), 570–603.

Hutton, V., & Sisko, S. (Eds.). (2020). *Multicultural responsiveness in counselling and psychology: Working with Australian populations*. Springer Nature.

Kleist, D. M. (2024, February 1–3). *"What's in a name?" Professional identity language of counselors who work with couples and families* [Conference presentation]. 2024 IAMFC World Conference, St. Petersburg, Florida, United States.

Lebow, J. L. (2021). Attending to the larger system in systemic therapy and family research. *Family process, 60*(4), 1079–1082.

Martín-Baró, I. (1994). *Writings for a liberation psychology.* (A. Aron & S. Corne, Eds.). Harvard University Press.

McDowell, T. (2015). *Applying critical social theories to family therapy.* Springer. https://doi.org/10.1007/978-3-319-15633-0

McDowell, T., & Hernández, P. (2010). Decolonizing academia: Intersectionality, participation, and accountability in family therapy and counseling. *Journal of Feminist Family Therapy, 22*(2), 93–111.

McDowell, T., Knudson-Martin, C., & Bermudez, J. M. (2019). Third-order thinking in family therapy: Addressing social justice across family therapy practice. *The Family Process, 58*(1), 9–22. https://doi.org/10.1111/famp.12383

McDowell, T., Knudson-Martin, C., & Bermudez, J. M. (2022). *Socioculturally attuned family therapy: Guidelines for equitable theory and practice.* Routledge.

Nichols, M. P., & Davis, S. D. (2017). *Family therapy: Concepts and methods* (11th ed.). Pearson.

Ratts, M. J., Singh, A. A., Nassar-McMillan, S., Butler, S. K., & McCullough, J. R. (2016). Multicultural and social justice counseling competencies: Guidelines for the counseling profession. *Journal of Multicultural Counseling and Development, 44*(1), 28–48.

Rober, P., & De Haene, L. (2014). Intercultural therapy and the limitations of a cultural competency framework: About cultural differences, universalities and the unresolvable tensions between them. *Journal of Family Therapy., 36*(S1), 3–20. https://doi.org/10.1111/1467-6427.12009

Singh, A. A., Nassar, S. C., Arredondo, P., & Toporek, R. (2020). The past guides the future: Implementing the multicultural and social justice counseling competencies. *Journal of Counseling and Development, 98*(3), 238–252. https://doi.org/10.1002/jcad.12319

Sisko, S. (2020). Key principles for multicultural perspectives and responsiveness in counselling and psychology. In V. Hutton & S. Sisko (Eds.), *Multicultural responsiveness in counselling and psychology: Working with Australian Populations* (pp. 287–296). Springer Nature.

Sprenkle, D. H., Davis, S. D., & Lebow, J. (2009). *Common factors in couple and family therapy the overlooked foundation for effective practice* (1st ed.). Guilford Press.

Sue, D. W., Arredondo, P., & McDavis, R. J. (1992). Multicultural counseling competencies and standards: A call to the profession. *Journal of Multicultural Counseling and Development, 20*(2), 64–88. https://doi.org/10.1002/j.2161-1912.1992.tb00563.x

Teh, Y. Y., & Winley, D. (2021, May 6). *24 most influential articles on social justice and diversity in family therapy: A collaboration between Family Process and the Journal of Family Therapy 1980–2019.* https://onlinelibrary.wiley.com/doi/toc/10.1002/(ISSN)9999-0009.24most-influential-articles

Tervalon, M., & Murray-Garcia, J. (1998). Cultural humility versus cultural competence: A critical distinction in defining physician training outcomes in multicultural education. *Journal of Health Care for the Poor and Undeserved, 9*, 117–125. https://doi.org/10.1353/hpu.2010.0233

Wampler, K. (2018). Addendum to: The profession of couple, marital, and family therapy (CMFT): Defining ourselves and moving forward. *Journal of Marital and Family Therapy, 45*(1), 19.

Watts Jones, T. D. (2016). Location of self in training and supervision. In K. V. Hardy & T. Bobes (Eds.), *Culturally sensitive supervision and training* (pp. 16–24). Routledge.

Wyatt, R. (2008). Kenneth V. Hardy on multiculturalism and psychotherapy. *Psychotherapy.net.*

Zhu, P., Luke, M., & Bellini, J. (2021). A grounded theory analysis of cultural humility in counseling and counselor education. *Counselor Education and Supervision, 60*(1), 73–89.

CHAPTER 9

Cultural Responsiveness in Community Counselling

John J. S. Harrichand, Joy M. Mwendwa, and Sravya Gummaluri

Introduction

Our world continues to experience the impact of COVID-19. As of December 2, 2022, the World Health Organization's (WHO, 2022) Online Dashboard reported 640,395,651 confirmed cases and 6,618,579

J. J. S. Harrichand (✉)
College of Education, The University of Texas at San Antonio, San Antonio, TX, USA
e-mail: john.harrichand@utsa.edu

J. M. Mwendwa
Counselor Education & Family Studies, Liberty University, Lynchburg, VA, USA
e-mail: jmmaweu@liberty.edu

S. Gummaluri
Graduate School of Education, The George Washington University, Washington, DC, USA
e-mail: gsravya@gwmail.gwu.edu

S. Sisko (ed.), *Culturally Responsive Psychotherapy, Counselling & Psychology*, Palgrave Texts in Counselling and Psychotherapy,
https://doi.org/10.1007/978-3-031-81831-8_9

deaths globally. According to Cullen et al. (2020, p.1), society's psychological reactions following an infectious disease outbreak like COVID-19 result in "maladaptive behaviors, emotional distress, and defensive responses." These challenges are expected to further compromise the lives of those already experiencing mental health concerns in our communities. In addition to demands for increased medical care, WHO's alarming statistics have critical implications for our overall health and well-being at both individual and societal levels (Pfefferbaum & North, 2020).

Takakjy (2020, para. 1) shared that regardless of the clinical setting, "counselors practice…in community with others…[and] must be aware as counselors of the issues that affect the communities where we practice." The implications of global, socio-cultural, and environmental stressors, both new and old, present novel opportunities for counsellors and psychologists in agency and community counselling settings seeking to intentionally respond in culturally appropriate ways, with the hope of improving mental health services (Moreno et al., 2020). Community counselling provides a comprehensive framework for counsellors and psychologists to address these challenges (Lewis et al., 2011). This framework is culturally responsive when grounded in multiculturalism and social justice-centred principles such as decolonisation, intersectionality, anti-oppressive practice, cultural humility, self-awareness, engagement and connection, and advocacy (Ratts et al., 2016b; Sisko, 2021). This chapter will discuss these principles in relation to community counselling using the RESPECTFUL Model (D'Andrea & Daniels, 2001) and demonstrate key concepts using a case study to inform and support counsellors and psychologists seeking to be culturally responsive in a changing world.

Historical Background

The United States (U.S.)

According to Gladding and Newsome (2018), over the past four decades, employment opportunities for professional counsellors have increased significantly. Before the Community Mental Health Act of 1963 (Title II, Public Law 88–164) was passed, counsellors primarily worked in educational settings. The Community Mental Health Centers Act, envisioned by President Kennedy and signed into law in 1963, sought to create 1,500 federally funded mental health centres nationwide, under the supervision of the National Institute of Health (Erickson, 2021). The Act sought to create new treatment centres for individuals who had previously been housed in unsafe, and sometimes inhumane, state institutions and public hospitals, while also providing services to individuals within their local communities (Neukrug, 2024).

Today, clinical mental health counsellors work in a variety of clinical environments, including government-funded agencies, hospitals, rehabilitation centres, family service organisations, shelters for domestic violence victims, probation settings, and faith-based organisations. Counsellors working at these mental health centres can find employment in various areas, including outpatient counselling, short-term inpatient services, day treatment for individuals with serious mental health issues, medication checks, and emergency services to name a few. Counsellors often work with individuals of all ages dealing with issues from developmental transitions to severe mental disorders, experiencing moderate to severe impairment. Therefore, it is crucial for them to have knowledge of evidence-based treatments (EBP), the *Diagnostic and Statistical Manual, Fifth Edition, Text Revision* (DSM-5-TR; American Psychiatric Association [APA], 2022), the *International Classification of Diseases, 11th Revision* (ICD-11; World Health Organization [WHO], 2019), and psychopharmacology (Gladding & Newsome, 2018; Neukrug, 2024).

Community mental health centres (CMHCs) were intended to offer a wide range of care, but they often fell short of meeting the community's needs (Gladding & Newsome, 2018). This gap in services led to many individuals not receiving the treatment they required, resulting in higher rates of homelessness and rehospitalisation. According to the National Institute of Mental Health (NIMH), more than one-fifth of U.S. adults live with a mental illness, i.e., in 2021 this fraction represented approximately 57.8 million Americans (NIMH, 2023). Sadly, even coordinated service delivery methods fall short of meeting a community's mental health needs. Ensuring adequate support for everyone in need of mental health assistance remains a significant challenge for community mental health service providers (Gladding & Newsome, 2018).

The aim of *community-based mental health*, also known as *community behavioural health*, is to create a comprehensive care system in collaboration with the community, service providers, and payers. According to Gladding and Newsome (2018) the following principles help guide community mental health practices:

- Services should be accessible and culturally sensitive to those seeking treatment.
- Services should be accountable to the entire community, including at-risk and underserved populations.
- Services should be comprehensive, flexible, and coordinated.
- Continuity of care should be assured.
- Behavioural health care needs to be holistic and personalised to meet individual needs.
- Prevention and early intervention are the most essential services provided.
- Treatment providers should use a multidisciplinary team approach to care.

The European Union (EU)

Semrau et al. (2011) noted that, following various mental health treaties, action programs, and plans within the European Union (EU) during the 1990s and early 2000s, a significant milestone in the development and reform of mental health policies across Europe was the 2005 Mental Health Declaration for Europe and the Mental Health Action Plan for Europe. In these documents, all European health ministers recognised mental health as a priority, emphasised the need for evidence-based policies, defined a broad scope for these policies, committed to their development, implementation, and reinforcement, and proposed twelve action areas and milestones to be achieved by 2010. Action items included a commitment to develop community-based mental health services, reduce the reliance on large mental institutions, and integrate mental health services into primary health care.

According to Semrau et al. (2011), most European countries (around 83%) have mental health policies in place, covering approximately 89% of the region's population. Similarly, almost all countries (over 95%) now have mental health legislation, covering 90% of the population. Additionally, specific policies and plans for developing community mental health services, downgrading large mental hospitals, and integrating mental health into primary care have been developed in at least two-thirds of European countries. However, significant differences in policies remain between countries (Semrau et al., 2011). While many countries have updated their policies to align with contemporary ideals of mental health service provision—approximately half of the countries with mental health policies have adopted new or updated existing policies since 2005—others have outdated policies that need improvement. Furthermore, although around 40% of countries with mental health legislation have updated or adopted new legislation since 2005, about one-quarter still have legislation that is over ten years old. Newer date were not available at the writing of this chapter.

Today, Hipple Walters et al. (2020) noted that many European countries tackle mental health concerns and promote well-being through specialised programs and practices focusing on community-based and accessible mental health services. While these initiatives benefit various stakeholders in mental healthcare, there is currently no systematic way to disseminate quality, practical information about effective practices to other stakeholders across Europe—a significant concern for community mental health providers. The *EU Compass for Action on Mental Health and Well-being* seeks to address this gap through various methods. Its mission is to collect, monitor, exchange, analyse, and disseminate information on mental health policies and stakeholder activities to enhance mental health and well-being in Europe. These efforts aim to provide insight and guidance to other stakeholders in mental healthcare, improving the delivery of healthcare and well-being services and the overall health and well-being of European residents (Hipple Walters et al., 2020).

Australia

Australia is frequently ranked among the world's top healthcare systems, but these assessments often overlook mental health care (Rosenberg & Harvey, 2021). One major reason for this mixed performance is the limited commitment to community mental health care. Community-based mental health care in Australia gradually developed during the twentieth century, especially after World War II (Meadows et al., 2012). This era saw the uncoordinated growth of community clinics and psychosocial support services from the charitable and welfare sectors. Australia was one of the pioneers in national mental health strategy, publishing its first National Mental Health Policy in 1992 (Australian Health Ministers, 1992). This progressive document emphasised the rights and civil liberties of consumers and carers, and aimed to close long-term psychiatric institutions, allowing individuals with persistent mental illnesses to live in the community. Australia committed to this policy through five national mental health plans, the latest of which was signed in 2017, along with a second National Policy (Australian Government, 2008; Rosenberg & Harvey, 2021).

Despite this commitment, by 2017–2018, there were still 1,613 beds in psychiatric hospitals across five states, costing $565 million, or just under 10% of total state mental health spending. Half of these beds are in New South Wales (Productivity Commission, 2020). Funding changes have added confusion about the goals of mental health reform, with tools like Activity Based Funding seen as incentivising hospital care over community care (NSW Mental Health Commission, 2017). Some argue the core issue is a lack of acute mental health hospital beds (Allison & Bastiampillai, 2015). The average stay in a public hospital mental health unit has decreased from 15.1 days in 2010–2011 to 13.1 days in 2017–2018 (Productivity Commission, 2020). Despite policy focus since 1992, mental health expenditure has remained relatively unchanged, from 7.3% of total health spending in 1992–1993 to 7.6% in 2017–2018, even though mental illness accounts for around 12% of the total disease burden. This funding gap complicates mental health reform (Australian Institute of Health and Welfare, n.d.-a).

Several mental health-related services in Australia are funded by different levels of government and individuals, with services delivered by both government and non-government providers (Australian Institute of Health and Welfare, n.d.-b). For instance, the Australian Government funds consultations with specialist medical practitioners, general practitioners (GPs), psychologists, and other allied health practitioners through the Medicare Benefits Schedule (MBS). It also supports other primary mental health services through the Primary Health Networks and provides assistance for psychosocial disabilities via the National Disability Insurance Scheme. Access to psychiatrists, psychologists, and other allied health professionals may be subsidised through initiatives like the Better Access initiative, depending on eligibility. State and territory governments offer mental health services through public hospitals, including emergency departments, residential mental health care, and community mental health care services. Government and non-government providers support population mental health crisis and support services, such as Lifeline and Beyond Blue, and mental health care is available in private hospitals (Australian Institute of Health and Welfare, n.d.-b).

Rosenberg and Harvey (2021) shared that without a national consensus on community mental health, various models have emerged. Typically, states and territories offer community mental health services through teams of health professionals. These teams operate under names like community crisis teams, home care teams, early psychosis intervention teams, youth mental health teams, and residential rehabilitation units (Rosenberg & Harvey, 2021). Effective community-based treatment involves 24-hour crisis intervention and ongoing care, assertive and intensive community case management, professionally supervised residential treatment and rehabilitation, and recovery-oriented vocational opportunities for individuals with mental illnesses. Evidence suggests that such community-centred care is more cost-efficient and effective than hospital-centred care, especially when community services are integrated with primary health care and hospital-based services (Rosenberg & Harvey, 2021).

According to the Parliament of Australia (2005), consumers and carers advocate for a holistic vision of community mental health care, that includes:

- Managing medical and non-medical treatment with a focus on recovery
- Equipping people with mental illness to live independently
- Providing access to accommodation, employment, and social activities
- Maintaining mental health centres offering support services and information
- Offering outreach services and home-based assistance
- Providing case management that recognises the episodic nature of mental illness
- Ensuring timely access to various levels of assistance and intervention
- Responding quickly to acute illness episodes
- Offering respite care to alleviate the burden on families and carers

Our review of the literature indicated that the approach to community counselling varies by geographical location. For example, the U.S., a society that prides itself on individualism, promotes individual counselling practice to a greater extent than group/couple/family counselling. On the other hand, although Australia is a highly individualistic society, when it comes to mental health, there seems to be a greater focus on community counselling practices, which may in large part stem from the way it honours its Indigenous origins. Still, formal literature is lacking to corroborate these observations. The application section of this chapter will highlight this reality.

Impact on the Counselling Profession

Before addressing the impact of community counselling on the counselling profession, it is important to operationalise the term *community counselling*. According to Lewis et al. (2011)

> Community counseling is a comprehensive helping framework that is grounded in multicultural competence and oriented toward social justice. Because human behavior is powerfully affected by context, community counselors use strategies that facilitate the healthy development both of their clients and of the communities that nourish them. (p. 9)

According to Sue et al. (2022), three key attributes define a culturally competent helping professional. Firstly, this professional is continually working to become aware of their own assumptions, values, biases, preconceived notions, and personal limitations. Secondly, they actively strive to understand the worldview of their culturally diverse clients. Thirdly, they are committed to developing and practising intervention strategies and skills that are appropriate, relevant, and sensitive to their clients' cultural differences.

Community counsellors require a broader understanding of what defines healthy human development (Lewis et al., 2011). They seek to enlarge people's choices by expanding human capabilities and functioning. At all stages of development, the three essential capabilities for human development are for people to lead long and healthy lives, to be knowledgeable, and to have a decent standard of living (Lewis et al., 2011). Without these basic capabilities, many choices are unavailable, and many opportunities remain out of reach. However, human development encompasses more than these basics: it includes essential areas of choice highly valued by people, such as political, economic, and social opportunities for creativity and productivity, as well as enjoying self-respect, empowerment, and a sense of belonging to a community. This conceptualisation of human development aligns well with counselling, as it emphasises expanding people's choices and building their capabilities. The alignment with the community counselling model is particularly strong, given its focus on empowerment and fostering a sense of belonging within the community (Lewis et al., 2011).

Counselling theories that emphasise the connections between individuals and their environments have become central tenets of twenty first-century counselling. This shift is due to the increasing recognition of the environment's power to nurture or limit human development (Lewis et al., 2011). People continually interact with their surroundings in ways that can either help or harm them. As individuals grow, they depend on their interpersonal environment for learning and support, meeting their needs primarily through interactions with others. However, the environment can also negatively impact them, stunting growth and limiting development (Lewis et al., 2011).

Given the significant influence of the environment, counsellors who adopt the twenty first-century paradigm understand that promoting their clients' psychological development without addressing their social systems is often ineffective. Effective counsellors believe that all their clients have the potential for growth towards complex and fulfilling lives. These counsellors have always known they can best facilitate growth through respectful, positive, and empowering relationships and methods. According to the community counselling model, a client's progress depends not only on the quality of direct services provided by the counsellor but also on the support from the larger community environment (Lewis et al., 2011).

Therefore, the impact of community counselling is evident from the standpoint of the community counsellor who understands the difference between a person who merely exists and someone who lives zestfully resides in the support and opportunities provided by their environment. Within Australian culture, it seems that there are more intentional efforts to move from acknowledging universal healthcare to focusing on mental health, which has not always been the case for the U.S. As such, the U.S. can learn from Australia, as they seek to move the dial forward on mental health. We echo Ng et al.'s (2023) position that the global professional counselling community must engage in systematic discussions on preparing counsellors, educators, and leaders to advocate for the inclusion of counsellors as valued members in interdisciplinary work settings. Integrating counsellors into interdisciplinary contexts is crucial for advancing the counselling profession, locally and globally (Ng et al., 2023). Moreover, recognising professional counsellors as qualified professionals would significantly enhance access to mental health services in every community. The next section highlights challenges to community counselling. We begin by examining the U.S., followed by the EU, and conclude with a closer examination of Australia.

Challenges Related to Community Counselling

The United States (U.S.)

According to Phillips (2023), growing recognition of the importance of mental health has led to the demand for licensed mental health counsellors in recent years, particularly since the onset of the COVID-19 pandemic. Unfortunately, the U.S. is experiencing a severe shortage of these professionals, leaving many individuals and families without the necessary support. This shortage is having a widespread impact on the healthcare system, making it increasingly difficult for those with mental health issues to access the care they need (Phillips, 2023). The reasons for this shortage are complex and multifaceted, but Phillips (2023) lists five key contributing factors. 1) *Lack of Funding*: The government allocates limited funding for mental health services and counselling, forcing many providers to rely on private insurance or self-pay to cover their services. 2) *Poor Reimbursement Rates*: Mental health providers often receive inadequate reimbursement from insurance companies and government programs, discouraging them from entering or remaining in the field. 3) *Low Retention*: The current number of mental health professionals falls short of meeting the population's needs. This is partly due to low reimbursement rates, but also because mental health professions are not particularly attractive to younger generations due to the stigma associated with them. 4) *Increased Demand and Limited Access*: The rising demand for mental health services is outpacing the supply of providers. Clients, especially in rural areas, often face limited access to care due to a lack of public transportation or proximity to mental health facilities. Additionally, mental health providers frequently choose not to work in rural areas due to poor reimbursement rates and low pay. 5) *Ageing Workforce*: Many mental health professionals in the U.S. are nearing retirement age. Low retention rates mean that as these professionals retire, they are not being replaced by younger professionals at the same rate, exacerbating the shortage in the field. It is crucial to address this shortage to ensure that individuals suffering from mental health issues can receive the care they need (Phillips, 2023).

The European Union (EU)

The increasing occurrence of mental health disorders in Europe and a rising focus on human rights in treatment have led to the widespread adoption of community-based mental health (CBMH) interventions throughout the region (Remy et al., 2023). Nonetheless, the execution of these interventions differs notably between Western and Eastern European nations due to variations in societal structures, healthcare systems, and the unique design and implementation approaches of the interventions (Remy et al., 2023), presenting a range of challenges and disparities (Bernardo & Alvarez del Vayo, 2021), some of which mirror those of the U.S. One of the main barriers is the financial burden on clients. In many countries, mental health care is not adequately covered by public health systems or insurers, forcing individuals to pay out of pocket for services. This financial strain is particularly evident in countries like Romania, Slovakia, Estonia, and Croatia, where the cost of a single counselling session can equate to several days' wages. In contrast, countries like France have more affordable private consultations, but still, the lack of public funding limits access for lower-income individuals (Bernardo & Alvarez del Vayo, 2021).

Additionally, the stigma surrounding mental health and a lack of understanding about mental health issues further complicate access. Cultural barriers and conservative community values in rural areas often make it difficult for mental health counsellors to integrate and provide care effectively. This is exacerbated by a shortage of mental health counsellors in many regions, leading to long wait times and limited availability of services (Bernardo & Alvarez del Vayo, 2021). Rural areas lack mental health counsellors, making it difficult for residents to receive timely and adequate care. The prevalence of mental health issues is comparable between rural and urban areas, but the impact of additional stressors, like unemployment and poverty, is more pronounced in rural settings (Bernardo & Alvarez del Vayo, 2021). According to Bernardo and Alvarez del Vayo (2021) and Remy et al. (2023), to address these issues, it is crucial for European countries to increase funding for mental health services, improve public health coverage, and reduce the stigma associated with mental health care. Enhanced training for mental health professionals to work in diverse environments and promoting mental health awareness are essential steps towards improving access and quality of mental health care across Europe.

Australia

A scoping review by Kavanagh et al. (2022) outlined the disparities in mental health outcomes between urban, regional, rural, and remote areas of Australia, noting higher rates of mental health-related emergencies and suicide in remote regions, highlighting the need for research to document and address inequalities in accessing mental health services in regional, rural, and remote Australia. Access to mental health services is affected by various factors including social and geographical dimensions, workforce shortages, and resource constraints. The unequal distribution of healthcare professionals exacerbates health inequalities in rural areas (Kavanagh et al., 2022). Strategies such as the Rural Health Multidisciplinary Training program aim to address these disparities in Inner Regional to Very Remote areas of Australia. Telehealth has also shown promise in providing remote access to mental health services, particularly during the COVID-19 pandemic (Kavanagh et al., 2022).

A systematic review by Savaglio et al. (2022) focused on the impact of community mental health programs for Australian youth. According to Savaglio et al. (2022), about 14% of Australian youth experience a mental disorder annually. Psychological distress among 15–19-year-olds has risen from 19% in 2012 to 25% in 2019, and suicide is the leading cause of death for 15–24-year-olds. Certain groups, including those in out-of-home care, LGBTQIA+ youth, and Aboriginal and/or Torres Strait Islander youth, are particularly vulnerable to mental health issues due to various factors such as intergenerational trauma and marginalisation—all of which were exacerbated by the COVID-19 pandemic (Savaglio et al., 2022). Despite the increasing prevalence of mental health issues among youth, global access to mental health services remains low, with an estimated 50–60% of Australian youth not receiving necessary treatment (Savaglio et al., 2022). Personal-level barriers like stigma and cultural dissonance, along with system-level barriers such as limited awareness of available services and long waiting times, contribute to this treatment gap (Savaglio et al., 2022).

Community-based mental health services, delivered in natural environments like homes, schools, and community centres, offer a promising solution to these barriers. These services aim to increase accessibility, engagement, and flexibility while being low-cost or free for clients (Savaglio et al., 2022). In Australia, recent mental health service reforms have prioritised early intervention in the community, with initiatives like Headspace providing youth-focused, holistic care. However, some youth still face barriers to accessing these services, highlighting the need for more tailored community-based models to address severe mental health presentations and complex needs effectively (Savaglio et al., 2022). In response to these identified challenges, the following sections provide an overview and application of the six key principles for multicultural perspectives and responsiveness in counselling and psychology to community counselling settings (Sisko, 2021).

Application of the Six Key Principles for Multicultural Perspectives and Responsiveness in Counselling and Psychology to Community Counselling Settings

When engaging in community counselling services and serving diverse and marginalised clients, it is essential to approach counselling and wellness from a decolonial, intersectional, and anti-oppressive lens. The following section will outline the *Six Key Principles for Multicultural Perspectives and Responsiveness in Counselling and Psychology* (Sisko, 2021) in application to working with diverse and marginalised clients in community counselling agency settings. Several principles will be applied directly to migrant communities in consideration of the prevalence of this population in Australia (Blignault et al., 2022).

Principle 1: Decolonising Psychotherapy, Counselling and Psychology

Decolonising Psychotherapy, Counselling and Psychology addresses how colonial perspectives have historically been regarded as superior in the fields of psychology and counselling, often marginalising other viewpoints (Sisko, 2021). A decolonial approach in these fields acknowledges the harmful impact of colonialism, including power dynamics and privileges, and calls for a critical examination of existing power structures and hierarchies within the counselling profession. This approach is especially important in community counselling settings to effectively meet the mental health and wellness needs of marginalised clients. Traditional concepts of wellness in counselling, often defined through a dominant lens, have overlooked the diverse cultural histories and roots of wellness. Wellness in the counselling field has been defined as the integration of mind, body, and spirit, aiming for optimal health and well-being, allowing individuals to live fully within their human and natural communities (Gamby et al., 2021; Myers et al., 2000). Wellness movements have historical roots in India dating back to 3000 to 1500 BCE, highlighting the importance for counsellors to understand wellness in various cultural contexts (Gamby et al., 2021). Modern wellness practices have often been appropriated from Indian, Indigenous, and African traditions through European colonisation. Recognising this reality can help counselling professionals embrace social justice and decolonisation principles. Gamby et al. (2021) offered recommendations and a new wellness framework to better serve diverse and underserved populations in community counselling settings.

Decolonise Wellness Education
This recommendation challenges the colonial belief that only Western perspectives on wellness are valuable, asserting that non-Western wellness knowledge should not need validation through a Western lens (Gamby et al., 2021). To decolonise and promote wellness in community counselling, professionals must critically examine the origins and sources of their understanding of wellness and its impact. Counsellor educators, supervisors, and professionals need to reflect on their own concepts of wellness, considering if the theorists and literature they rely on represent wellness practices in marginalised communities. Gamby et al. (2021) suggested that counsellors ask: *(1) Do I consider both historical and current contexts when discussing wellness with clients and supervisees? (2) How can I support my clients' pursuit of wellness through social change informed by an understanding of wellness in marginalised communities?*

Acknowledge Context
Counsellors in community agency settings, particularly those working with underserved populations, must recognise how an individual's context affects their ability to achieve wellness. This awareness challenges the notion that all individuals have the control and resources needed for wellness, acknowledging the barriers they face (Bahls, 2011; Gamby et al., 2021). To incorporate this into decolonial practice, counsellors should consider clients' financial, environmental, familial, and historical contexts when discussing goals and wellness practices. Models such as the social determinants of mental health (SDMH) provide frameworks for understanding how factors like discrimination and poverty impact marginalised communities and contribute to adverse health outcomes (Pester et al., 2023). Using the SDMH, counsellors can better understand how these contexts influence clients' cognitive, behavioural, psychological, and emotional health, leading to more effective wellness practices in community settings (Gamby et al., 2021).

Integration of Collectivistic and Individualistic Wellness Factors
Wellness can be challenging for individuals within the dominant community, but those in marginalised communities face profound impacts due to factors like the social determinants of mental health (SDMH) and societal oppression. Issues such as sexism, racism, and homophobia make access to wellness even more difficult (Sisko, 2021). Consequently, marginalised individuals often have less control over their wellness (Bahls, 2011; Gamby et al., 2021). To address these barriers, counsellors should adopt alternative wellness narratives grounded in collectivism and community, rather than solely focusing on individual responsibility for wellness (Gamby et al., 2021; Harrichand et al., 2022).

Increasing Access and Equity to Self-Care and Wellness Practices
Counsellors must ensure accessible and equitable holistic wellness practices for clients, particularly those from marginalised communities (Gamby et al., 2021; Harrichand et al., 2022). By upholding social justice, counsellors can combat oppression and injustice in society, including in workplaces, schools, and mental health settings. Embracing cultural responsiveness and promoting multicultural values, counsellors can collaborate with communities to help marginalised clients access ethnoculturally appropriate referrals and services (Gamby et al., 2021).

Principle 2: Intersectionality

Intersectionality, a theory developed by Kimberlé Crenshaw (1991), explores the complex and multifaceted nature of multiple identities and how these intersect in marginalised individuals and communities (Sisko, 2021). This framework examines how systems of oppression and privilege overlap (Sisko, 2021). For those in the counselling profession—practitioners, researchers, educators, and policymakers—adopting an intersectional approach is crucial for understanding and addressing the overlapping experiences of multiple identities in marginalised groups (Sisko, 2021). An intersectional framework is essential for tackling oppression, power dynamics, and creating societal change, particularly for clients from marginalised communities. This approach is especially important in community counselling settings, where counsellors are likely to encounter migrants, as Australia is a major destination for migrants (Blignault et al., 2022). Employing an intersectionality framework helps provide deeper insight into how various determinants affect migrant health across different stages of migration (i.e., pre-, during, and post-migration; Gray et al., 2022). It highlights the compounded marginalisation experienced by migrants with intersecting identities, such as gender and migration status. For example, migrant women's health issues, including sexual health, are influenced by gender inequality in both the host and origin countries (Gray et al., 2022).

Principle 3: Cultural Humility

Cultural humility involves practitioners engaging in continuous multicultural learning through active self-critique and self-reflection (Sisko, 2021). It encompasses interpersonal and intrapersonal components (Davis et al., 2010; Sisko, 2021). The interpersonal aspect involves focusing on others and refraining from displays of superiority, while the intrapersonal aspect involves maintaining an accurate self-view (Sisko, 2021). In counselling and psychology, culturally humble practitioners explore their clients' cultural identities and lived experiences (Sisko, 2021). This emerging framework in multicultural counselling emphasises acceptance and respect for others' cultural backgrounds (Cabell et al., 2024; Hook, 2015).

Developing cultural humility requires:

1. A lifelong commitment to multicultural learning and self-reflection.
2. Awareness of power dynamics and imbalances.
3. Challenging and holding institutions and systems accountable for addressing power differentials (Cabell et al., 2024).

According to Hook (2015), counsellors' engagement in cultural humility positively impacts the therapeutic alliance and therapy outcomes. Summers and Nelson (2023) noted, to enhance cultural humility, counsellors can reflect on questions such as:

1. What are my core cultural values and where do they originate?
2. How do I experience power, privilege, and/or marginalisation in my daily life?
3. What is my level of awareness and comfort when discussing cultural differences and social injustices?

One framework to enhance cultural humility when working with migrant groups, such as refugees, is the Multicultural Orientation

Framework (MCO), where cultural humility is one of the three main components (Adams & Kivlighan, 2019). The MCO framework aids counsellors in increasing cultural responsiveness and improving treatment outcomes for marginalised groups like refugees (Adams & Kivlighan, 2019). By adopting cultural humility in therapy, counsellors can better understand how refugees are affected by various sociocultural factors such as prejudice, xenophobia, family dynamics, language, ethnicity, discrimination, and conceptualisations of illness, all of which impact wellness, mental health prognosis, and participation in treatment (Adams & Kivlighan, 2019; Bemak & Chung, 2021; Cabell et al., 2024; Hyun et al., 2023). Counsellors using cultural humility through the MCO framework can explore how displacement and forced migration impact refugees' psychosocial functioning, exacerbating traumatic experiences and mental health disorders such as PTSD, depression, anxiety, financial insecurity, and acculturative stress (Adams & Kivlighan, 2019; Bemak & Chung, 2021). Additionally, counsellors must recognise the diverse experiences within the refugee population (Adams & Kivlighan, 2019; Harrichand et al., 2025). This curious and other-oriented perspective allows counsellors to learn about each refugee client's unique lived experiences (Adams & Kivlighan, 2019). Furthermore, counsellors can incorporate cultural humility in therapy by broaching conversations about potential cultural beliefs regarding mental health, counselling, and definitions of wellness (Adams & Kivlighan, 2019). When working with refugees, cultural humility helps counsellors actively listen to their clients' narratives, empowering them and advocating for their overall wellness and safety (Adams & Kivlighan, 2019; Harrichand et al., 2025).

Principle 4: Psychotherapist, Counsellor and Psychologist Self-Awareness

Psychotherapist, Counsellor and Psychologist Self-Awareness is foundational to multicultural counselling and culturally responsive practice (Sisko, 2021). Self-awareness involves being conscious of one's thoughts, feelings, beliefs, behaviours, and attitudes, and understanding how these factors are shaped by one's developmental and social history (Sisko, 2021). According to the 2018 Psychotherapy and Counselling Federation of Australia (PACFA) Code of Ethics, self-awareness requires counsellors to understand their worldviews and biases and their impact on clients and communities (Sisko, 2021). Principle 4, Counsellor Self-Awareness, is closely linked to Principle 3, Cultural Humility, emphasising the need for counsellors to continually be aware of their evolving biases and values when working with marginalised communities (Sisko, 2021).

To develop self-awareness, counsellors can engage in transformational learning activities such as personal counselling, clinical supervision, and research (Sisko, 2021). Anti-oppressive and culturally responsive clinical supervision is particularly beneficial in fostering self-awareness in both supervisees from marginalised and dominant communities. Psychoeducation through videos and reading materials focused on refugees and immigrants during supervision can help counsellors develop critical consciousness and reflect on their attitudes, biases, strengths, and ambivalence towards these populations (Peters & Luke, 2022; Snow et al., 2020, 2021). Supervisors can encourage self-awareness in supervisees by asking reflective questions, such as: *(1) What are my thoughts on migrants like immigrants and refugees coming to Australia? (2) How do I think the government should respond to immigration, and how do I feel about the government's current response? (3) Do I have any migrants in my social or counselling circles, and how do I treat them?* These questions help counsellors uncover biases and understand systemic issues affecting migrants' wellness (Rung, 2023; Snow et al., 2020). Additionally, supervisors modelling humanistic counselling skills like genuineness, empathy, and warmth can help counsellors apply these in their work with immigrant and refugee clients (Harrichand et al. 2025; Snow et al., 2021). Reflecting on past and current reactions to refugees and immigrants equips counsellors to use cultural humility in therapy, providing ethical and multiculturally competent services to marginalised populations (Snow et al., 2021).

Principle 5: Engagement and Connection

Engagement and Connection emphasises the ongoing nature of multiculturalism and the importance of continuous reflexivity and training. Immersing oneself in diverse communities, personally and professionally, is crucial for understanding and building relationships with diverse clients (Sisko, 2021). This principle highlights that engaging in mutual relationships with diverse clients can help mental health practitioners understand and disrupt power dynamics, thereby confronting privilege and oppression (Sisko, 2021). It is essential for counsellors to actively incorporate clients' cultural values and beliefs into all aspects of therapy rather than merely observing (Hwang, 2016; Sisko, 2021). This active engagement represents multiculturalism in action, as counsellors not only learn about the client's cultural background and identities but also integrate this knowledge into treatment.

Counsellors must actively incorporate knowledge of clients' cultural identities into their practice. This can be achieved through equity-focused engagement with marginalised clients, such as migrants, by (1) enhancing therapist self-awareness, (2) understanding the intersection of therapist and client worldviews, and (3) participating in counselling and advocacy interventions that are oriented towards social justice (Bartlett et al., 2022; Ratts et al., 2016a). Culturally responsive counsellors can immerse themselves in diverse communities by forming partnerships with organisations that serve these communities (Blignault et al., 2022). Such community partnerships foster trust between counsellors and the communities they aim to understand and support (Blignault et al., 2022).

An example of an Australian program serving culturally and linguistically diverse (CALD) Arabic migrant and refugee communities is the CALD Mindfulness Program. This program engages in research on mindfulness-based interventions (MBIs) for this population (Blignault et al., 2022). The CALD Mindfulness Program helps counsellors address barriers to mental health care in migrant populations by destigmatising mental health, supporting migrants in coping with stress, and connecting them to mental health services (Blignault et al., 2022). By creating and participating in such programs, counsellors can build connections and relationships with diverse communities, promoting relational safety and culturally responsive counselling in the therapeutic space.

Principle 6: Activism with and on Behalf

Activism with and on Behalf underscores the necessity of engaging in social justice as a vital component of sustaining cultural responsiveness and multiculturalism (Sisko, 2021). To achieve this, counselling must be coupled with advocacy for clients (Ratts, 2017; Sisko, 2021). Counsellors need a critical consciousness of the complexities of socialisation systems, hierarchies, privilege, oppression, and power to fully conceptualise wellness within marginalised and non-dominant communities (Peters & Luke, 2022; Sisko, 2021). This principle emphasises the importance of developing counsellor skills to engage in activism that creates structural and systemic change, thereby helping marginalised individuals and communities gain autonomy over their lives and well-being (Sisko, 2021) both within and outside the therapeutic space.

The Multiphase Model of Psychotherapy, Counseling, Social Justice, and Human Rights (MPM) serves as an example of a culturally responsive model for counselling professionals working with migrant communities such as refugees (Bemak & Chung, 2017). This model comprises five phases: (1) mental health education, (2) group, individual, or family psychotherapy, (3) cultural empowerment, (4) Indigenous healing, and (5) social justice and human rights (Bemak & Chung, 2017). The sequence of these phases can be tailored to best meet the client's needs. For instance, phase three, cultural empowerment, can help refugee clients overcome cultural barriers and heal from trauma by connecting with cultural elements that empower them to engage in self-advocacy (Bemak & Chung, 2017). Counsellors can implement this phase by addressing immediate stressors such as acculturation challenges—access to language training, medical care, housing, social services, transportation, and employment—before tackling presenting mental health concerns (Bemak & Chung, 2017). Cultural empowerment can also assist clients in processing experiences of racism and discrimination, and help clients build skills to address these issues in the host country (Bemak & Chung, 2017).

Moreover, phase five of the MPM addresses refugee concerns related to social injustice, human rights violations, lack of access to essential services and resources like housing and employment, and discrimination within legal systems to improve their quality of life. This phase can include educating migrant clients about their rights in Australia for themselves and their children (Bemak & Chung, 2017). Such education empowers migrant clients, within and outside the therapeutic setting, aiding in areas such as the immigration process and employment settings. Overall, models like the MPM are critical for counsellors aiming to engage in activism on behalf of diverse and marginalised clients in community counselling settings, addressing oppressive systems that impact the mental health and well-being of clients in marginalised communities. Below, we integrate the elements of this chapter using a case study analysis to demonstrate cultural responsiveness in action.

The Case of Angela Baraka

Angela Baraka is a 23-year-old international student majoring in Biomedical Engineering. She was one of ten students awarded a distinguished national scholarship for being the top-ranking student in her country after completing the national exam. This scholarship, part of a program facilitated through partnerships between African presidents, their respective Ministries of Education, and developed countries, allowed her to study at a university in England. Angela aspires to become a medical engineer to help design and procure necessary technological equipment for her country and the broader East African Community (Burundi, Congo, Kenya, Rwanda, Somalia, Sudan, Tanzania, Uganda).

Ms. Baraka comes from a large, close-knit community that includes her nuclear and extended family, as well as city and rural family members. She also has support from stakeholders in the government, private STEM sector, and religious circles, who have all supported her journey as a girl-child in STEM. Upon receiving the news of her scholarship, her former public high school and local church held celebrations and dedication services. These events honoured her efforts and those of her family, while also praying for her success as she moved to a foreign country. Fundraising efforts during these events helped Angela with her move and settlement in England. Although Angela felt encouraged and honoured to be the first woman in her community to pursue a degree in this field, she was also overwhelmed by the uncertainty of moving alone to a foreign country. She understood the sacrifices her family made, including selling property and dedicating time and resources to her education.

After moving to England in 2019, Angela excelled in her first semester. She formed a small support network primarily composed of other international students and an East African Community (EAC)-born counsellor she met during orientation, although she had only contacted her once for writing support. In 2020, the COVID-19 pandemic disrupted global schooling, and Angela's school required students to vacate the dorms. Unable to leave the country due to travel restrictions and financial constraints, Angela moved in with friends, joining four other international students in a two-bedroom apartment. She lost her 20-hour-a-week job due to pandemic restrictions but found work as a babysitter for a nurse living in the same building.

The living situation was challenging, and Angela often felt homesick. She was grief-stricken by the deaths of people she knew due to COVID-19, including a close relative who was her godmother. Unable to attend the funeral, Angela felt isolated and overwhelmed by her circumstances. Around the same time, she discovered she was pregnant and feared her family's reaction, particularly given their religious beliefs that shunned pregnancy outside of marriage. Angela felt a deep sense of shame and isolation, exacerbated by a disconnect from her doctor, her unborn child, and her community during a prenatal care visit.

The nurse at her flat shared information about a birthing centre offering an Indigenous-focused prenatal wellness program. During her intake session, Angela expressed her feelings of loneliness, shame, and homesickness. She missed the communal prenatal care practices of her home community, where women would support each other during and after pregnancy. In her community, a helper (usually a relative) would live with the pregnant woman until the baby was born and almost weaned. Angela had firsthand experience of this tradition when she stayed with her recently deceased aunt during her cousin's birth.

The birthing program consisted of new mothers from diverse political, religious, and cultural backgrounds. As the program commenced, Angela found comfort in hearing the validation of her grandmother's wisdom concerning prenatal and postnatal care. Elements of the wellness movement that resonated deeply with her included:

- *Singing to baby*—Angela recognised the value of talking, praying, and singing to her child. She remembered her grandmother advising new mothers to build a bond with their unborn children, creating a connection that extends beyond the womb. Embracing this practice, Angela was pleasantly surprised by how many Swahili songs she recalled. As she began singing to her baby, she shared with her counsellor and the group that she started to feel more connected not only to her child but also to the women in her family. Her collectivistic background emphasised the importance of connection and the wellness it brought.
- *Honouring the naming process*—Angela embraced the realisation that the life growing within her womb belonged not only to her but also to her village and community. Deeply rooted in her cultural heritage, she understood the sacred nature of naming, both for herself and for her baby. Her wish was for family members to contribute potential names while she sought the name of her child in her sacred space. The counsellor and group members supported her non-English

naming tradition with openness and respect, encouraging her to follow this meaningful process.

- *Nutrition and birth-plan development discussions*—In a previous session, Angela mentioned her unusual craving for rocks, recalling how she observed many expectant women in her village licking specific rocks during her childhood. Her counsellor responded with empathy, acknowledging Angela's experience and offering psychoeducation on "pica," a condition where individuals crave non-food items. The counsellor highlighted that during pregnancy, pica could be linked to a deficiency in calcium. They also took proactive steps by connecting Angela with a culturally responsive nutritionist and encouraging her to discuss calcium supplementation with her doctor during her next prenatal visit. Additionally, the counsellor and doula collaborated to educate Angela and other new mothers on the importance of creating a Birth Plan within the birthing system, emphasising its role in ensuring personalised and informed childbirth experiences
- *Zoom births and support*—Due to COVID-19 restrictions, the counsellor advocated for Angela to access telehealth services, including counselling and Indigenous wellness group sessions online, as well as online doula services. As Angela began to experience the benefits of these virtual activities, the counsellor suggested that she consider inviting her mother, other influential women in her life, and chosen family members to participate in online blessings/naming ceremonies and ZOOM® birthing sessions. This way, her loved ones could still be part of these events, if she wished. This suggestion uplifted Angela's spirits, prompting her to envision how her biomedical engineering background could be used to connect patients who are unable to meet in person or live in rural areas with their supportive communities during childbirth and postnatal care.
- *Contextualising counselling techniques and activities*—At the birthing centre, the counsellor integrated counselling techniques and activities through a culturally respectful approach. These included role-playing conversations and psychodramas such as family sculpting, where Angela sculpted her family from her own perspective, not influenced by the counsellor or dominant cultural views. This allowed Angela to explore both joys and feelings of shame in a supportive environment. The counsellor also encouraged Angela to engage in journaling exercises, where she envisioned conversations with her

grandmother, mother, aunt, and future child. These writings focused on what Angela was experiencing, lessons she wished to pass on, the strength and dreams that shaped her life and heritage, and other personal reflections relevant to her journey. Throughout these sessions, the counsellor supported Angela in expressing herself authentically by suggesting she write in her heart language or mother tongue, Swahili, which resonated deeply with her.

Cultural Responsiveness in Action

Applying the RESPECTFUL model (D'Andrea & Daniels, 2001; Harrichand et al., 2020) to Ms. Baraka we see: *Practicing advocacy and cultural humility*—The counsellor collaborated closely with Angela to advocate for her needs as a new mother navigating a birthing system in a new country. Providing Angela with relevant, evidence-based psychoeducation was integral to their approach. The counsellor practiced cultural humility by reflecting on their own values, increasing self-awareness while refraining from judgment. Instead, they encouraged Angela to engage in and honour her Indigenous wellness techniques. Additionally, the counsellor recognised Angela's intersectional identity as a newly single mother, a STEM student, an international student facing migrant stressors, and a marginalised individual due to COVID-19 factors.

- **Religious/Spiritual Identity:** Angela identifies as religious, with beliefs that prioritise familial contexts for children. The counsellor's self-awareness is crucial in ensuring they do not impose their own values on Angela's beliefs.
- **Economic Background:** Angela's economic situation is constrained, as she lost her job due to COVID-19 restrictions and can only work limited hours as an international student in England. Her family's ability to support her financially from abroad is limited, having already made sacrifices to send her to school on a scholarship. The counsellor advocates for resources to meet Angela's basic needs, including food, baby clothing exchanges, and potential scholarships for living expenses.
- **Sexual Identity:** Angela has not disclosed her sexual identity explicitly. However, being a new single mother challenges traditional gender roles in her cultural context. Advocating for childcare support is crucial to helping Angela navigate her varied roles effectively.

- **Psychological Maturity:** Despite being in her early twenties, Angela demonstrates maturity and a proactive approach to seeking counselling. She is open about the impact of cultural differences on her psychological well-being while embracing support that respects her Indigenous roots. A decolonising counselling approach fosters a non-judgmental space for Angela to connect with the Indigenous wellness practices of her African heritage.
- **Ethnic/Racial Identity:** Angela is from the East African Community and speaks Swahili. The scarcity of professional services that understand Angela's ethnic and racial identity underscores the importance of the counsellor's cultural humility and self-awareness in facilitating effective counselling.
- **Chronological Challenges:** Angela's decision to support her aunt during pregnancy, despite missing a semester in ninth grade, enriched her cultural experiences and strengthened their relationship. This upbringing has deepened Angela's appreciation for her people's pregnancy journey and Indigenous wellness practices. The counsellor employs decolonising interventions to address age-related issues and stressors relevant to Angela.
- **Traumatic Threats:** Angela has alluded to experiencing both shame and joy surrounding her pregnancy, though specifics remain undisclosed. A comprehensive assessment considering cultural factors is essential for the counsellor to implement culturally responsive strategies and seek appropriate resources for Angela's treatment.
- **Family Background and History:** Angela comes from a tightly knit nuclear and extended family rooted in a collectivistic background. She experiences conflicting emotions of shame and pride regarding having a baby outside of marriage and a family setting. The counsellor acknowledges these dynamics to support Angela effectively.
- **Unique Physical Characteristics:** Angela faced the stress of being pregnant during the COVID-19 pandemic, potentially complicating her healthcare access. The counsellor advocates for Angela's unique needs, such as telehealth support services, to mitigate these challenges.
- **Location of Residence and Language Differences:** Angela relocated to England from East Africa within the past year, adapting to new educational and support systems. The counsellor helps Angela navigate the intersectionality of being a pregnant new single mother in a foreign country with an unfamiliar birthing system and limited access to Swahili-speaking counsellors.

Conclusion

Applying the Six Key Principles for Multicultural Perspectives and Responsiveness in Counselling and Psychology is crucial for effectively serving diverse and marginalised clients in community counselling settings. By adopting a decolonial, intersectional, and anti-oppressive approach, counsellors can better meet the needs of these communities. Decolonising counselling practices involves challenging the dominance of Western perspectives and recognising the rich histories of wellness in various cultural contexts. Understanding and addressing the context of clients' lives, integrating collectivistic and individualistic wellness factors, and increasing access to equitable self-care practices are essential steps. Additionally, fostering cultural humility, enhancing self-awareness among counsellors, and engaging in meaningful connections with diverse communities further promote cultural responsiveness. Finally, activism and advocacy play a vital role in supporting clients' autonomy and well-being, ensuring that counselling practices contribute to systemic and structural change. By implementing these principles, community counselling agencies can create a more inclusive, equitable, and effective therapeutic environment for all clients.

References

Adams, M. C., & Kivlighan, D. M. (2019). When home is gone: An application of the multicultural orientation framework to enhance clinical practice with refugees of forced migration. *Professional Psychology, Research and Practice, 50*(3), 176–183. https://doi.org/10.1037/pro0000230

Allison, S., & Bastiampillai, T. (2015). Mental health services reach the tipping point in Australian acute hospitals. *Medical Journal of Australia, 203*(11), 432–434. https://doi.org/10.5694/mja15.00782

American Psychiatric Association. (2022). *Diagnostic and statistical manual of mental disorders* (5th ed., text rev.). Author.

Australian Government. (2008). *National mental health policy 2008*. http://www.health.gov.au/internet/main/publishing.nsf/Content/mental-pubs-n-pol08

Australian Health Ministers. (1992). *National mental health policy*. Canberra. http://www.health.gov.au/internet/wcms/publishing.nsf/Content/mentalhealth-mhinfo-standards-nmhp.htm/$FILE/nmhp.pdf

Australian Institute of Health and Welfare. (n.d.-a). *Mental health services in Australia: Expenditure*. Retrieved May 20, 2024, from https://www.aihw.gov.au/reports/mental-health-services/mental-health-services-in-australia/report-contents/expenditure-on-mental-health-related-services

Australian Institute of Health and Welfare. (n.d.-b). *Australia's mental health services*. Retrieved May 20, 2024, from https://www.aihw.gov.au/mental-health/overview/australias-mental-health-services

Bahls, C. (2011, October 6). Achieving equity in health [Policy brief]. *Health Affairs*. https://www.healthaffairs.org/do/10.1377/hpb20111006.957918/

Bartlett, A., Faber, S., Williams, M., & Saxberg, K. (2022). Getting to the root of the problem: Supporting clients with lived-experiences of systemic discrimination. *Chronic stress (Thousand Oaks, Calif.), 6*, 1–10. https://doi.org/10.1177/24705470221139205

Bemak, F., & Chung, R. C.-Y. (2017). Refugee trauma: Culturally responsive counseling interventions. *Journal of Counseling & Development, 95*(3), 299–308. https://doi-org.proxygw.wrlc.org/10.1002/jcad.12144

Bemak, F., & Chung, R. C.-Y. (2021). Contemporary refugees: Issues, challenges, and a culturally responsive intervention model for effective practice. *The Counseling Psychologist, 49*(2), 305–324. https://doi.org/10.1177/0011000020972182

Bernardo, A., & Alvarez del Vayo, M. (2021, March 9). Pay up or put it off: How Europe treats depression and anxiety. *Civio*. https://civio.es/medicamentalia/2021/03/09/access-to-mental-health-in-europe/

Blignault, I., Saab, H., Woodland, L., Giourgas, K., & Baddah, H. (2022). Promoting mental health and wellbeing in multicultural Australia: A collaborative regional approach. *International Journal of Environmental Research and Public Health, 19*(5), 1–21. https://doi.org/10.3390/ijerph19052723

Cabell, A., Burgess, D., Brown, E., & Medina, C. (2024). Counseling trainees' experiences working with Afghan refugees: Building cultural humility. *Counselor Education and Supervision, 63*(1), 41–57. https://doi.org/10.1002/ceas.12290

Crenshaw, K. (1991). Mapping the margins: Intersectionality, identity politics, and violence against women of color. *Stanford Law Review, 43*(6), 1241–1299. https://doi.org/10.2307/1229039

Cullen, W., Gulati, G., & Kelly, B. D. (2020). Mental health in the COVID-19 pandemic. *QJM: Monthly Journal of the Association of Physicians, 113*(5), 311–312. https://doi.org/10.1093/qjmed/hcaa110

D'Andrea, M., & Daniels, J. (2001). RESPECTFUL counseling: An integrative multidimensional model for counselors. In D. B. Pope-Davis & H. L. K. Coleman (Eds.), *The intersection of race, class, and gender in multicultural counseling* (pp. 417–466). SAGE.

Davis, D. E., Worthington, E. L., Jr., & Hook, J. N. (2010). Humility: Review of measurement strategies and conceptualization as a personality judgment. *Journal of Positive Psychology, 5*(10), 243–252. https://doi.org/10.1080/17439761003791672

Erickson, B. (2021). Deinstitutionalization through optimism: The Community Mental Health Act of 1963. *American Journal of Psychiatry Residents' Journal, 16*(4), 6–7. https://doi.org/10.1176/appi.ajp-rj.2021.160404

Gamby, K., Burns, D., & Forristal, K. (2021). Wellness decolonized: The history of wellness and recommendations for the counseling field. *Journal of Mental Health Counseling, 43*(3), 228–245. https://doi.org/10.17744/mehc.43.3.05

Gladding, S. T., & Newsome, D. W. (2018). *Clinical mental health counseling in community and agency settings* (5th ed., pp. 350–375). Pearson Education.

Gray, C., Crawford, G., Maycock, B., & Lobo, R. (2022). Exploring the intersections of migration, gender, and sexual health with Indonesian women in Perth, Western Australia. *International Journal of Environmental Research and Public Health, 19*(20), 1–16. https://doi.org/10.3390/ijerph192013707

Harrichand, J. J. S., Kirk, K. E., & Mwendwa, J. M. (2020). Deepa's discovery: An examination of intersectionality when multiple identities collide –Managing family roles, doctoral work, and clashing Eurocentric worldviews. In B. King & T. Stewart (Eds.), *Cases on cross-cultural counseling strategies* (pp. 192–218). IGI Global. https://doi.org/10.4018/978-1-79980022-4.ch010

Harrichand, J. J. S., Kirk, K. E., Vaishnav, S., Mwendwa, J. M., & Snow, K. C. (2025). Immigrants, refugees, diasporas, and xenomisia. In J. M. Cook, & M. Clark (Eds.), *Multicultural & social justice counseling: A systemic, person-centered, and ethical approach.* (1st ed., pp. 210–235). Cognella.

Harrichand, J. J. S., Su, Y-W., Hyun, J., & Anandavalli, S. (2022). School counselors and refugee students: Application of the refugee well-being project intervention to address the social determinants of health. *Professional School Counseling, 26*(1b), 1–8. https://doi.org/10.1177/2156759X221106810

Hipple Walters, B., Heijdra Suasnábar, J., & Petrea, I. (2020). *Good practices in mental health & well-being: Mental health services in the community.* European Union. https://health.ec.europa.eu/system/files/2018-03/2018_goodpractices_en_0.pdf

Hook, J. N. (2015). Engaging clients with cultural humility. *Journal of Psychology and Christianity, 33*(3), 277–280. https://www.proquest.com/scholarly-journals/engaging-clients-with-cultural-humility/docview/1609199862/se-2

Hwang, W. C. (2016). Culturally adapting evidence-based practices for ethnic minority families. In N. Zane, G. Bernal, & F. T. L. Leong (Eds.), *Cultural, racial and ethnic psychology book series. Evidence- based psychological practice with ethnic minorities: Culturally informed research and clinical strategies* (pp. 289–308). American Psychological Association. https://doi.org/10.1037/14940-014

Hyun, J., Harrichand, J. J. S., Anandavalli, S., Su, Y.-W., & Yoon, E. (2023). Culturally responsive counseling, cultural humility, and empathy with Asian Americans and Pacific Islanders. In L. Summers & L. Nelson (Eds.),

Multicultural counseling: Responding with cultural humility, empathy, and advocacy (pp. 68–88). Springer. https://doi.org/10.1891/9780826139535.0006

Kavanagh, B. E., Beks, H., Versace, V. L., Quirk, S. E., & Williams, L. J. (2022). Exploring the barriers and facilitators to accessing and utilising mental health services in regional, rural, and remote Australia: A scoping review protocol. *PloS one, 17*(12), e0278606, 1–14. https://doi.org/10.1371/journal.pone.0278606

Lewis, J. A., Lewis, M. D., Daniels, J. A., & D'Andrea, M. J. (2011). *Community counseling. A multicultural-social justice perspective* (4th edn, pp. 1–22, 53–89, 226–250). Brooks/Cole Cengage.

Meadows, G., Farhall, J., Fossey, E., Grigg, M., McDermott, F., & Singh, B. (Eds.). (2012). *Mental health in Australia: Collaborative community practice* (3rd ed.). Oxford University Press.

Moreno, C., Wykes, T., Galderisi, S., Nordentoft, M., Crossley, N., Jones, N., Cannon, M., Correll, C. U., Byrne, L., Carr, S., Chen, E. Y. H., Gorwood, P., Johnson, S., Kärkkäinen, H., Krystal, J. H., Lee, J., Lieberman, J., López-Jaramillo, C., Männikkö, M., Phillips, M. R., et al. (2020). How mental health care should change as a consequence of the COVID-19 pandemic. *The Lancet. Psychiatry, 7*(9), 813–824. https://doi.org/10.1016/S2215-0366(20)30307-2

Myers, J. E., Sweeney, T. J., & Witmer, J. M. (2000). The Wheel of Wellness counseling for wellness: A holistic model for treatment planning. *Journal of Counseling & Development, 78*(3), 251–266. https://doi.org/10.1002/j.1556-6676.2000.tb01906.x

National Institute of Mental Health (NIMH). (2023). *Any disorder among adults.* Retrieved May 20, 2024, from www.nimh.nih.gov/health/statistics/prevalence/any-mental-illness-ami-among-us-adults.shtml

Neukrug, E. (2024). *Foundations of clinical mental health counseling: Professional and clinical issues* (1st ed., pp. 63–85). Cognella.

Ng, K.-M., Harrichand, J. J. S., Litherland, G., Ewe, E., Kayij-Wint, K. D., Maurya, R. K., & Schulthes, G. (2023). Interdisciplinary collaboration challenges faced by counselors in places where professional counseling is nascent. *International Journal for the Advancement of Counselling, 45*, 155–169. https://doi.org/10.1007/s10447-022-09492-y

NSW Mental Health Commission. (2017, July). *Review of transparency and accountability of mental health funding to health services.* Retrieved May 20, 2024, from https://nswmentalhealthcommission.com.au/sites/default/files/documents/funding_review_web.pdf

Parliament of Australia. (2005). *A national approach to mental health – from crisis to community.* Retrieved May 20, 2024, from https://www.aph.gov.au/Parliamentary_Business/Committees/Senate/Former_Committees/mentalhealth/report/index

Pester, D. A., Jones, L. K., & Talib, Z. (2023). Social determinants of mental health: Informing counseling practice and professional identity. *Journal of Counseling and Development, 101*(4), 392–401. https://doi.org/10.1002/jcad.12473

Peters, H. C., & Luke, M. (2022). Principles of anti-oppression: A critical analytic synthesis. *Counselor Education and Supervision, 61*(4), 335–348. https://doi.org/10.1002/ceas.12251

Pfefferbaum, B., & North, C. S. (2020). Mental health and the Covid-19 pandemic. *New England Journal of Medicine, 383*(6), 510–512. https://www.nejm.org/doi/full/10.1056/nejmp2008017

Phillips, L. (2023, May). A closer look at the mental health provider shortage. *Counseling Today.* https://www.counseling.org/publications/counseling-today-magazine/article-archive/article/legacy/a-closer-look-at-the-mental-health-provider-shortage

Productivity Commission. (2020). *Report on government services 2020.* https://www.pc.gov.au/research/ongoing/report-on-government-services/2019/health/mental-health-management

Ratts, M. J. (2017). Charting the center and the margins: Addressing identity, marginalization, and privilege in counseling. *Journal of Mental Health Counseling, 39*(2), 87–103. https://doi.org/10.17744/mehc.39.2.01

Ratts, M. J., Singh, A. A., Butler, S. K, Nassar-McMillian, S, & McCullough, J. R. (2016a). Multicultural and social justice counseling competencies: Practice applications in counseling. *Counseling Today.* https://ct.counseling.org/2016/01/multicultural-and-social-justice-counseling-competencies-practical-applications-in-counseling/.

Ratts, M. J., Singh, A. A., Nassar-McMillan, S., Butler, S. K., & McCullough, J. R. (2016b). Multicultural and social justice counseling competencies: Guidelines for the counseling profession. *Journal of Multicultural Counseling and Development, 44*(1), 28–48. https://doi.org/10.1002/jmcd.12035

Remy, M. L., Blijleven, P. S., Coetzer, J. A., & Bondarenko, N. (2023). Facilitators and barriers for implementation of community-based mental health interventions in Western and Eastern Europe - A systematic literature review. *European Journal of Social Work, 1–14.* https://doi.org/10.1080/13691457.2023.2229047

Rosenberg, S., & Harvey, C. (2021). Mental health in Australia and the challenge of community mental health reform. *Consortium Psychiatricum, 2*(1), 40–46. https://consortium-psy.com/jour/article/view/44

Rung, D. L. (2023). COVID-19 and policy-induced inequalities: Exploring how social and economic exclusions impact 'temporary' migrant men's health and wellbeing in Australia. *International journal of environmental research and public health, 20*(13), 1–15. https://doi.org/10.3390/ijerph20136193

Savaglio, M., O'Donnell, R., Hatzikiriakidis, K., Vicary, D., & Skouteris, H. (2022). The impact of community mental health programs for Australian youth: A systematic review. *Clinical Child and Family Psychology Review, 25*, 573–590. https://doi.org/10.1007/s10567-022-00384-6

Semrau, M., Barley, E. A., Law, A., & Thornicroft, G. (2011). Lessons learned in developing community mental health care in Europe. *World Psychiatry, 10*(3), 217–225. https://www.ncbi.nlm.nih.gov/pmc/articles/PMC3188777/

Sisko, S. (2021). Key principles for multicultural perspectives and responsiveness in counselling and psychology. In V. Hutton & S. Sisko (Eds.), *Multicultural responsiveness in counselling and psychology* (pp. 287–296). Palgrave.

Snow, K. C., Harrichand, J. J. S., & Mwendwa, J. M. (2021). Advocacy and social justice approaches with immigrants and refugees in counsellor education. *Canadian Journal of Counselling and Psychotherapy (Online), 55*(1), 7–27. https://doi.org/10.47634/cjcp.v55i1.68482

Snow, K. C., Mwendwa, J. M., & Harrichand, J. J. S. (2020). Getting personal with immigrants and refugees: Advocacy and social justice counseling concerns. In M. Pope, M. Gonzalez, E. Cameron, & J. S. Pangelinan (Eds.), *Social justice and advocacy in counseling: Experiential activities for teaching* (1st ed., pp. 132–137). Routledge. https://doi.org/10.4324/9781315180687-34

Sue, D. W., Sue, D., Neville, H. A., & Smith, L. (2022). *Counseling the culturally diverse: Theory and practice.* John Wiley & Sons.

Summers, L. M., & Nelson, L. (2023). Counseling With cultural humility, empathy, and responsiveness. In L. Summers & L. Nelson (Eds.), *Multicultural counseling: Responding with cultural humility, empathy, and advocacy* (pp. 23–30). Springer. https://doi.org/10.1891/9780826139535.0003

Takakjy, D. (2020, April 15). The counselor's role in community outreach and resiliency building. *Counseling Today.* https://ct.counseling.org/2020/04/the-counselors-role-in-community-outreach-and-resiliency-building/

World Health Organization. (2019). *International classification of diseases for mortality and morbidity statistics* (11th Revision). Author. https://icd.who.int/en/

World Health Organization. (2022). *WHO Coronavirus (COVID-19) dashboard.* Author. Retrieved December 2, 2022, from https://covid19.who.int/

CHAPTER 10

… Final Thoughts

Susan Sisko

Introduction

In this final chapter I will bring forward some thoughts about cultural responsiveness in counselling and psychology practice. Although this is not a comprehensive review of the edited collection, I will highlight some thoughts and impressions.

When I began to consider putting together this book project it was with the belief that cultural responsiveness is extremely critical to teaching, research, supervision, and practice in psychotherapy, counselling, and psychology. As you might imagine, I come away from this project with even more conviction on the importance of cultural responsiveness in the professions. It has been a meaningful and enlightening experience to work with the authors and to read through the chapters they developed. I was stirred by their knowledge, specific examples and case studies based on their area of expertise. I had asked each author to include pertinent post-modern constructs related to teaching, research, supervision, and practice as they considered their writing, which they clearly and thoughtfully

S. Sisko (✉)
School of Health, University of Canberra, Canberra ACT, NSW, Australia
e-mail: Susan.Sisko@Canberra.edu.au

S. Sisko (ed.), *Culturally Responsive Psychotherapy, Counselling & Psychology*, Palgrave Texts in Counselling and Psychotherapy,
https://doi.org/10.1007/978-3-031-81831-8_10

achieved. The following thoughts focus on colonisation broadly and the impacts on education and practice and what a decolonised position in education and practice could look like.

Colonisation

> Colonialism is a practice of domination, which involves the subjugation of one people [by] another. One of the difficulties in defining colonialism is that it is hard to distinguish it from imperialism. Frequently the two concepts are treated as synonyms. Like colonialism, imperialism also involves political and economic control over a dependent territory. The etymology of the two terms, however, provides some clues about how they differ. The term *colony* comes from the Latin word *colonus*, meaning farmer. This root reminds us that the practice of colonialism usually involved the transfer of population to a new territory, where the arrivals lived as permanent settlers while maintaining political allegiance to their country of origin. *Imperialism*, on the other hand, comes from the Latin term *imperium*, meaning to *command*. Thus, the term *imperialism* draws attention to the way that one country exercises power over another, whether through settlement, sovereignty, or indirect mechanisms of control. (Mignolo, Loc 2909)

The "Spoils" of the Best Navy

Having a powerful navy was a significant factor in the success of the main colonisers from the fifteenth century forward. The ability to project naval power across vast oceans allowed European powers to explore, conquer, and control distant territories. The most prominent colonial powers—Portugal, Spain, the Netherlands, France, and the United Kingdom—had some of the most advanced and powerful navies during the height of their colonial expansions. Colonial powers benefitted from the extraction of resources such as minerals, spices, and agricultural products and the establishment of profitable trade routes. The colonies provided strategic military and naval bases, enhancing the geopolitical influence of the colonial power. The colonisers exploited indigenous labour for agricultural, mining, and infrastructure projects, significantly benefiting their economies. Colonialism often imposed a set of values that reflected the beliefs, norms, and interests of the colonising powers. These values were typically rooted in Eurocentric and Western ideologies and had significant and lasting impacts on the colonised societies.

The immediate and long-term impacts of colonisation meant that the colonised peoples often faced economic exploitation, land dispossession, and forced labour. Colonial powers frequently suppressed indigenous cultures, languages, and religions, leading to long-term cultural dislocation. Colonisation also disrupted social structures and traditional ways of life, leading to lasting social and political upheavals. Many "post"-colonial societies continue to grapple with economic disparities, underdevelopment, and dependency on former colonial powers. Arbitrary borders drawn by colonial powers and the legacy of divide-and-rule policies have contributed to ongoing conflicts and political instability in many regions. Colonial powers often regarded European culture, language, religion, and social norms as superior to those of the colonised peoples. This led to the marginalisation and suppression of indigenous cultures, traditions, and knowledge systems.

Colonisers imposed belief in the superiority of the white race and the inferiority of non-white races. This ideology justified the subjugation and exploitation of colonised peoples and laid the groundwork for systemic racism that persists today. In fact, colonisation can be understood as the root of racism. "Every [colonising] empire tells itself that it is unlike all other empires, that its mission is not to plunder and control but to educate and liberate" (Said, 2003). Yet, there was no evidence that colonised peoples were seeking education or liberation by these European or Western countries.

Colonial economies were structured to benefit the colonising powers through the extraction and export of resources, often at the expense of local economies and communities. This included the establishment of plantations, mines, and other forms of resource exploitation that relied on the labour of the colonised populations. Missionary activities were a significant part of the colonial enterprise, with the aim of converting indigenous peoples to Christianity. This often involved the suppression of indigenous religions and spiritual practices, and the imposition of Western religious values and moral codes. Colonial powers often imposed patriarchal values that reinforced male dominance and limited the roles and rights of women. These gender norms disrupted existing gender relations in many societies and contributed to long-lasting gender inequalities.

Efforts to reclaim and revitalise indigenous cultures, languages, and identities are ongoing, but the impact of colonial cultural suppression remains significant. The fear of decolonisation arises from a variety of reasons, including uncertainty about the future, potential loss of power and privilege, economic concerns, and cultural changes. Those who have historically benefitted from colonial structures, such as political elites, landowners, and certain ethnic groups, may fear losing their power, status, and economic advantages. Institutions that have been shaped by colonial legacies may resist change due to entrenched interests and the potential upheaval of existing power dynamics. There is often a fear that decolonisation could lead to economic instability, as the shift away from colonial economic structures might disrupt current systems of production, trade, and finance. People may fear losing their cultural identity or being forced to adopt new cultural norms that feel alien or imposed. Changes in education systems and language policies aimed at decolonisation can be perceived as threatening to the established cultural and social norms. Decolonisation involves significant social, political, and economic changes, which can create anxiety and fear about the unknown.

Addressing these fears requires careful and inclusive planning, clear communication about the goals and benefits of decolonisation, and efforts to build trust and consensus among stakeholders. Ensuring that decolonisation processes are just and aimed at creating inclusive and sustainable futures is crucial for overcoming resistance and fostering positive change. In the next sections I will briefly offer suggestions to decolonising education, training, and practice in psychotherapy, counselling, and psychology.

Decolonisation

Education and Training

Eurocentric and colonial knowledges have been privileged in education and are designed and treated as the core foundations in psychotherapy, counselling and psychology, while historically, different perspectives have been seen as deviations. Decolonising education and training include recognising the colonial impact and the power and privilege that remains associated with that. As described in Chap. 1 of this book, we cannot wholly separate from our foundations, but we need to progress education and training beyond that and include indigenous, diverse, and postmodern knowledges. It is important to understand connections across cultures and emphasise the importance of communication, empathy, and shared experiences to foster cross-cultural relationships, thus, allowing for these connections to promote mutual understanding and respect in a globalised world (Krause, 1998).

At a systemic level this includes, but is not limited to:

Curriculum Revision

- Integrate indigenous knowledge, non-Western theories, postmodern and diverse cultural perspectives throughout the core curriculum.
- Include courses that address the history and impact of colonisation on mental health and counselling practices.
- Diverse cultural resources including textbooks and media.

Inclusive Faculty Recruitment

- Actively recruit and retain faculty members from diverse cultural backgrounds who bring different perspectives and experiences to the program.

Community Partnerships

- Build partnerships with local indigenous and diverse communities to incorporate their input and perspectives into mental health education and training.
- Develop students' opportunities for diverse community-based learning and culturally immersive experiences.

Training and Workshops

- Provide ongoing training and professional development for faculty and students on cultural responsiveness, anti-racism, and decolonising practices.
- Include workshops led by indigenous and culturally diverse experts.

Further, educational institutes need to develop flexible learning modalities to include postmodern and transformational learning practices. Cultural critic, feminist theorist, and educator bell hooks extensively discussed the concept of transformational learning in her works. In her book, *Teaching to Transgress: Education as the Practice of Freedom*, hooks introduced the concept of engaged pedagogy. This approach encourages teachers to be fully present and emotionally involved in the learning process, creating a reciprocal relationship with students. Engaged pedagogy emphasises holistic education, addressing the intellectual, emotional, and spiritual dimensions of students. hooks emphasised that education should be an emancipatory and transformative process, rather than merely a means of transmitting knowledge (hooks, 1994).

Unfortunately, the current standard of education does not often reflect value in transformational learning. Large tertiary institutes have become education businesses with focus on the bottom-line and less on engaging pedagogy or developing holistic education. Class sizes can be huge, especially in undergraduate courses, where often students do not meet their educators in person, but they learn through pre-recorded lectures or online material only. Engaged pedagogy and holistic education is more demanding to develop and facilitate than current education practices. It takes more time and possibly money, more attention to the processes of engagement and the relationship between people than the current standard of education offers.

However, the very essence of education within the counselling profession is to support the development of students to become self-aware and critically reflective people as they train to become counsellors and psychologists. It may be difficult (but not impossible) to move this mountain in one fell swoop, but I believe we can remain committed to transformational learning and engaged pedagogy. The classroom can be made a democratic setting where everyone feels responsible and safe to contribute to a central goal of transformative pedagogy, opening dialogue about inclusion, intersectionality, and diversity. Each person brings is a legitimate position of knowledge through lived experiences and their diverse stories. Creating small group structures and using strategies where every person has a chance to share and speak.

As an example, one of my favourite educational activities is that I ask the students develop a *Cultural Genogram,* which is a framework for individuals to reflect on and articulate the varying intersections (e.g., age, sex, gender identity, religious beliefs, ethnicity, and so forth) of their personal story. Following that process, the student is asked to consider how these intersections have been experienced as privileges or as oppressions for them overtime. Once the student has had adequate time to reflect, they would share their cultural genogram in small groups. In doing this they open themselves up to other students, share their lived experiences as well as developing empathy, building rapport, understanding and insight by hearing the stories of people who may be different from themselves. Mind you, this is not always comfortable or welcomed by students who prefer didactic ways of learning, as they too may be resistant to engaged pedagogy. As hooks says, "there can be, and usually is some degree of pain involved in giving up old ways of thinking and learning new approaches. I respect that pain" (hooks, 1994, p.43).

Clinical Practice

Wake, Woke and Cultural Responsiveness

To be awakened means to cause one to stop sleeping. Woke is the past tense and past participle of wake. However, in the current social and political climate the term "woke" has garnered significant attention and debate in recent years. The term "woke" has evolved over time, but it was originally rooted in African American Vernacular English (AAVE) and it means being aware of and attentive to issues of race and social justice, issues with the roots in colonisation. Today woke broadly refers to being aware of social injustice and inequities, particularly those related to race, gender, and other groups who are often marginalised in society. It suggests a heightened awareness of systemic oppressions and a commitment to challenging and address these inequities.

In positive terms woke is intrinsically linked to cultural responsiveness as it fosters awareness, empathy, advocacy, and inclusive practices that are essential for addressing the needs of all people but especially important for diverse cultural groups and promoting social justice. In less positive terms "wokeism" can be seen as a threat to conservative or traditionalist values. This perceived threat arises from challenges to cultural norms, political and economic principles, educational content, and religious beliefs. An example of this is described in Chap. 6 by Camilo and Owen within the school counselling sector. They described campaigns against school counsellors with suggestions that school counsellors are *indoctrinating* students if issues related to sexual identity or race are discussed by the student in therapy. The campaign and, in some cases, lawmakers are introducing legislation proposing to limit interactions between students and helping professionals. This seems very risky to withdraw skilled counselling support from individuals, in this instance students, who may be wrestling with a myriad of significant issues.

Developing culturally responsive psychotherapists, counsellors, and psychologists supports a position that demonstrates empathy, non-judgement, acceptance, and understanding for all people attending therapy. This allows people who are attending therapy to express their pain, suffering, and concerns openly and freely and to be confident that their lived experience will be respected. The focus on the counsellor's self-awareness, critical reflection, cultural humility, and an intersectional approach are about setting aside any personal values, beliefs, or biases of the counsellor to fully allow the individual to express themselves in therapy. This is particularly important as it fosters trust, enhances communication, improves understanding, and reflects the diversity of each person. These factors collectively contribute to more effective cultural responsiveness and respective therapeutic outcomes. This is the cornerstone of the therapeutic process and is rather the opposite of indoctrination.

The Six Principles identified in *Multicultural Responsiveness in Counselling and Psychology* Sisko (2021) for developing cultural responsiveness include counsellor self-awareness, cultural humility, and understanding intersectional framework as some of the main tenets of the culturally responsive counsellor.

Counsellor Self-Awareness and Critical Reflection

Counsellor self-awareness refers to the ongoing process of understanding one's own beliefs, values, biases, and emotions, and recognising how these personal aspects can impact the counselling relationship and therapeutic process. Pieterse et al. (2013) define self-awareness as a "state of being conscious of one' s thoughts, feelings, beliefs, behaviours, and attitudes, and knowing how these factors are shaped by important aspects of one's developmental and social history" (p. 191). Critical reflection in counselling involves a deeper level of analysis where counsellors critically examine their own practices, the broader context of their work, and the systemic factors that influence the therapeutic environment.

Counsellors and psychologists' need to engage in ongoing self-examination and self-assessment of their own responses and reactions to be able to work effectively with their clients. When counsellors and psychologists are challenged because of working with clients, they need to develop reflexivity and openness to understand how their own values might influence the therapeutic process. Approaches to developing self-awareness of counsellors and psychologist include engaging in transformational learning activities that may include personal development through group and individual counselling, supervision, ongoing reading, and research.

Cultural Humility

Counsellor self-awareness is directly linked to cultural humility. Tervalon and Murray-Garcia (1998) described the concept of cultural humility as therapists engaging in self-reflection, self-critique, and as lifelong learners in multicultural perspectives. This includes the counsellor self-awareness of their own values and bias to avoid bringing those into the counselling room. Davis et al. (2010) identified definitions of humility including both intrapersonal and interpersonal components. The intrapersonal dimension describes individuals who are humble and demonstrate an accurate view of self. The interpersonal dimension describes individuals who maintain a position of being focussed on others rather than being self-focussed. For example, the culturally humble counsellor and psychologist is interested in and open to exploring the client's cultural background and experiences. They do not assume that their knowledges or theories are more valuable than the position of their client's worldview and experiences. It is very much about valuing and respecting each client's unique cultural identity, including their values, beliefs, and practices. Cultural humility empowers clients through validation of their cultural experiences and perspectives.

Intersectionality

Intersectionality in counselling refers to an approach that recognises and addresses the multiple, interconnected social identities and related systems of oppression or discrimination that clients may experience. This concept, originally developed by Kimberlé Crenshaw, emphasises the importance of understanding how different aspects of a person's identity (such as race, gender, sexuality, class, ability, etc.) intersect and interact to shape their experiences and mental health. Rodó-de-Zárate (2014) describes intersectionality as developing out of a growing recognition that it is not possible to separate out a person's identities and explain them through a singular framework. As such, counsellors need to adopt an intersectional framework that recognises the complex and cumulative ways in which multiple experiences of identity combine, overlap, or intersect for individuals but especially in the experiences of marginalised individuals or groups. To address the inequities experienced by individuals who intersect with multiple forms of marginalisation, counsellors and psychologists must be able to make linkages between client identity, marginalisation, and privilege (Ratts, 2017). Intersectionality is not only about focussing on multiple identities, but it is also about addressing societal changes in response.

Culturally Responsive Psychotherapy and Counselling in Practice

As a result of colonisation, the groundwork was laid for systemic racism, gender inequality, and loss of cultural identities and languages of the colonised peoples. Colonisers imposed their superiority and the forced subjugation and exploitation of colonised peoples. Through colonisation an imposed set of values that reflected the beliefs, norms, and interests of the colonising powers was accepted. Postmodernism, including social justice movements, began to challenge these Eurocentric norms and values.

Postmodernism, as a philosophical and cultural movement, challenges the ideas of objective truth, universal narratives, and single perspectives, instead advocating for the recognition of multiple realities, subjective experiences, and the deconstruction of established norms. Postmodernism emphasises the existence of multiple, coexisting truths and realities, rejecting the idea of a single, objective truth. Culturally responsive psychotherapy and counselling acknowledges that clients come from diverse cultural backgrounds and with different worldviews, beliefs, and experiences. Culturally responsive counselling respects and validates the unique cultural context of each client, recognising that there is not only one way to approach counselling.

Postmodernism challenges the grand narratives or universal theories that claim to explain all aspects of human experience. Culturally responsive counselling moves away from applying universal theories and methods that may not be relevant or effective for all clients. Further, it deconstructs dominant therapeutic models to adapt and create approaches that are culturally relevant and sensitive to the client's individual context.

Postmodernism values subjective experiences and the individual's perspective as central to understanding human behaviour and society. Culturally responsive counselling places the client's personal and cultural experiences at the forefront of the therapeutic process while encouraging clients to share their stories and perspectives, using these as the basis for understanding and intervention.

Postmodernism critiques established power structures and hierarchies, advocating for a more egalitarian approach while highlighting the importance of giving voice to marginalised and oppressed groups. Culturally responsive counselling recognises and addresses the power imbalances in the counsellor-client relationship and in broader societal contexts and advocates for social justice and works to empower clients by acknowledging and addressing systemic oppression and discrimination they may face.

Postmodernism values the integration of diverse perspectives and the coexistence of different viewpoints as enriching and necessary for a comprehensive understanding. Culturally responsive counselling incorporates knowledge from various cultural traditions and practices into the therapeutic process as well as seeks to understand and integrate the client's cultural background, values, and practices into counselling.

Culturally responsive psychotherapy and counselling embodies postmodern principles by recognising and valuing the multiplicity of clients' cultural realities, deconstructing dominant therapeutic models, emphasising subjective experiences, challenging power structures, and being flexible and adaptive in approach. This alignment with postmodernism allows for a more inclusive, respectful, and effective counselling practice that honours the diverse cultural contexts of clients.

Conclusion

I could go on, but I will stop here. Although this is the conclusion of this book, I do hope that this book adds to the journey of educators, researchers, supervisors, students, and practitioners in developing culturally responsive practice in counselling and psychology.

I extend my appreciation to my colleagues and chapter authors of this book. Further, I extend a depth of gratitude to all the educators, researchers, supervisors, and practitioners who have bravely gone before and forged the way forward in decolonising counselling theory and practice to push for postmodern culturally responsive practices.

References

Davis, D. E., Worthington, E. L., Jr., & Hook, J. N. (2010). Humility: Review of measurement strategies and conceptualization as a personality judgment. *Journal of Positive Psychology, 5*, 243–252.

hooks, b. (1994). *Teaching to transgress, education as the practice of freedom*. Routledge.

Krause, I.-B. (1998). *Therapy across culture*. Sage.

Pieterse, A. L., Lee, M., Ritmeester, A., & Collins, N. (2013). Towards a model of self-awareness development for counseling and psychotherapy training. *Counselling Psychology Quarterly, 26*(2), 190–207. https://doi.org/10.1080/09515070.2013.793451

Ratts, M. J. (2017). Charting the center and the margins: Addressing identity, marginalization, and privilege in counseling. *Journal of Mental Health Counseling, 39*(2), 87–103. https://doi.org/10.17744/mehc.39.2.01

Rodó-de-Zárate, M. (2014). Developing geographies of intersectionality with relief maps: Reflections from youth research in Manresa, Catalonia. *Gender, Place & Culture, 21*(8), 925–944. https://doi.org/10.1080/0966369X.2013.817974

Said, E. (2003, July 20). Blind imperial arrogance. *Los Angeles Times.*

Sisko, S. (2021). Key principles for multicultural perspectives and responsiveness in counselling and psychology. In *Multicultural responsiveness in counselling and psychology: Working with Australian populations.* Palgrave. 978-30-30554-26-2.

Tervalon, M., & Murray-Garcia, J. (1998). Cultural humility versus cultural competence: A critical distinction in defining physician training outcomes in multicultural education. *Journal of Health Care for the Poor and Undeserved, 9*, 117–125. https://doi.org/10.1353/hpu.2010.0233

Index

S. Sisko (ed.), *Culturally Responsive Psychotherapy, Counselling & Psychology*, Palgrave Texts in Counselling and Psychotherapy,
https://doi.org/10.1007/978-3-031-81831-8

S

T

U

V

Y

The manufacturer's authorised representative in the EU is Springer Nature Customer Service Centre GmbH, Europaplatz 3, 69115 Heidelberg, Germany. If you have any concerns regarding our products, please contact ProductSafety@springernature.com

Printed and bound by CPI Group (UK) Ltd, Croydon, CR0 4YY
30/09/2026
02225560-0001